Twentieth Century Reporting
At Its Best

1964 ★★★

Twentieth Century

REPORTING

At Its Best

by

Bryce W. Rucker

★ ★ ★

Foreword by

FRANK LUTHER MOTT

THE IOWA STATE UNIVERSITY PRESS
AMES, IOWA, U.S.A.

About the Author

BRYCE W. RUCKER, director of the journalism graduate program and director of journalism research at Southern Illinois University, has a solid background in both practical and theoretical journalism. A native of West Virginia, Dr. Rucker completed his undergraduate work in journalism at the University of Kentucky. He earned the M.S. degree at the University of Wisconsin and the Ph.D. degree at the University of Missouri. He has taught a variety of journalistic subjects at the University of Missouri, the University of Texas and Southwest Texas State College, and has worked in public relations, as a special correspondent and in many advisory capacities. Dr. Rucker is a co-author of *Modern Journalism* (Pitman) and has contributed to the *Journalism Quarterly* and other publications.

© 1964 The Iowa State University Press.

All rights reserved.

Composed and printed by
The Iowa State University Press,
Ames, Iowa, U.S.A.

Second Printing, 1967

Library of Congress Catalog Card Number 64–13371

Dedicated to **American reporters, the world's greatest press corps**

Foreword

EZRA POUND once wrote, "Literature is news that stays news."

A good news story does not lose its freshness with the passage of time. Any doubter can verify this by digging out the files of Dana's *New York Sun* of the 1870's and looking over the front pages of that paper. How readable! How interesting! How hot off the fire! These stories, nearly a century old now, still have a kind of inner vigor and reality that has kept them alive even on yellowing and forgotten pages.

It is a pity that the best writing of this kind should be so evanescent. I have been accustomed to say to my classes that the journalist writes on water. No, let us abandon the figure, with its plaintive connotations, and admit frankly that the news-paperman writes for a newspaper, and that newspapers are designed and doomed for quick destruction. Moreover, events follow upon each other's heels at such a rate that today's news story inks out yesterday's.

One way to prevent such quick forgetting is to gather to-gether for publication between covers some of the best news stories of various periods. This Dr. Rucker has done in the present volume. He has chosen a period illustrating con-temporary developments of news writing and not covered by any other general anthology. His headnotes will be helpful to the general reader, to the student, and to the practising reporter.

I cannot close this little preface without suggesting that the liberal and unprejudiced critic will find in many of these stories undeniable literary values. In varying degrees they challenge the reader's thinking, exhibit underlying significances in human life and contemporary problems, make a restrained appeal to the emotions, and display writing styles that are admirable for their purposes and in their places.

FRANK LUTHER MOTT

Introduction

WRITING EXCELLENCE stands out above all else in the stories in this collection, because that was the sole criterion used in their selection. Each piece in its own way glistens brightly as the best of American journalism. Note how each writer communicates clearly, creates an appropriate mood, relates his news skillfully.

One might ask, "What makes these stories the best?" Specific comments accompanying each article cite strengths. Generally speaking, however, the same ingredients that make any writing excellent are evident here. Most important, this involves using vivid, powerful, accurate verbs and crisp, specific nouns. These writers consistently used them to achieve interesting texture, toughness, temper. Repeatedly, these skilled writers selected nouns and verbs which fit the news event at hand, rather than threadbare, indefinite ones appropriate to a myriad of similar events.

This isn't to advocate discarding adjectives and adverbs. They contribute, too. But a wise writer realizes the most muscular adverb can't strengthen a cream puff verb. Nor can the most apt adjective revive a tired, general noun.

Hence, skilled writers select all words meticulously, including adjectives and adverbs and conjunctions as well as nouns and verbs. They reject the tired, the general, the vague, realizing freshness contributes to excellence.

Simplicity in sentence, paragraph, and story structure also heightens communication. These writers know when to use change of pace in sentence length and structure to avoid monotonous, singsongy, juvenile prose. None of these longer sentences, however, commits a writing sin condemned as early as 1888 by ex-newspaper reporter Samuel L. Clemens (Mark Twain):

> . . . At times he may indulge himself with a long one (sentence), but he will make sure that there are no folds in it, no vagueness, no parenthetical interruptions of its view as a whole. When he is done with it, it won't be a sea-serpent with half of its arches under the water; it will be a torchlight procession.[1]

Writers evidenced imagination, a golden touch, in many of these stories. Repeatedly they showed keen insights and selected similes, metaphors, examples, anecdotes, etc., which heightened communication.

Even a cursory study of these stories reveals their clear organization. Note how one writer used a straightforward narrative chronological framework, another blended expertly direct quotations with summaries and paraphrases into an easy-to-understand story, still another constructed punchy story summaries of unpretentious simplicity.

Skilled reporting, too, contributes to the greatness of these stories. Some are reports of matters of great moment. Others of less significance still reflect prodding in depth.

All of this and more make these stories a valuable guide to anyone who wishes to write well, be he a highly experienced newsman, a beginner, or one who aspires to a journalism career. This collection also stands as a challenge to all who would demean newspaper writing as poor, inexpert, crude. For these pieces will stand the test of closest scrutiny and compare favorably with the best contemporary writing regardless of form.

These 55 stories are the elite of those published since the end of World War II. They are the distillate, the condensation from an exhaustive study of thousands of stories in hundreds of America's greatest newspapers. Articles selected are from 25 newspapers and the then three American-based world news services. Some won prizes. But that is coincidental as none of the limitations imposed on those selecting prize-winning stories influenced this anthology.

---

[1] Letter from Samuel L. Clemens, Hartford, Conn., Oct. 15, 1888, to an unidentified clergyman.

The writer is deeply indebted to the many editors, publishers, reporters, and others who "nominated" news stories. Even so he accepts full responsibility for all decisions. He is further indebted to the newspapers and news services by whose gracious permission these articles have been reprinted.

Thanks, too, go to Dr. Frank Luther Mott, dean emeritus of the University of Missouri School of Journalism, for his numerous suggestions and continuing interest, and to Dr. Earl F. English, dean of Missouri School of Journalism, for his encouragement. And, most of all, my gratitude goes to a patient family, to my wife, Betty; and children, Bryce Calvert and Linda Sue.

Contents

[*xiii*]

Contents xv

Twentieth Century Reporting
At Its Best

REPORTING
AT ITS BEST

Nuclear Energy and Outer Space

HISTORIANS NO DOUBT will evaluate the mid-Twentieth Century largely in terms of what we have accomplished with the twin challenges and opportunities of nuclear energy and space exploration. How phases of these two continuing stories were reported, then, seems a fitting starting point for this collection. Let's consider first space exploration.

The Western world had become rather blasé about space flight by the time Leroy Gordon Cooper manually guided his "Faith 7" space craft to a Pacific Ocean splashdown on May 16, 1963. Yes, his 22-orbit flight, the finale of the single-man Mercury series, was the news of the day, as had been lesser flights by Alan B. Shepard, Jr., Virgil Grissom, John H. Glenn, Jr., Malcolm Scott Carpenter, and Walter M. Schirra, Jr.

Boy, What A Ride

None of these, however, evoked quite the same drama as did Shepard in his suborbital flight down the Atlantic a short two years previously.

American space scientists, still smarting from an apparently commanding Soviet lead, lost the race to be first with manned space flight. For it was 23 days after Yuri Gagarin became the world's first astronaut that Shepard rode an American rocket into outer space. True, Gagarin flew farther, once around the earth, yet his flight was shrouded in secrecy. Americans, literally riding co-pilot via radio and television, flew with Shepard on his 302-mile arch down the Atlantic.

It really wasn't much of a flight by present standards and might be compared by future sophisticates to the sputterings of Henry Ford's first Model T. But all who heard and saw will long remember the drama of this long-awaited attempt to catch up to the Soviets.

Ralph Dighton faced up to the challenge of recounting this epic flight with all the drama of the moment yet kept it in perspective as the first of possibly many and more daring space explorations. To paraphrase the astronaut, "Boy, what a Story!"

Note the crisp word choice, "plucked" (par. 3), "knifed" (par. 27); the varied sentence structure; the smoothness with which Shepard's quotations were dovetailed into a free-flowing chronology. The writer also wove voluminous factual background information, including distances and times of Gagarin's flight, into his story without disrupting the story's meter.

This story maintains interest throughout by wringing full mileage from the few usable quotes available. Structurally, the writer relied largely on chronological tellings.

By Ralph Dighton
The Associated Press, May 5, 1961

CAPE CANAVERAL, Fla.—Steel-nerved Alan B. Shepard, Jr., rode a rocket into space today, exclaimed "What a beautiful sight" as he looked down on the earth, and then dropped to a safe landing in the Atlantic ocean.

To the wiry, 37-year-old navy commander, the historic adventure obviously was no more frightening than many earlier flights he had made in experimental aircraft.

"It's a beautiful day," he told marines on the helicopter that plucked his space capsule out of the water after a soaring flight 115 miles above the earth and 302 miles southeast from the Cape Canaveral launching pad.

Then his nonchalance gave way to excitement as he declared:

"Boy, what a ride!"

Out Escape Hatch

Only 19 minutes after the Redstone rocket booster blasted off at 9:34 a.m. (EST), Shepard climbed out the escape hatch of the space craft and was picked up, to be transferred to the deck of the aircraft carrier Lake Champlain.

"I don't think there's much you'll have to do to me, Doc," America's first space man remarked to one of the physicians waiting anxiously to determine if Shepard suffered physical or psychological harm in his flight out of the atmosphere.

Shepard had radioed from the weightless void of space that he could see, through his periscope, the entire east coast of the United States.

Shepard's blazing, 5,000-mile-per-hour flight was only the beginning of American exploration of space, said Hugh Dryden, deputy administrator of the National Aeronautics and Space Administration.

Soon, Dryden said, an astronaut will orbit the earth and later travel to the moon and back.

Crewmen of the Lake Champlain were told not to speak to Shepard. Doctors and psychologists want him to tell his story without having it colored by ideas conveyed to him on his return.

Excellent Condition

Shepard later was reported in "excellent physical condition" and in "fine spirits."

The report was made by doctors who examined him on this ship.

Army Capt. Jerry Strong, one of the doctors, reported:

"There is nothing we can determine that is in any way abnormal after the flight."

The successful shot followed the orbiting of the earth by a Russian astronaut 23 days ago.

The Russian, Yuri Gagarin, the first space traveler, was shot into a 188-mile-high orbit and returned to earth 108 minutes later.

Today's suborbital shot does not match the Russian achievement but is a major step toward orbiting an American, which the National Space Agency plans to do later this year.

Space Chores Possible

The purpose of today's flight was to determine if man can perform useful chores in space.

Shepard proved conclusively it could be done.

He reported constantly throughout the flight that

he was able to do certain tasks, such as pushing levers and buttons and operating manual controls.

All the way through he told the control center at Cape Canaveral by radio that everything was okay.

During the flight, Mercury officials said that Shepard was reporting facts and figures just like a test pilot would.

Shepard's reports on the "beautiful sight" came only three minutes following launch, after a periscope in the capsule protruded to give the space pilot a view of the earth.

Shepard had entered his space cabin at 5:18 a.m., after a final medical examination and a breakfast of filet mignon, two poached eggs, sherbet and peaches.

Countdown Delayed

He remained there four hours, 16 minutes, during a countdown that had been delayed several times by technical troubles and weather.

The slender rocket, stretching 83 feet tall with the capsule and 15½ foot escape tower on top, flew a true course as it knifed into a clear sky under the anxious eyes of thousands who crammed into Canaveral to watch as America for the first time committed a man into space.

As the missile accelerated, forces six times the pull of gravity pushed the astronaut against his couch.

At 141 seconds after launch, the capsule separated and the escape tower—designed to jerk the capsule free and parachute it safely to earth in case of trouble —was jettisoned.

Automatic controls then flipped the 9-foot-tall capsule over 180 degrees so the blunt heat shield base led the way, with the pilot riding backwards.

About four minutes after launch, Shepard tumbled, as if over a precipice, into a weightless world—an exhilarating experience that lasted about five minutes.

As swiftly as it came, the weightless feeling left and Shepard once again was gripped by G forces— twice those he had experienced on acceleration—as the capsule plunged back toward earth.

11 G's During Re-entry

The pilot reported he was subjected to 11 G's during the re-entry period.

Ten minutes after launch, at an altitude of 40,000 feet, a small parachute opened to stabilize the space craft.

At 10,000 feet, a 63-foot main chute unfurled to lower the capsule into the water, presumably with no more force than if it had fallen off a 14-foot wall.

Recovery ships in the area reported they sighted the large red and white parachute as it lowered the capsule toward the sea.

Two helicopters from the Lake Champlain rushed to the scene. One lowered a hook to raise the capsule upright. It was on its side in the water.

When this was done, Shepard climbed out an escape hatch and was pulled into the other helicopter.

A few minutes later he was on the deck of the carrier.

Examinations

After his initial medical check Shepard was taken by helicopter to a hospital on Grand Bahama island, about 75 miles southwest of the recovery site.

He is expected to remain there at least 48 hours for extensive examination and psychological tests.

Then he will be flown to Washington, probably Sunday or Monday, for a hero's welcome at the White House from President Kennedy.

He will remain in Washington about 36 hours and then will return to Cape Canaveral for further tests.

These will include simulation flights in a mock capsule, so that medical men can compare the results of similar mock flights which he made before today's real thing.

Clad in his silvery space suit, Shepard stepped out of the helicopter aboard the Lake Champlain, went briefly to the capsule and picked up his space helmet which he had left behind.

He said "Thank you" to Lt. George Cox, Eustis, Fla., the co-pilot, who also snagged the space-chimp, Ham, from the ocean.

Spit and Polish Welcome

It was a real spit and polish welcome usually reserved for high brass admirals.

The capsule touched down on a platform emblazoned with red, white and blue bunting.

Seamen shouted and whooped when they first saw the orange parachute appear northeast of the carrier. The sailors had heard Shepard's voice over the ship's loudspeaker announcing he had reached 20,000 feet coming down.

You could see the splash clearly from the ship and five helicopters were in the immediate area, perhaps only a mile away, reports said.

The capsule was picked up about four miles east northeast of the carrier.

When Shepard arrived on Grand Bahama island he jauntily strode into hospital seclusion.

Grinning broadly, he shook hands with and slapped the backs of two other astronauts, Virgil Grissom and Donald Slayton.

They asked how it went and he said everything went fine.

Shepard threw back his head and laughed and seemed in high spirits.

Shepard walked a few yards from the car to the hospital and was put in bed immediately. He landed here about 3½ hours after his blastoff from Cape Canaveral.

First U.S. Moon

Americans, long accustomed to being first in technological advances, were collectively jolted from a long siege of complacency on Oct. 4, 1957. The event: the Soviet Union successfully launched the world's first satellite. Sputnik I cost the United States heavily in international prestige, leading some to predict an irreparable setback in our efforts to woo and win the masses in uncommitted nations.

The federal government almost immediately launched a frenzied crash program to catch up. Then a second blow fell; the Soviet Union on Nov. 3 launched Sputnik II, a husky 1,120-pound satellite reportedly with a dog aboard.

In December the United States sought to enter the interplanetary flight race with a Vanguard three-stage rocket. Amid much fanfare and full international publicity the Navy rocket barely lifted off the pad before erupting into a fiery tangle. This brought further recriminations with louder demands to catch up regardless of cost.

It was against this backdrop that the Army successfully launched a Jupiter-C satellite bearing a 29.7-pound baby moon. Success at last!

This Associated Press story captured much of the "jubilation" of a grateful nation. More than this, however, the reporter made understandable a mass of complex data, couched largely in a strange, new lunar language. Brief, easy-to-digest sentences, often one to a paragraph, move rapidly, methodically through the mountain of data. Structurally, the story is near perfect despite pressing deadlines; it deals with each subdivision of the event in logical order before moving on to the next. Note the summary of specifics in the first five paragraphs; then the official announcement and celebrations. Next it returns to the center of interest, the satellite launching. The writer in effect takes the reader by the hand and traces the launch chronologically, so clearly his eyes become the reader's.

Virtually every word appears measured as if the writer had taken time to search thesauri until he had found in each instance the perfect word, perfect in accuracy yet fully understandable to the masses: "firm orbit" (par. 2), "clusters of small rockets" (par. 5), "huge splash of flame" (par. 13).

The Associated Press, Jan. 31, 1958

CAPE CANAVERAL, Fla.—The Army launched its Jupiter-C satellite tonight and within 113 minutes the artificial moon had completed its first flight around the world.

The Explorer satellite was in firm orbit, so perfectly on course that it may remain aloft as long as 10 years.

The satellite orbit takes it within 230 miles of the earth at its lowest point and 2000 at the peak of its course. Its speed is 19,400 miles per hour.

The tube of metal, more than 6 feet long, was launched at 10:48 p.m. (EST).

The 70-foot-long Jupiter-C launching vehicle sent the satellite into space, and clusters of smaller rockets provided the added speed necessary to push it into an orbit.

Two hours later, President Eisenhower made the first announcement that an orbit had been established.

Issued by Hagerty

The announcement, from the President's vacation quarters at Augusta, Ga., was issued by the White House Press Secretary, James Hagerty.

The official confirmation that a U.S. satellite was roaming the sky in company with the Soviet Sputnik II touched off a wave of jubilation among persons associated with the launching project.

At Huntsville, Ala., where the Jupiter-C was built, the Army's group of scientists organized a celebration immediately after the launching, and they were among the first to spread the word definitely that an orbit had been achieved.

Here at the missile test center, there were also festive groups who had waited up for the President's announcement.

The new satellite is swinging around the earth once every 113 minutes.

The Jupiter-C, 70 feet tall, thundered off its launching pad only an hour and a quarter after it had been exposed to view.

The missile was off to a beautiful launching. It rose slowly at first in a huge splash of flame with a roar that could be heard for miles.

Gleams in Searchlights

The giant missile, gleaming white in the searchlights, continued to climb upward with terrifically increasing pace into a sky dotted with a few white clouds. The missile soared on upward in the light of a pale moon.

There were many stars in the sky and it was difficult to determine which was the missile and which was a star.

After the missile disappeared from sight, another light was seen high in the sky. It could not be determined whether this was another stage of the missile or whether the vehicle had merely reappeared through another layer of clouds.

Newsmen watching the launching shouted and cheered as though at some exciting sports game.

Even before the missile was launched, its form,

heretofore secret, could be easily made out in the searchlights playing on it.

Bucket Starts Spinning

It was tall and slender and snow-white up to the stubby end of the Redstone first-stage rocket. On top of that stage sat a round bucket which, about 11 minutes before launching, was seen to start spinning.

Above the spinning bucket—containing a number of smaller sized rockets—the slender satellite itself protruded for several feet.

The satellite was like polished silver in the floodlights marked with parallel stripes of dark brown color running barber-pole fashion down the sides. These stripes were layers of zirconium oxide applied to minimize the temperature changes.

Furious, Fiery Trail

The Redstone first-stage rocket was scheduled to burn out some two minutes after leaving the stand, and shortly thereafter would fall away. This separation, visible on some previous Jupiter-C launchings, was not discernible on this occasion.

The rocket vehicle itself on taking off demonstrated that it was one of the most powerful rockets ever launched here. Its furious red fiery blast extended far beneath it as it pushed its way up into the sky.

The giant missile became fully visible to watchers on the beaches some miles away about an hour before launching, when the crane surrounding it was rolled back.

Fumes Drift Out

It stood there minute after minute, with fumes of liquid oxygen drifting out from it like steam from a simmering kettle.

As the minutes raced by and it became more and more likely that at last the U.S. would launch a satellite vehicle, tension grew among the large group of watching newsmen.

Assembled for the event were more than two dozen motion picture and still-camera units clustered together at one good observation point. One observer said it was the most elaborate array of photographic equipment that had ever been assembled for a single news event.

From time to time action could be seen in the launching area indicating progress in the steady approach toward a firing.

Rod Removed

A rod beside the vehicle was removed and the missile itself grew whiter in the floodlights as frost accumulated more thickly on the frigid surface of its liquid oxygen tanks.

At the moment the rocket engine was started there was a sharp flash of fire. Almost immediately this expanded to a huge orange balloon of flame accompanied by an earth-shaking roar.

Unlike some other big ballistic missiles, the Jupiter-C is not lashed down until it can build up power but is permitted to start climbing immediately.

And that was exactly what this one did.

It sprang into the air and moved up with a speed almost matching that of much lighter and smaller missiles.

The thunder of the rocket engine was so terrific that observers could only shout at each other and even then could not make themselves understood.

The watchers waved their arms and pounded each other on the back as the missile surged skyward.

The Jupiter-C climbed vertically for what appeared to be an extremely long period, by contrast with ballistic missiles that have been fired here recently.

Some moments after take-off sparks could be seen trailing back in the rocket's path.

These were fragments of burned graphite and represented the erosion of carbon vanes inside the missile which extended into the jet blast and provided means of guidance.

There was none of the cloud of steam or water which surrounds the launching of other large missiles. This was true because the Jupiter-C was "dry launched"—did not use the pool of water which is employed by other missiles to protect the launching area.

As the missile struggled away from the launching pad, chunks of frost dropped from its icy surface.

Far up in the sky, minutes after the missile's flame had disappeared, the upper stages of the rocket were expected to reach a course horizontal to the earth and to signal that information to the ground.

Waiting at a control station at the cape was Dr. Ernst Stuhlinger, director of research projects for the Army Ballistic Missile Agency. At the proper moment Stuhlinger pushed the button that was to ignite the upper stages of the rocket and sent it to orbital velocity.

Friends said Stuhlinger recently became a father. They said his wife told him, "Okay, I had my little satellite. Now you have yours."

The new satellite, a tube 80 inches long and 6 inches in diameter and weighing 29.7 pounds, was expected to complete a trip around the world every 113 minutes.

The Navy tried to send the Vanguard satellite aloft in December. The three-stage rocket rose only a few feet, toppled and destroyed itself in flames.

Sputniks Launched

That vehicle contained in its nose a 6.4-inch sphere weighing only about 3¼ pounds.

A Vanguard rocket launching planned for March may use a 20-pound instrumented sphere 21 inches in diameter and later Vanguard satellites may be even larger.

Russia launched the world's first man-made moon, the Sputnik I, last Oct. 4. On Nov. 3 the Reds put up the 1120-pound Sputnik II with a live dog aboard.

Sputnik I reach a maximum altitude of 560 miles, and kept orbiting until early this month when it spun closer and closer to earth and finally disintegrated.

The second Red satellite was reported to have reached an altitude of 1056 miles. Its dog passenger died not long after its launching, but the satellite itself is still circling the earth.

Yeast to be Sent

The Navy has plans to put yeast cells aboard the Vanguard satellite as an experiment on the effect of space flight on living organisms.

The Army said there was no living matter in the Jupiter-C satellite.

Some two minutes after the launching the mighty Rocketdyne engine of the five-ton first stage was expected to exhaust the last of its liquid propellants, a combination of liquid oxygen and either alcohol or kerosene.

After the first stage burned out, the explosive bolts that linked the Redstone first stage to the upper stages were set to discharge. This enabled the spent Redstone—a metal tube 6 feet in diameter and more than 60 feet long—to fall away.

Inside the spinning bucket sat the tiers of smaller rockets of the upper stages, like bottles spinning around in a washer.

As the Jupiter-C climbed and accelerated, the rate of spin of the upper-stage rockets increased.

Once it was free of the dead Redstone, the upper part of the Jupiter-C went on silently toward the stars, its rocket load still spinning like mad.

At an altitude of 200 or more miles the vehicle was "programed" to arch over to the horizontal.

Then, when a "level" course parallel to the earth's surface was achieved, the rocket clusters were fired.

"And that is why we had to spin those rockets," an Army officer explained.

"If any one or more rockets should fail to fire properly, we would still have a uniform thrust so long as they were spinning.

"If these high speed rockets were stationary in their bucket, the failure of some of them to perform could throw the satellite far out of its orbit course."

Rocket experts said that any deviation from the horizontal greater that 1 per cent could prevent the establishment of an orbit.

The Army satellite had two radio transmitters, each weighing about two pounds, aboard. They were:

1—the standard Vanguard transmitter with an output of 60 milliwatts, capable of being received on 108.03 megacycles, by the Vanguard minitrack network and by amateur radio operators. It was expected to continue broadcasting for two to three weeks.

2—A long-range, low-powered—10 to 29 milliwatts —microlock transmitter operating on a frequency of 108 megacycles and likely to last for two to three months.

H-Bomb vs. The Pacific

Reports of vast, powerful nuclear explosions must transport the reader to the scene—let the explosion's searing heat burn him, bright flash blind him momentarily, awesome force lash him.

Bob Considine did just that in his description of the United States' first air drop of a hydrogen bomb. Considine relied largely on strong verbs, vivid adjectives, specific nouns to inject power into his story. Note, on the other hand, his somewhat subdued over-all tone. This veteran International News Service reporter had long since learned that a "shouting" end-of-the-world, breathless presentation interferes with clear communication. His story achieves strength through a dramatic, fairly measured pace, aided by brief sentences.

He injected factual information—10 million tons of TNT (par. 4), high-flying B-52 intercontinental jet (par. 2)—skillfully, unobtrusively. Note how Considine described in terms highly meaningful to a New York reader: "equal to that of several Empire State Buildings" (par. 3), "boxes so numerous they would fill Yankee Stadium, Ebbets Field and the Polo Grounds" (par. 5). This technique helps reduce to understandable proportions that which soars beyond the grasp of the human mind. For who can visualize the explosive force of the mass of 10 million tons of TNT?

Over-all story structure, in keeping with the action inherent in the news event, is chronological and repeat chronological with appropriate insertions of background and scene information. Chronological fragments appear in paragraphs 10 to 13, 14 to 16, 18 to 23, and 24 to 30. This pattern will be discussed more fully later.

By Bob Considine
International News Service, May 21, 1956

ABOARD USS MOUNT McKINLEY—The United States touched off its first air-dropped hydrogen bomb with a nightmarish explosion over the Bikini Atoll Isle of Namu today, proving America now has a thermonuclear thunderbolt it can hurl anywhere on earth.

The monstrous eruption of the super-missile, released from a high-flying B-52 intercontinental jet bomber at 5:51 a.m., rocked and seared a wide mid-Pacific expanse, and its deadly radioactive aftercloud was wafted by winds over ocean wastes to the north.

Thousands of Feet

The fearful air burst at a height of thousands of feet—equal to that of several Empire State Buildings—was triggered only a few weeks after Russia trumpeted a boast it had won the race to be first to detonate a "package" H-bomb dropped from a plane.

The force of the fabulous blast from America's first aerial hydrogen missile was measured in several megatons, and one unofficial estimate said it was equal to about 10 million tons of TNT. A megaton equals the energy released by the explosion of 1 million tons of TNT.

Today's tremendous H-bomb eruption was equivalent to a blast from TNT piled in boxes so numerous they would fill Yankee Stadium, Ebbets Field and the Polo Grounds.

It shook a big section of the earth and was undoubtedly recorded on some seismographs around the globe.

Ghastliest of Weapons

Revealing a new dimension in America's defense arsenal, today's explosion of history's ghastliest mass destruction weapon hoisted its devastating power several thousand feet above the mid-air point of the blinding burst itself.

The fantastic spectacle was witnessed by newsmen and civil defense officials from aboard the communications ship Mount McKinley, 34 miles off the target Isle of Namu, in the first public showing of an American hydrogen test.

The enormous blast immersed America's huge Eniwetok Proving Ground in a tidal wave of light and scalding heat which, aboard the Mount McKinley felt as though the door of a nearby blast furnace had been suddenly opened.

The aerial unleashing of man's newest and virtually indescribable weapon spread a chameleon-hued fireball at least four miles across the stilled watery horizon toward which the shielded eyes of the observers were tensely trained.

Then the ensuing mushroom cloud began ballooning overhead until it had climbed to the awesome height of more than 100,000 feet—about 20 miles.

The spreading umbrella of peach color, and now golden and now gray, measured at least 50 miles in breadth at 55,000 feet.

Could Blow Away City

There the great upper level winds took charge. By the time the mushroom had reached 100,000 feet, in a sky which the rising sun had turned into a gloriously pale blue, the span across the top of the lethal cloud was 100 miles or more.

The mammoth flashing explosion itself would have turned to cinder and blown away any great city on the globe. And it would have erected its own breathtaking "monument" over the desolate ruin below. That "monument," over Bikini Atoll, first took the shape of a pillar of light that the unaided human eye could not confront without risk of blindness.

It stretched up from below the horizon to at least 20,000 feet in the air, and it was infinitely hotter than the sun which gives life to our planet.

In an instant, the brazen fireball changed color to a grayish orange and out of its peak sprouted the mushroom formation of rising radioactive debris—symbol of these tense swaddling years of the atomic age.

With shattering force, America now had "trumped" the card played by Communist Party boss Nikita Khrushchev when he claimed recently that Russia already had dropped and detonated an aerial H-bomb.

A great galleon of a cloud sailed between our observers' ship and the violently growing mushroom, helping to bring an uncertain darkness back to this ocean waste which only moments before had literally writhed in light and heat.

Cloying Silence

For the observers' eyes, at least, "the bomb" had gone and the oppressive silence that had surrounded the phenomena of the light, heat and the hellish apparition grew more cloying.

"Brace yourselves; brace yourselves for the shock wave!" the iron throats of the Mount McKinley's "bullhorn" loudspeakers brayed.

And then, just two minutes and 53 seconds later,

the voice and the shudder of "the bomb" was heard as the shock wave hit the Mount McKinley.

There was no Jovian thunder clap; no roughing up of some 7,000 men at the rails of the task force ships at sea off Bikini.

Rather, it was the voice of a giant from some forgotten childhood tale—clearing his hairy throat and clumping off to his lair.

The great curtain of cloud stayed roofed between our ship and the drama taking place on the horizon. But it could not obscure the spectacle very long for the exploded bomb, code-named "Cherokee," was racing for heaven like the proverbial homesick angel.

The peach and cream colored eminence of the mushroom peeked with deceptive coyness over the top of the charcoal "stem," and soon the whole incredible plateau of that eerie man-made edifice had shown itself—swirling and heaving and growing with an inborn vigor that was stupefying to behold.

"It's still a million degrees centigrade, even up that high," a scientist remarked on the bridge of the Mount McKinley.

His was the only voice that had been heard since a seaman had said in an awed and faraway voice:

"Oh, dear God, what that would have done to my home town."

As the expanding mushroom rose to its full, stratospheric height, lacy vapor trails from the friskier of 34 planes engaged in "Operation Redwing" now began to appear, going in and coming out of the radioactive cloud.

Invisible Needles

It looked like invisible needles sewing an enormous powder puff to the blue heaven with threads of wool and silk. It brought, however, a realization that for the men in these planes the sampling and testing of the mushroom had only begun.

For others—notably the seven-man crew of the eight-jet B-52 H-bomber named "Barbara Grace" which will live in history for this perilous performance—the day's work was over.

These seven staunch men, commanded by Maj. David M. Critchlow, 36, made their get-away from the deadly effects of the bomb they dropped from about 55,000 feet, and safely brought the "Barbara

Grace" back to the Eniwetok Island airstrip, 200 miles away.

Also safe was a group of 10 scientists and technicians who were the closest humans to "Ground Zero"—Namu Islet where the H-bomb burst over a bullseye target drawn with coral and asphalt.

These experts were buried in the deep recesses of a thick-walled steel and concrete bunker on Enyu Isle, only 20 miles from Namu.

From the bunker, crammed with a maze of intricate recording devices, Dr. Gaelen L. Felt, leader of the party, reported laconically by radio that a strong air blast shook his post but that no other effects of the blast were noted.

Many Miles Away

The method by which the B-52 drop plane escaped the wrath of the cataclysmic wallop it delivered on Namu remained a secret. But it was presumed that as soon as the bomb was safely away from the huge bomber's belly, the "Barbara Grace" banked abruptly and "poured on the coal" in speeding away as fast as it could.

It may have put 20 miles between itself and the target before the H-bomb air burst went off, and perhaps twice again that distance farther before the shock wave reached the plane.

All of the joint task force seven aircraft flying in the Bikini area at the time the oft-postponed H-bomb detonation finally occurred got away from the effects of "the shot." This was the official announcement issued by Rear Adm. B. Hall Hanlon, "Operation Redwing" commander, one hour after the big blast.

The planes which took part in the historic, complex experiment were believed to include the 1,000-mile-an-hour F-101-A jet which had been assigned to streak high over the fireball that arose from the thermonuclear detonation.

Possible Casualty

The only possible casualty thus far reported in the operation, involving a total of 1,300 officers and men of Hanlon's task force, is Capt. Paul Crumley, listed as missing after bailing out from a jet plane early last Friday just before "H-hour" was postponed for the ninth time.

In the end, the momentous "Cherokee" drop operation, originally slated for May 8, was precision itself! The planes, ships and endless spread of recording devices were in their assigned positions and functioning properly.

The bomb itself was released at the precise scheduled moment of 5:51 a.m. It was a visual drop triggered by Major Critchlow's navigator-bombardier, Maj. Dwight E. Durner, 37, of Charlotte, Mich. The highly sensitive H-bomb was armed in flight by the B-52's navigator weaponer, Maj. Floyd A. Amundsen, 36, of Grand Forks, N. D.

The absence of untoward incident in the great experiment was reflected in the radio message from the brilliant 34-year-old Dr. Felt to Admiral Hanlon.

"I have nothing of particular interest to report," the scientific task group commander radioed from Enyu.

Later Dr. Felt and his nine men would venture out of their drop dugout and be picked up by two helicopters and flown as close to radioactive Namu Islet as possible. They will wear protective clothing for safety from deadly gamma and beta rays in case they are forced down on contaminated land or water.

The powerful vacuum movement that followed the detonation was believed to have sucked up much of tiny Namu and some scientific equipment on the target isle, and probably also some of the monkeys and rabbits which had been placed around "Ground Zero" for test purposes.

Part of the Cloud

All became part of the cloud that ascended three times higher than Mount Everest. In that cloud was the equivalent of millions of pounds of radium-like matter. Only about three pounds of radium have been refined from pitchblende since its discovery by the Curies more than a half century ago.

Beneath the H-bomb's mushroom cloud and on the surface of the Pacific sat three of the United States Navy's strangest vessels—refitted Liberty ships called "Yags."

Their profiles were featured by huge "bird baths" with which to catch "hot" debris from the radioactive cloud, and "dumb waiters" to bring these samples below decks. The ships also were fitted with a dozen big marshmallow-like "hornets' nests" to catch deadly rays from the unleashed hydrogen bomb.

No living soul was seen aboard the three ships as they followed the mushroom cloud north and northwest across the ocean wastes. All personnel of the vessels were shielded far below decks in little control and sampling rooms by tons of concrete and many cubic yards of sea water.

Carefully Charted

The multimillion-dollar bomb was dropped, at long last, after the go-ahead signal was given by weathermen who had carefully charted vagrant Pacific winds and visibility conditions.

The many postponements of "Cherokee" during the past 14 days were due to south-blowing winds which might have spilled radioactive fallouts on units of the task force and some 1,500 people of the Marshall Islands south of Bikini.

This morning the winds were moving generally northeast—over empty Pacific waters and isles—and the clouds failed to obscure the bullseye target made of coral and asphalt on tiny Namu.

Then the order was given to the B-52 H-bomber's seven-man crew, commanded by Major Critchlow to carry out its history-making, danger-laden mission.

The eight-jet planes took off without untoward incident from the Eniwetok Island airstrip at 3:45 a.m.

Saucers, Science And Sex

Long before Buck Rogers-inspired space flight fantasies were taken seriously by most Americans, we were exposed to wierd tales of flying saucers invading our atmosphere. Few were the newspapers that failed to receive calls from impressionable youngsters reporting their first "sighting." Then came the inevitable; the believers organized, elected officers, and held conventions.

Picture the dilemma of Los Angeles *Times* reporter James Hubbart when assigned to cover one such gathering. Hubbart, an imaginative reporter, saw in the Amalgamated Flying Saucer Clubs of America, Inc. convention a drama not unlike those made popular in Gilbert and Sullivan operettas. As you read this gem see how he used the Gilbert and Sullivan theme to report, tongue-in-cheekishly, the mutual hoax conventioneers seemed to enjoy playing on each other.

Rather than mar your enjoyment by detailed diagnosis, let me merely suggest that you note carefully two things other than the theme—the selection of individuals to be included in the piece and the workmanship interweaving of carefully selected direct quotations with summaries.

By James Hubbart
Los Angeles Times, July 12, 1959

The saucers that fly in the
   Spring, Kla-La,
Breathe promise of merry
   sunshine,
As we merrily dance and we
   sing, Kla-La,
We welcome the hope that
   they bring, Kla-La,
Of a summer of roses and
   wine;
Of a summer of roses and
   wine.

With no apologies to Gilbert and Sullivan, 2,000 flying saucer believers opened a two-day convention at the Statler Hotel yesterday to ponder the latest prophecies from outer space.

They paid $5 a head, earth money, to hear about trips to the Stars, to Venus and Mars; of Clarion scows, cosmic powwows and saucers and science and sex.

They heard tape recorded messages from such interplanetary personalities as Monka and Merku, Ashtar of Venus, La-Lur, Soltec and, of course, Kla-La.

Kla-La, according to the chief earthbound go-be-tween, Richard Miller of Van Nuys, whooshes down occasionally from another solar system and ap-parently is the Aldebaranian equivalent of Gilbert and Sullivan's Lord High Executioner.

In any event, everybody was spellbound by it all.

Photographer Is Founder

The convention was put together under the banner of the Amalgamated Flying Saucer Clubs of America, Inc. Most of its members claim to have seen, booked passage on or communicated with mysterious space conveyances.

The founder of the organization is Gabriel Green, 35, onetime photographer with the Los Angeles school system.

The purpose of the convention, he explained, is to demonstrate that superior creatures from outer space "will establish the kingdom of heaven on earth."

Some delegates sported uniform shirts, cryptic in-signia or other trappings emblematic of their cult.

The most notable of these was Harold J. Byer, of 16728 Flanders St., Granada Hills. He wore an aerial helmet, a uniform with five-star epaulettes and a badge proclaiming him as national executive direc-tor of the Robot Rangers.

"It's a youth organization," Byer confided from be-hind his cigar. "We take up where the Boy Scouts and the Girl Scouts leave off."

Somebody Watches

Fifty storytellers spent yesterday afternoon re-lating experiences with flying saucers or their occu-pants. Although their tales and theories differed, they held one belief in common, namely:

Somebody up there is watching us.

"All the planets have changed orbits," declared George L. Robertson of Inglewood. He displayed maps to prove it. "That's why we have flying saucers. We're in their territory."

The conclave was not altogether harmonious. Dan Martin, of St. Louis, Detroit and Mexico, leveled an accusing finger at the other delegates.

"They're 99% fakes," he charged.

Martin, 61, who said his Mormon wife divorced

him and then tried to have him committed to a mental institution for his beliefs, admitted he has never seen a flying saucer.

"But I rode in one," he added solemnly, "I was lifted into the spaceship on a ray that neutralized gravity."

Martin said it was a Venusian vehicle with a Mercurian crew that entertained him at a luncheon of fruit salad and wine.

He predicted the earth will shift on its axis in 1964. In his words:

"A gigantic nuclear explosion in the vicinity of the North Pole will break up the arctic icecap. The ice will float south, throw the earth out of balance and cause it to tip upright."

Sorta Like Red Cross

Spacemen will descend after the calamity to rehabilitate the planet "just as the Red Cross does in a disaster," Martin said knowingly.

He challenged other convention speakers to prove their saucer claims. He said he could verify his.

"The public is tired of all these fantastic stories," Martin noted.

At least one visitor to yesterday's session was really out of this world.

She was Miss Angel McCall, 16, who appeared as an emissary from Venus. She was wearing a futuristic costume and a four-hour make-up job that included rhinestone eyebrows, jewel-tipped eyelashes and blue face powder.

Accompanying her was Lawrence Milton Boren, founder-director of the World of Tomorrow Foundation. He explained that Miss McCall will have a featured role in his forthcoming outer-space musical, "From Venus With Love."

The convention will conclude today with reports on "Spiritual Significance of the Space Ships," "Universal Vibration," "Meeting With Lazarus," and other out of this world topics.

CIVIL RIGHTS

MONUMENTAL CHANGES have been wrought during the past two decades. So much so many of us experienced a scintillating wooziness as the earth spun at an increasingly freightening pace. Real or fancy? Who can say. None can deny, however, the fantastic rate with which travel speeds have increased, the diminishing time spans between international political crises, the tremendous rate of European economic growth.

These were at snail pace, however, when compared to American social changes, especially as concerns civil rights. Yet many protest that these few birthrights won have been grudgingly granted with rear guard actions forcing an inch-by-inch battle. When compared to accomplishments of decades past, though, even the most outspoken supporter of civil rights must agree much has been gained.

This has been and will continue to be a bitter controversy, little understood by those of us on the sidelines. Even so, few can view this dispassionately.

Newspapers reflected much of the heat and fury generated by a minority and its allies battling for a better life. Ray Sprigle of the Pittsburgh *Post-Gazette* in 1948 donned appropriate dress and assumed the role of a Negro to expose the plight of Negroes in the deep South. Others followed his lead. But it was the United States Supreme Court ruling in 1954 that "separate but equal" educational facilities were unequal, and so unconstitutional, that provided the basis for radical change.

How Far From Slavery?

Newspaper reporters throughout the country wrote reams of civil rights copy. Which stories represent the best? A difficult decision. One chosen was the first in an 18-part series by probably the most skilled Negro newspaperman alive. It rates tops by any measure. Ambassador Carl T. Rowan, then a Minneapolis *Tribune* staff writer, revisited his native South in the winter of 1950–51. The series appeared in the *Tribune* during February and March, 1951.

This piece gains much of its strength by (1) explaining logically why the writer felt challenged to undertake this highly unpleasant assignment and (2) treating the subject unemotionally, yet forcefully. Certainly Rowan proves again the power of understatement. Rowan's story is so conversational one experiences this, rather than merely reads it.

By Carl T. Rowan
The Minneapolis Tribune, Feb. 26, 1951

McMINNVILLE, Tenn.—Nearly eight years ago I boarded a Jim Crow train and left this central Tennessee town of 6,000.

On my first trip out of Dixie I was answering the call of the United States Navy. As it turned out, it also was the call of opportunity, for my hello to arms was farewell to the south in which I was born and reared.

I have just returned to this farm-industrial community—this time by Jim Crow bus. It was like rolling back the time.

Negro youths still lean against the First National Bank building at Main and Spring streets, as I once did hour upon hour. There was no place to go, nothing to do—except wait for a white man to come along and agree to our previously-conspired demand of 25 cents an hour to mow a lawn, clean a basement or unload a boxcar of 100-pound bags of cement.

There was the colored section town. It was the same squalor, the same unpainted frame dwellings huddled along narrow, hole-filled streets. Scores of houses still lacked window panes.

The same paths led through weedy backyards to smelly, wooden privies.

My return also was to keep a promise to a white southern sailor who found in 1943 that he was a stranger in his native land.

I propped my head on my hand and dozed that October in 1943 as my dirty, smoky Jim Crow coach rolled across Kentucky and southern Illinois. I was bound for Topeka, Kan., and a navy V12 unit. Upon arrival I found that I had been snatched completely from the segregated world. I was in a unit of 335 sailors, 334 whites.

Among those sailors was Noah Brannon, a music lover from Brownsville, Texas, who wanted to be a minister. I loved music, too, so Brannon and I quickly became piano pals.

But I was the first Negro whom Brannon had known on an equal basis. His first racial question, asked as if he were startled, was: "Where is that overpowering odor they told me all Negroes have?"

Brannon proved to be even more uninformed about Negroes.

"Until I met you, Carl, I didn't even know Negroes had last names. We always called them 'Aunt Susie' or 'Uncle Charlie'," he confessed.

Tell Little Things

Brannon was amazed to learn that in McMinnville, my home town, I couldn't (and still can't) get a drink of water at a drugstore unless the fountain clerk could find a paper cup. No Negro drinks out of glass.

In the summer of 1944, eight months after we had met, Brannon abruptly stopped playing "I'll Be Seeing You." We were about to part. He turned to me and said:

"You plan to be a writer after the war. Sometime, why don't you just sit down and tell all the little things it means to be a Negro in the south, or anywhere where being a Negro makes a difference. It all was right before my eyes. You probably can't get a drink of water in Brownsville, either, but I'd never have known it.

"If you're a southern white person you see these things and you don't. You're taught not to care. It's something that exists because it exists.

"Don't preach, but tell it all," Brannon pleaded,

"for there must be many people in the south with big hearts and little knowledge of this thing."

So I have returned to the south, where the color of my skin counts above all things. I have returned to keep a promise, to make a report to the Noah Brannons of the south and north on what it means to be a Negro.

But much has happened in the south since Noah Brannon and I shared torch tunes and laughed at racial myths that date to before slavery.

The Negro's lot is better in some big and some small ways. Aided by the federal courts, he has made progress toward equality of educational opportunity, but complete equality is far away still.

Much 'Old South'

In every state but Mississippi, Negroes now vote in tens of thousands—although in rural areas of many states they still do not get the ballot.

In other fields—employment, health, equality at the hands of the law—change comes at snail's pace.

But there are many changes in the south—social and economic changes. Southerners already speak with pride of "The New South."

Is there a new south for the Negro? Five minutes across the Mason and Dixon line answered that.

I took a plane as far south as Nashville, Tenn. At the Louisville, Ky., airport I went to a candy stand. One white soldier was there and the attendant waited on him. By this time other whites reached the stand. The attendant passed me going down the counter and waited on whites. When she passed me going up the counter, I walked away.

This was the old racial protocol system I had known since I was 6. I knew I would be served only after all whites had been waited on. I was acutely aware that I was in Dixie again.

If there were any doubts, my arrival at Nashville dispelled them. In 1945, my last time in the Nashville airport, there was no segregated seating. This time, as I stepped into the building, I noticed a sign painted on the wall. Just above two chairs, it read: "FOR COLORED PASSENGERS ONLY."

There also were four toilets, one for white and one for colored men; then one was marked, "WHITE LADIES," the other "COLORED WOMEN."

I walked to the local office of the Hertz U-Drive-It system. I had asked the airline to see that I had a car waiting.

Can Never Be Sure

"I'm Rowan of the Minneapolis *Tribune*," I said to the attendant, "I believe you have a car waiting for me."

"You . . . you're Rowan?" he replied.

"That's right, Carl T.   I believe Eastern Airlines wired from Chicago."

The attendant tossed some keys to a Negro porter who sat nearby.

"Bring up car 42," the attendant ordered.

A few minutes later I was driving a 1950 Chevrolet. I was surprised—but the Hertz agent didn't know it. I was laughing, laughing at the serious "Oh, no" I got for an answer when I jokingly asked the porter if car 42 came equipped with a time bomb.

But Jim Crow signs in an airport and a courteous attendant in the Hertz office were typical of the unpredictable south. They illustrate what it is like to be a Negro. It is a life of doubt, of uncertainty as to what the reception will be from one town, even one building, to another.

As I drove that rented car through cracker-barrel hamlets and along highways that snaked across fields laden with shocks of dead cornstalks and cotton plants browned by winter's chill, I realized that I had come face to face with doubt. Doubt as to which filling station would allow me to buy gasoline and also use the toilet. Doubt as to which restaurant would sell me food—even to take out.

I remembered that to give any report to America's Noah Brannons, I was to cover some 6,000 miles of the south. For my own safety, I would have to erase some of the doubt.

Things to Remember

I would have to remember to wear a tie on the bus from Nashville to McMinnville—in this area a Negro fares better if he looks educated and willing to demand the few rights he possesses.

I would have to remember NOT to wear a tie in several small towns in Georgia, Mississippi, Louisiana—a Negro still can get killed in these towns for "dressing and acting like white folks."

Also, I would have to remember the words of Prof. Merle R. Eppse when I drove the Hertz car to Tennessee A & I State college, a Negro school.

"Where did you get the car?" he asked.

"From Hertz U-Drive-It," I replied as if I rented one daily.

"Well I'll be damned," he snorted. "Every time we try to rent a car they send a truck—they figure that's all a Negro can use.

"But you meddlin' damyankees come down here and upset our way of life," he added, tongue in cheek.

Still, I would have to remember that Eppse could be right. Despite my 18 years in the south, I might be considered just another "meddlin' damyankee."

The Noah Brannons would have to answer that one.

Kentucky Town Tensely Awaits Integration Crisis

How can those who are a thousand miles away understand the emotional tension inherent in admitting Negroes to a previously all-white southern school? Moreover, who among us can write objectively and informatively of these tensions. One man could and did—Francis A. Sugrue of the New York *Herald Tribune.*

As you read Sugrue's almost poetic article, note the contrast he paints of a sleepy, quiet, rather typical border-area community, outwardly calm, yet seething with an explosiveness which might well erupt into bloodshed. Only the most skilled of writers could rise to such heights as did Sugrue.

What makes his story great? Many things. Let's begin with the first paragraph where, as elsewhere, repetition enhances drama: "you could taste it—taste the" and the repetition of "and." His birds and choirs don't merely sing, they "challenged the silence" (par. 2). He stole a trick from forums he no doubt had covered for an approach, "Let's examine the issues" (par. 9, 10). This apparently stimulated his news sources, certainly more so than the usual reporter questions posed with a block-on-the-shoulder attitude. Then Sugrue got out of the way and let his sources speak.

This story treats with understanding the prejudices, fears, and over-simplified solutions suggested. All of his sources come through as believable people. How better could you describe a slow-talking man with foot on an ash can other than a "leisurely like fellow" (par. 17)? And he put his finger on the basic concern—integrated schools may lead to intermarriage (par. 22, 23, 24). Sugrue returned to his basic "quiet on the surface but violence welling up" theme at the end.

Yes, this is the work of a master writer. It reflects great skill as a news gatherer, too; above all Sugrue observed keenly the whole of the community and sliced off a generous portion for us to savor.

By Francis A. Sugrue
New York Herald Tribune, Sept. 10, 1956

CLAY, Ky., Sept. 9—It was so still today in this sleepy little town in the western Kentucky mine fields that you could taste it—taste the dark, hidden tensions and the possible violence and the hint of evil things to come tomorrow morning if one Negro woman again insists on bringing her two young children to the elementary school in Clay.

Only the birds were in riot today, chirping under the blue skies as though they had never had a chance to sing before. Only the birds and choirs in the churches challenged the silence, but tomorrow the birds won't be heard and the churches will be empty if Mrs. James Gordon again drives into town to enroll her two children, James Henry, ten, and Teresa, eight, in the third grade. The people of Clay are united by one common rule—"no colored children are going to school with white children."

And on Friday they showed that they meant it when Mrs. Gordon first came to the school with her children and was turned back by a crowd of miners, farmers, and townspeople. No word was spoken. There was no need for words. There was an abundance of understanding between Mrs. Gordon, the Kentucky Negro, and her white Kentucky neighbors. Reporters and camera men came in later to find out what had happened, but they didn't stay too long because they were advised that "you better not let the grass grow under your feet, reporters." The photographers were given hard-as-steel advice that they had better pack their cameras and make tracks out of town.

Mrs. Francele H. Armstrong, editor of the Henderson *Gleaner and Journal,* wrote a story for the *Herald Tribune* describing how a man told her that a woman would "take care of her" and would "beat up my camera and me."

Warned to Stay Out

Clay became something of a newspaper man's no-man's-land where reporters were to be treated as aliens without passports.

When this reporter decided to go into Clay he was advised by others who had been there that it would be unpleasant—that it wouldn't be worth while.

And with this little warning ticking in his head he was a trifle apprehensive when he stepped out of the car and looked up and down the main street of Clay, a nice little town with television antennas reaching into the sky from neat little houses along the streets, every one with a car in its front yard. From each door along main street a veranda hung over the sidewalk to protect the people from the sun.

It was a wonderful blue-sky day, as pleasant as the sound of the name of Kentucky itself. But there was perspiration on the reporter's neck where the sun seemed to beat with a special meanness just for him. He looked up and down the red brick sidewalk and found four men sitting on a bench in front of a store that had a sign "Police Station and Clerk's Office" marked on the window. They were staring back at him. And there was but one thought in their eyes.

The Real Issues?

It was like a scene in a movie where Spencer Tracy, Gary Cooper, Alan Ladd and even Frank Sinatra are in a tough spot, but then Tracy knows jujitsu, Cooper is reputedly a handy guy with his fists and Alan Ladd is one of the quickest shots alive. And Frank Sinatra can sing. But this reporter had his last fight when he was twelve because, fortunately, he has never been challenged since then. There was a wayward tickling amusement in his mind. At so many forums, discussions and round-table conferences a man inevitably rises and says, "Now what are the real issues here? Let's examine them."

The reporter pictured himself going up to the men and saying just that—"What are the real issues here, let's examine them"—and watching the astonishment on their faces, their nostrils flaring out as they expressed their dislike for the stranger.

But they didn't react that way. They just looked at the red brick sidewalk. One of them, a neatly dressed man wearing a light summer shirt and a black-faced watch on his arm—and you could see that it was a strong arm—said:

"The issue is that the trouble is that everybody wants to mind everybody else's business. You came all the way from New York. What for? Because you're so nosy. The issue is that we don't want nigger children going to school with our white children. That's the issue."

Patience, Patience

He didn't have to say it. You could feel the real issue is what happens to one of these men physically when he thinks of a Negro child going to school with a white child. He feels a hot wind in his stomach, a shiver along his heart that may even go to the border of his soul, or deeper still, and may be a conviction so strong as his belief in God. It is difficult to describe this problem accurately when you look at it squarely—when you look at a Southerner's face who doesn't want colored children to go to school with his children.

The answer may only be patience, patience that may take longer than all the chapters in the Book of Job.

There was a man with an overgrowth of beard and a middle tooth missing and a red shirt and a pipe in his pocket. He said, "Don't you know those niggers don't want to go to school down here? They know they've never been any niggers right in this town. They all live outside of town. They know they shouldn't go to school here. That woman's getting a bundle of dollars for this and all the other niggers know it."

And a man in gray chinos spoke up. He had clear blue eyes and a friendly laugh. He said, "You know the other niggers in her community won't have anything to do with her for sending her children here, causing trouble. Her husband's going to stay home tomorrow and beat her up. The violence that happened up at the school was when one woman started tearing the hair of another woman because she let her children stay in school when the Negroes were coming."

A man with a cigarette in his mouth and a foot on an ash can, a leisurely like fellow, was the next to talk. "Heard you been having a little trouble up in New York," he said. "I've been reading something about kidnappings and throwing acid in people's face and all things like that." That's all he said.

Price of Peace

All the men agreed there wouldn't be any violence if they are allowed to handle this thing in their own way. No one would get hurt and "the National Guard had no business threatening to come in to protect the niggers if they wanted to go to school."

There will be no violence, of course, if they are allowed to handle it their own way, but the Negroes won't get to school either.

Down the street singing was coming from the General Baptist Church, so the reporter decided to drop in. They were singing "The Price of Redemption Is Paid." The part of the service known as the "recognition of visitors" had come. And the reporter sitting in the back pew was forced to stand up and give his name. And a member of the congregation gave him a fulsome welcome and said it was too bad there wasn't somebody at the door to welcome him in person.

When the service was over, a man who was obviously a respectable, God-fearing church-goer had this to say: "Reporters are not welcome here. The people here are tense. They'll be tense tomorrow if those colored people try to go to school. The colored people are equal before God, all right, but that doesn't mean they have to go to school together. We just don't want 'em to the same school. I'll pay three times the taxes to see that colored folks get good schools, but not together. There could be trouble if they force this thing. The storekeepers will close up shop and go out and help the towns-people keep them out."

Heart of the Problem

But another man in front of the church, a polite young man, put his finger on the heart of the problem. He is a man with young children and he said "God would not have made some people white and some people black if he wanted them to live together and intermarry. He wouldn't have done it. I'd just as soon send my children to a rundown, dilapidated school as to send them to a nice modern school if niggers are going to be in it. I'd be mad as all get out if my daughter came home with a colored fellow and said, 'This is my husband,' or my son came home with a colored girl and said, 'This is my wife.' Maybe they should be getting married. I don't know. But I don't think God meant it that way."

And that about summed it up. What the people fear is that going to school together will eventually lead to intermarriage.

After the service, the pastor, the Rev. M. L. Clark, was friendly. He said the townsfolk had been libeled by being called rioters by newspapers. His feeling about the colored situation was this: "God made the colored people and the white people equal. There's no doubt about that. I don't want to see colored people mistreated. I want to see them get a good education. I want to see them go to the best of schools. But I don't think it's time for them to go to school together down here. If we could be sure when they went to school together this would not lead to intermarriage, then it would be all right. But that day hasn't come. I do not believe intermarriage between whites and the colored people is a good thing."

He gave just one warning. He said he knew the people down in this section, and he knew that they could be led but couldn't be forced.

It was a beautiful peaceful day in Clay, but there was no poetry here because so many of the people were trying to hide a thing they feared—a little red ball of violence that might burst into bloodshed.

When the school bell rings in Clay tomorrow, it will toll for the Negro children only if they are protected by the National Guard and the state police. And it isn't being too trite to say it may also be tolling for all Americans.

A Human Explosion

Passions erupted several times as Negroes sought equal educational opportunities—at Clinton, Tenn.; Nashville, Tenn.; Sturgin, Ky.; New Orleans, La.; Oxford, Miss.; and Little Rock, Ark., to mention a few. Of these, Little Rock probably hit home hardest even though other disturbances were more destructive and bloodier. And probably the best-written "violence" story was Relman (Pat) Morin's Little Rock coverage for The Associated Press. It earned for him a second Pulitzer Prize, his first was awarded for his Korean War coverage.

Arkansas Governor Orval E. Faubus gave renewed hope to segregationists by announcing Sept. 2, 1957, he had stationed National Guard troops at Central High School to prevent integration. The National Guardsmen remained at the school from Sept. 2 to 20, when a federal court ordered Governor Faubus to withdraw them. They were replaced on Monday, Sept. 23, by a large crowd, whose leaders had announced their determination to keep Negro students out. Thus was the stage set for the disorders which Morin reported.

He literally seated his readers on the 50-yard line with his descriptions of the crowds, small groups, individuals. His deft reporting shows us how the crowd, enflamed by the tears, shouts, and actions of a few key individuals, became a howling, shrieking, violent mob. As much as anything, this is a study in mob psychology.

What is even more remarkable about this story is that Morin dictated it by telephone, describing the scene as it unfolded. Yet it was printed with virtually no editing.

By Relman Morin
The Associated Press, Sept. 23, 1957

LITTLE ROCK, Ark.—It was exactly like an explosion, a human explosion.

At 8:35 a.m., the people standing in front of the high school looked like the ones you see every day in a shopping center.

A pretty, sweet-faced woman with auburn hair and a jewel-green jacket. Another holding a white portable radio to her ear. "I'm getting the news of what's going on at the high school," she said. People laughed. A grey-haired man, tall and spare, leaned over the wooden barricade. "If they're coming," he said, quietly, "they'll be here soon." "They better," said another, "I got to get to work."

Ordinary people—mostly curious, you would have said—watching a high school on a bright blue-and-gold morning.

Fraction of Second

Five minutes later, at 8:40, they were a mob.

The terrifying spectacle of 200-odd individuals, suddenly welded together into a single body, took place in the barest fraction of a second. It was an explosion, savagery chain-reacting from person to person, fusing them into a white hot mass.

There are three glass windowed telephone booths across the street from the south end of the high school.

At 8:35, I was inside one of them, dictating.

I saw four Negroes coming down the center of the street, in twos. One was tall and big shouldered. One was tall and thin. The other two were short. The big man had a card in his hat and was carrying a Speed Graphic, a camera for taking news pictures.

Kick, Beat

A strange, animal growl rose from the crowd.

"Here come the Negroes."

Instantly, people turned their backs on the high school and ran toward the four men. They hesitated. Then they turned to run.

I saw the white men catch them on the sidewalk and the lawn of a home, a quarter-block away. There was a furious, struggling knot. You could see a man kicking at the big Negro. Then another jumped on his back and rode him to the ground, forearms deep in the Negro's throat.

They kicked him and beat him on the ground and they smashed his camera to splinters. The other three ran down the street with one white man chasing them. When the white man saw he was alone, he turned and fled back toward the crowd.

Nicely Dressed

Meanwhile, five policemen had rescued the big man.

I had just finished saying, "Police escorted the big man away—."

At that instant, a man shouted, "Look, the niggers are going in."

Directly across from me, three Negro boys and five girls were walking toward the side door at the south end of the school.

It was an unforgettable tableau.

They were carrying books. White bobby-sox, part of the high school uniform, glinted on the girls' ankles. They were all neatly dressed. The boys wore open-throat shirts and the girls ordinary frocks.

They weren't hurrying. They simply strolled across perhaps 15 yards from the sidewalk to the school steps. They glanced at the people and the police as though none of this concerned them.

Can Never Forget

You can never forget a scene like that.

Nor the one that followed.

Like a wave, the people who had run toward the four Negro men, now swept back toward the police and the barricades.

"Oh, God, the niggers are in the school," a man yelled.

A woman—the one with the auburn hair and green jacket—rushed up to him. Her face was working with fury now.

Her lips drew back in a snarl and she was screaming, "Did they go in?"

"The niggers are in the school," the man said.

"Oh, God," she said. She covered her face with her hands. Then she tore her hair, still screaming.

She looked exactly like the women who cluster

around a mine head when there has been an explosion and men are trapped below.

Billy Clubs Swinging

The tall, lean man jumped up on one of the barricades. He was holding on to the shoulders of others nearby.

"Who's going through?" he roared.

"We all are," the people shrieked.

They surged over and around the barricades, breaking for the police.

About a dozen policemen, in short-sleeved blue shirts, swinging billy clubs, were in front of them.

Men and women raced toward them and the policemen raised their clubs, moving this way and that as people tried to dodge around them.

A man went down, pole-axed when a policeman clubbed him.

Tears Streaming

Another, with crisp curly black hair, was quick as a rat. He dodged between two policemen and got as far as the schoolyard. There the others caught him.

With swift, professional skill, they pulled his coat half-way down his back, pinning his arms. In a flash they were hustling him back toward the barricades.

A burly, thick-bodied man wearing a construction worker's "hard hat" charged a policeman. Suddenly, he stopped and held both hands high above his head.

I couldn't see it, but I assume the officer jammed a pistol in his ribs.

Meanwhile, the women—the auburn haired one, the woman with the radio, and others—were swirling around the police commanding officers.

Tears were streaming down their faces. They acted completely distraught.

Pure Hysteria

It was pure hysteria.

And they kept crying, "The niggers are in our school. Oh, God, are you going to stand here and let the niggers stay in school?"

Then, swiftly, a line of cars filled with state troopers rolled toward the school from two directions. The flasher-signals on the tops of the cars were spurting red warnings.

The troopers, big, thin-waisted men in broad-brimmed hats, moved inside the barricades with the policemen.

In an instant, they had the crowd—not wholly under control—but well away from the school.

The roaring and howling went on, but it was futile now. Nobody tried to charge the lines again.

In a first-floor window, a high school boy kept a small camera pointed out toward the street. The upper floor windows were packed tightly with other students, watching.

Turn on Newsmen

Then the people—still wearing the savage, snarling mob's mask—turned on reporters and photographers. It was a gesture of frustration for the wild rage and hysteria that had galvanized them.

A boy leaped high in the air, caught a telephone wire leading from one of the booths to the main line, and swung up and down, trying to break it. The booth, with a reporter inside, teetered wide and came close to falling over.

Francis Miller, a *Life* magazine photographer, was coming out of the crowd. His arms were filled with camera equipment. He never had a chance to defend himself.

A man rushed toward him, and crashed his fist full in Miller's face. He went down, blood pouring from his mouth.

In the next few minutes, they beat up four others. They had said earlier, "We ought to wipe up the street with these Yankee reporters."

Now, with no one else to attack, they started.

I passed through the milling, swirling crowd, trying not to walk too fast, nor too slow. Nothing happened.

When I looked back from a block away, it was relatively quiet.

It was an explosion.

How The Night Exploded Into Terror

"The City of Birmingham has reached an accord with its own conscience," three Negro leaders said in announcing a four-point racial truce in that Alabama city. Peace came after five weeks of Negro demonstrations, resulting in more than 2,200 Negro arrests. Police had resorted to fire hoses and dogs to control the unrest.

The truce, negotiated with white business leaders, was announced Friday, May 11, 1963, amid fanfare as a great interracial victory. Then came Saturday night, May 12. All hell broke loose after white segregationists bombed a Negro human rights leader's home and a Negro motel. But let's let Charles Portis of the New York *Herald Tribune* Service tell it.

As you read his crisp, tightly-written story note these strengths: (1) the story moves chronologically from the preliminaries through the climax and to the "all quiet," (2) simple, forceful language communicates clearly, (3) sentences and paragraphs are pointedly brief, (4) Portis, rather than blaming anyone, recounted the event unemotionally so the reader understands fully. On the latter point, see how he clearly portrayed the role of the state police system without resorting to name calling (par. 33–40, 61–65, and 67–69).

By Charles Portis
New York Herald Tribune Service, May 13, 1963

BIRMINGHAM, Ala.—It was a hot night. Down in the Negro section of town, around the A. C. Gaston Motel, the beer joints and barbecue stands were doing a good Saturday night business.

Within a three-block area more than 1,000 Negroes were milling about.

Over at Bessemer, 12 miles away, the Ku Klux Klan was having an outdoor rally in the flickering light of two flaming, 25-foot crosses.

On hand were 200 hooded men, including the imperial wizard himself and a couple grand dragons and about 900 Klan supporters in mufti.

There were a lot of bugs in the air, too, knocking their brains out against the crosses and falling into open collars.

For a month, through all the Negro demonstrations here, little was heard from the tough white element in the Birmingham area—very likely, the toughest in the South.

Everyone wondered why.

The explosion came Saturday night, literally.

Earlier in the day, the Rev. Wyatt Walker, Dr. Martin Luther King's executive secretary, asked the police to place a watch on the Gaston Motel because some white men had been observed "casing it."

At 7:30 p.m., a call came through the motel switchboard, warning that the motel would be bombed that night. It was a straight tip.

At 11:32 p.m., some night riders tossed two bombs from a car onto the front porch of the Rev. A. D. King's home in the suburb of Ensley. The front half of the house was ripped apart, but no one was injured.

Mr. King is Martin Luther King's brother.

The night riders then sped four miles across town to the motel headquarters for the Negro leaders, and threw another bomb.

It blasted a four-foot hole through the brick wall of one of the bedroom units. Three Negro women inside were sent tumbling—including one about 80 years old—but they were not seriously injured.

That did it.

The Negroes in the area, many of them just leaving the beer joints at midnight closing, went into a frenzy of brick-throwing, knifing, burning and rioting that took four hours to stop.

It was the worst night of terror in the South since the battle of Ole Miss last fall. More than 25 persons were injured and property damage was estimated at many thousands of dollars.

A Dull Whoomp

Reporters staying at the Tutwiler Hotel, four blocks away from the Negro motel, heard the midnight explosion—a dull whoomp—and got there a few minutes later.

Only about 35 city policemen were on the scene and they were standing in a small perimeter, arms over their heads, catching a volley of rocks and bottles from a Negro mob that was cursing and closing in on them.

Mr. Walker was catching it from them, too, as he moved about, pleading for calm.

"Please, please. Move back. Throwing rocks won't help," he said. "This is no good. Please go home. It does no good to lose your heads."

"Tell it to (Police Commissioner) Bull Connor," they shouted back to him, "This is what non-violence gets you."

Some of the rioters were attacking the police cars, smashing the windows with chunks of cinder blocks and cutting the tires with knives.

One group kicked over a motorcycle and set it afire. Some others got around a paddywagon and tried to upset it but it was too heavy, so they just batted the windows in.

Patrolman J. N. Spivey found himself alone and encircled. Someone stabbed him in the shoulder and back.

Capt. Glenn Evans and a deputy sheriff managed to pull him free. They were kicked and punched in doing it.

Help arrived soon in the form of a Negro civil defense unit with helmets and billy clubs, and more white police. These emergency Negro officers took just as much abuse and pummelling as the whites.

The city's armored car came shortly before 1 a.m. Its menacing appearance provoked the mob anew.

"Let's get the tank," they yelled. "Bull, you — —, come on out of there."

The safety commissioner was not in the "tank" though this idea persisted throughout the night. No one seems to know where he was.

The little white riot vehicle roared back and forth under a hail of rocks to scatter the crowd, and it mounted the sidewalk once and made a headlong pass down it, sending the reporters diving for the dirt.

Two blocks away, in a quiet zone, a gang of white boys threw rocks and smashed the windows of Negro ambulances on their way to the motel. Police removed them from the scene early, though.

At 1:10 a.m. Col. Al Lingo, director of the Alabama Highway Patrol, arrived, itching for action.

He and a lieutenant sprang from their car with 12-gauge pump shotguns at the ready, and moved toward the crowd.

"I'll stop those — —," he said.

"Wait, wait a minute now," said Birmingham Police Chief Jamie Moore, intercepting him. "You're just going to get somebody killed with those guns."

"I damn sure will if I have to," said Lingo.

"I wish you'd get back in the car. I'd appreciate it."

"I'm not about to leave, Gov. Wallace sent me here."

He finally did go back to the car, jabbing a couple of Negroes with his gun on the way, but was to be heard from again before the night was over.

The 16th St. Baptist Church, the starting point of all the recent demonstrations, is a block away from the motel. For a while it was thought the church was burning, but it turned out to be a taxicab that had been turned over and set afire in front of the church.

The Rev. A. D. King arrived at 1:45 a.m. and joined Mr. Walker and a number of other Negro leaders in trying to quell the riot.

He climbed atop a parked car in the motel courtyard and gathered an audience of about 300 Negroes.

"We have been taught by our religion that we do not have to return evil for evil," he told them. "I must appeal to you to refuse any acts of retaliation for any acts of violence. . . We're not mad with a soul . . . my wife and five children are all right. Thank God we're all well and safe."

'We Shall Overcome'

As he spoke and prayed, and as the gathering sang, "We Shall Overcome," a white grocery store was burning on the corner a block away.

Firemen trying to put it out were undergoing a barrage of rocks from the mob. After a few minutes they had to retreat and let the fire go.

They pulled away so fast that they had to leave a hose in the street. It lay there, burning strangely in the no-man's-land.

At 2:30 a.m., another grocery store directly across the street blazed up. Then two frame houses on either side of the store caught fire, then a third, a two-story house. The firemen could not get in because of the rocks and it appeared the whole block would go.

"Let the whole . . . city burn, I don't give a damn," said one of the rioters.

"We have just spoken with the President's press secretary, Andrew Hatcher, and he asked you to return to your homes," announced one of the Negro leaders. "Please go to your homes. This is no answer."

At 3:05 a.m., with a police guard of about 75 men, the firemen returned to the blazing houses with two trucks and went to work again.

The rocks and bricks were still flying, but a line of Negro leaders kept the rioters out of throwing range of the firefighters.

In this scrap, Police Inspector William Haley caught a brick on the forehead which gave him a severe cut. He continued to work, blood running down his face into his eyes, calling, "Get back, get back, you must get back."

But after a time he became so weak he had to be carried away.

Patrolman Halted

This infuriated the city policemen standing nearby and one of them started toward the Negroes with a shotgun.

When Mr. King tried to stop him, he knocked the minister out of the way with his gun.

But a police lieutenant grabbed the angry patrolman and ordered him back. A few minutes later another policeman advanced on the mob, and sighted his pistol across his left arm.

Again the lieutenant stepped in and stopped him.

By this time there was only a small pocket of rioters left, young men in their teens and twenties, confined to 15th St. between 6th and 7th Avs.

This group set fire to yet another grocery store. The blaze was stopped by Negro Civil Defense workers.

It was pretty much all over at 3:40 a.m. when the state troopers began clubbing Negroes sitting on their porches. They had been sitting there all along, taking no part in the fight, just watching.

"Get in the house, damn it, get, get," shouted the troopers, punching and pounding them with their nightsticks.

And so the battle ended with the state policemen,

who had played only a very minor role in the acutal quelling of the riot, rapping old Negro men in rocking chairs.

Calls Chief 'Boy Scout'

Col. Lingo and his men had been chafing all week at the moderation and restraint of Chief Moore and his city police.

"Moore is a——Boy Scout," said Col. Lingo.

When daylight began to break at 4 a.m., there were no Negroes in sight.

The only sound to be heard was the screaming of sirens and more and more state troopers poured into the city, with their shotguns and carbines with fixed bayonets.

The police, about 1,000 of them, cordoned off a 3-by-7-block area around the motel, allowing no one to leave or enter the area.

Shortly before 6 a.m. a state police sound vehicle cruised about downtown warning individual Negroes to "Get off the Goddamn streets, get."

But someone put a stop to that. After all, it was Sunday and Mother's Day and there were the church-goers to think about.

After that the city was deathly silent. No one was seen on the streets for several hours—until church time.

It was a sparkling morning, and around the post office the air was fragrant with magnolia blossoms.

PART 3 ──────────── ★★★

Man Against the Elements—
NATURAL DISASTERS

ADVERSITY OFTEN BRINGS out the best or worst in man. He may find his greatest humanitarian self or sink abysmally, because law and order often are overburdened, if not disrupted, by nature on the rampage.

Nothing short of war can duplicate the bewilderingly hopelessness of weather gone berserk. Few other events call forth such team effort to help the suffering, protect a community's property, quell looting. Communicating all of this and casualties and damage requires skillful reporting and writing. Just as adversity brings out the best in most people, it often inspires reporters to give their all. It is little wonder then that some of the most powerful of all writing typically grows out of covering natural disasters.

Udall Dies In Its Sleep

A tornado the night of May 25, 1955, all but obliterated Udall, Kan. So electric was Ted Thackrey's relatively brief article, dictated from a telephone booth at the scene, that Udall became known nationally as the little Kansas prairie town that "died in its sleep." Thackrey fortified his powerful lead with a second paragraph only slightly less vivid. He wisely repeated this "town that was" theme (par. 5, 7, 9).

Return to the third paragraph where the last two brief sentences, the second almost as if an afterthought, heighten the drama. His simile in which he compared the water tank to a paper cup (par. 8) pictures graphically the wind's incomprehensible power. This story doesn't run out of steam. It continues to deliver through the final sentence, which, incidentally, lets us share the surprise of those who "stumbled on" the debris that once was Udall. Final toll: 87 dead, 143 injured in a town of some 500 population.

By Ted Thackrey
International News Service, May 26, 1955

UDALL, Kan.—This quiet prairie town died in its sleep last night.

A tornado whooshed through it like a biblical sword of wrath. In less than a minute, 60 years of growing was cut down to the sod.

Scott Mathews, 25, the town barber, was sleeping in a bunk at the rear of his shop. He can't be found. Neither can the shop.

George McGregor and his wife were sleeping in the rear of the main street cafe they ran. Their cafe is gone, but they managed to escape with their lives.

Only Shells Remain

Their luck was remarkable. All homes were shredded to splinters. Only the shells of stores and office buildings stand above the hip-level mess of kindling strewn across the area where Udall used to stand.

Fifty-six bodies were dragged from the debris. Possibly a dozen more bodies may be found. And from a population of 500 persons, no one has been found who was not injured in some way. Everyone has been taken to neighboring communities.

Aside from search crews, only the missing dead remain in Udall—truly a ghost town.

The funnel of smashing winds knocked out electric wiring and telephone service. A water tank which held the town's water supply high atop a skeletal steel tower was twisted inside out like a paper cup.

Few Saw Twister

The time of the catastrophe was set by the town's lone telephone operator. Operators along the circuit in other towns lost contact with her at 10:29 p.m. Her body was located at dawn.

Few residents can be found who actually saw the twister hit. Motorists stumbled on the horror when they found flat darkness where Udall should have been.

Tornado Resembles A-Bomb

The nation "watched" the funnel of a devastating tornado dance its death-dealing fandango over Dallas April 2, 1957. We saw through the observing eyes of Gladwin Hill, *The New York Times* correspondent, in Dallas to cover a heated senatorial election.

Simply, methodically, Hill organized his story into two chronological narratives (par. 1–8, 10–end). Through his eyes we see the tornado as "a huge vacuum cleaner" (par. 4) and "a giant's leg, pulling the great black cloud behind it" (par. 14). Debris looked like "some gigantic flock of birds" (par. 6), more specifically, panels careened "aloft like prehistoric pterodactyls" (par. 7).

Phrasing throughout is descriptively rich, including "fleeting festoons of eerie white flashes" (par. 8), the tornado "seemed to stride inexorably across the countryside" (par. 14).

Hill drew heavily on simile and personification, so much so the tornado becomes a living, breathing monster, rife with disagreeable personality traits.

By Gladwin Hill
The New York Times, April 3, 1957

DALLAS, Tex., April 3—I watched a tornado rip across this city of 700,000 people today.

For nearly a half hour the black, towering whirlwind moved with nerve-wracking deliberation from the southwest outskirts of the metropolis to its northeastern section.

It was a massive column of destruction, suggestive in its ferocity of an atomic bomb.

As it moved, its up-rushing, spiralling shaft of air smashed structures and sucked up the debris like a huge vacuum cleaner.

Near the top of the column, the debris was whirled outward. Roofs and sides of buildings spun crazily through the air.

For a moment the debris would be in small pieces, looking as if the whirlwind had stirred up some gigantic flock of birds, or released a storm of clay pigeons.

A moment later, the tornado would demolish some big structure, sending great panels careening aloft like prehistoric pterodactyls.

Hits Power Lines

Intermittently, the tornado would hit electric lines causing fleeting festoons of eerie white flashes from short circuits.

I watched the holocaust from the third floor of The Dallas Morning News Building in downtown Dallas, which the tornado circuited, by a margin of only a mile or two.

Shortly before 4 p.m. reports reached the paper's news room of nascent tornadoes about 30 miles away.

All we could see on the horizon was a great black cloud to the southwest, seemingly only a few thousand feet above the ground.

But about 4:15 p.m. as the cloud moved closer, the characteristic funnel-shaped tail, reaching all the way to the ground, began forming.

It would solidify for a few moments, then dissolve, then re-form, as if the tornado were struggling to achieve full growth and accomplish destruction.

Observers Hold Breath

As hundreds of observers in the building held their breaths, the towering black spout—probably no more than a few hundred feet wide—seemed to stride inexorably across the countryside, like a giant's leg, pulling the great black cloud behind it.

Its bursts of destruction alternated between flurries of small debris, flashes of light and fleeting moments of large-scale destruction.

It took about 30 minutes for it gradually to swing

around, over the southwestern suburbs, through West Dallas, finally seeming to dissipate over the northwestern outskirts of the city.

For a number of minutes it threatened to swing into the heart of the downtown area. Observers gritted their teeth as an intermittent procession of cars and trucks, apparently oblivious to the overhanging danger, continued to course along several main thoroughfares in its path.

As the tornado slowly disappeared, somebody exclaimed: "That must have gone right over my house" —and dashed for a telephone.

In the wake of the monstrous visitation, the city lapsed into a brief unfamiliar silence. It was soon broken by the screech of sirens.

Audrey's Awful Toll

Coverage of a multi-facet weather disaster often requires team reporting. True, one man may fit the pieces together, but the pieces are provided by possibly a dozen or more reporters. Thus was written *The* (New Orleans) *Times-Picayune* major story on hurricane Audrey and its aftermath.

Study this story for its broad scope—deft presentation of conditions at various localities, reports of dead and injured, care of refugees, and property damage at key locales. All was tied into a story bundle which flows smoothly. Much can be learned from this polished lead with its wise word choice and tight editing.

The (New Orleans) Times-Picayune, June 29, 1957

Grim misery cloaked the coastland of Southwest Louisiana Friday as the haggard living searched for the dead and dying left by a monster tidal wave, the stepchild of hurricane Audrey.

Survivors of the tragedies of Cameron, Pecan Island, Creole, Black Bayou, Grand Cheniere and Holly Beach mourned their dead. The toll in that area was estimated at 100 Friday night by Maj. Gen. Raymond F. Hufft, state director of civil defense, a downward revision from the 150 he predicted earlier. Hundreds more were missing.

While the survivors mourned, a massive search and rescue operation moved into action, seeking to save the hundreds of victims known to be still in the area of death and destruction.

Coast Guard boats probed into the flooded coast and airplanes droned over the splintered houses to seek out survivors. Some were seen still clinging to the debris, waving desperately for aid. Helicopters dipped down to pull many to safety. The pilots of other types of aircraft, unable to land, flew helplessly on.

Destruction Almost Complete

Destruction in the area from Cameron to Pecan Island is almost total, reports indicated. Some pilots said the devastation is "indescribable."

"There probably is not one in 25 homes that once were there still standing," one said. "The only way it is apparent that homes had been there are the pillars and sometimes a concrete slab."

Coast Guard and private boats, by Friday afternoon, had made the tortuous route from Lake Charles to the Cameron area and back with loads of survivors. These were shuttled by bus from the landing to the already overflowing shelters. More than 20,000 persons are already being cared for by volunteers.

And at Grand Cheniere, the Coast Guard sent its boats scudding through the debris to begin rescue operations. The community, some 20 miles east of Cameron, was "solidly hit" and completely flooded, a spokesman said.

Three of the four occupants of a light plane thought crashed in the Grand Cheniere area were found by an Air Force helicopter pilot. All the victims of the crash were Negroes. Three bodies were found at the scene by the helicopter pilot, who said he believed a fourth was under the wreckage.

Need Food, Water

Some 70 to 80 persons stranded along farm roads in the Grand Cheniere area were reported "in dire need of food and water" by a Coast Guard pilot.

And a Coast Guard amphibious pilot advised headquarters in New Orleans that between 200 and 300 persons were scattered in small groups of 10 to 30 between Grand Cheniere and Creole.

Helicopters and a fleet of boats were dispatched to the area.

Some 350 survivors evacuated Pecan Island Friday after medical and parish authorities warned of a possible outbreak of disease.

Irby Herbert, Vermilian parish clerk of court and parish Red Cross chairman, said 116 persons were off the island by mid-afternoon and the remainder was expected to be gone by nightfall.

Calasier parish Civil Defense headquarters said at 4:45 p.m. that 750 to 1,000 persons are homeless in the Black Bayou area. They were trapped on rooftops and high ground without food or water.

Meanwhile, the remnants of the killer hurricane had torn through North Louisiana, Mississippi, Tennessee and were sending winds and sheets of rain northeastward into the Ohio Valley Friday night.

At the White House in Washington, President Eisenhower said he is dispatching Val Peterson, former chief of the federal Civil Defense Administration, to the hard-hit Cameron area.

Rescuers Move In

As the first shocking reports of terror and tragedy trickled in from the stricken area, the organized force of relief and rescue workers moved in to begin operations.

Some of the rescue teams reaching Cameron said that bodies were found floating in debris miles from the ravaged town. The area is accessible only by helicopter and boat. Roads were washed out.

Refugees began to stream into Lake Charles from the hardest hit areas. Thousands of evacuees already packed the rescue shelters set up there by the Red Cross. The tattered, distraught and bewildered crowd made a pathetic picture.

No one could estimate the number injured in the storm.

Lake Charles Mayor Sidney Gray said 25 to 30 ambulances were standing by along with state-owned and privately-owned vehicles, including wagons, to bring people into the city as they came in by boat from Cameron.

Damage in Millions

Oil companies whose rigs in the Gulf were destroyed by the gale said an estimate of $15,000,000 in damage would be conservative.

And Sheriff Jack Moss at Abbeville, just north of Pecan Island, said helicoptor pilots saw no trace of a herd of Brahman-bred cattle worth "millions."

Coast Guard planes from Galveston, Tex., flew over Cameron and said the town was in "shambles, inundated and showing evidence of tremendous destruction." One pilot said oil and gas wells in the area are damaged and "bubbling under water."

Texas National Guard units were moving 10,000 cots and 10,000 blankets into Lake Charles to assist the 400 Red Cross officials helping the refugees. Lawmen from cities along the Texas-Louisiana state line moved in to give aid.

The Red Cross, which sheltered 19,000 people Thursday night, said it is prepared to stay "several weeks" to assist the injured and help family rehabilitation.

President Acts

President Eisenhower ordered Civil Defense workers into the area and said full resources of military establishments in the vicinity have been made available for rescue work.

Meanwhile, helicopters and seaplanes were winging toward Cameron parish from outlying areas. Seven helicopters from Fort Sam Houston, Tex., another from Houston, Tex., and two seaplanes from a Texas oil company were already doing rescue and damage survey work in the flooded area.

Police in Orange, Tex., said they have asked for 12 more helicopters from a training school in San Marcos, Tex.

Eleven ambulances from the Orange area were dispatched to the Sulphur, La., police station to bring back injured.

Scores of boats, military and private, churned through canals and lakes en route to the devastated area.

The widespread operation had the makings of being the biggest rescue endeavor since the Galveston storm of 1900 which took 5,000 or more lives.

Refugees Tell of Tragedy

In Lake Charles, accounts of tragedy were being told and retold by refugees who escaped death in the hurricane flood.

One elderly woman, mumbling as she counted on her fingers, said she lost "all six of my children."

Mrs. Arvin Primeaux and her 28-year-old nephew chopped through the roof of their home and clung to bits of floating debris before he finally slipped beneath the water.

Four victims at Pelican Island were the small children of Stephen Broussard, 40-year-old oil worker.

He said he and his wife and seven children were swept across a 10-mile wide lake clinging to pieces of their smashed home. The dead children ranged in age from nine months to three and a half years.

Deputy Sheriff D. P. Vincent, arriving in Lake Charles with other bedraggled survivors at Cameron, said: "It's hard to tell how many died. So many families talk of losing families of six or nine."

Abel LaBlanc, whose two children are missing, said a 15-foot tidal wave hit their home.

Pecan Island Damage Heavy

A survivor from Pecan Island said "everything was washed away and just floated around." Tides were reported at seven to eight feet and still getting higher.

Deputy Sheriff Al Moss of Vermilion parish said about 150 persons stayed in the Pecan Island area "and we're afraid 85 per cent of them are lost."

Mrs. Olga Corner, 46, an island storekeeper, estimated the height of the tidal wave at 10 to 15 feet.

Residents said the island had about 90 houses and about 10 of them were swept a mile into the marshlands toward White Lake by the hurricane. Those remaining standing were splattered with mud and sea slime.

Jesse Bourgue, 60, said 27 persons huddled in his wooden house as it took the horrifying trip. He said the occupants clung to the attic while the water lapped at the ceiling under their feet. When the storm subsided, he said, two boys swam back through the marshlands to report all were safe.

About 100 islanders took refuge in an old wooden frame high school and a two-story gymnasium— havens in previous storms.

Bodies of dead cattle, horses and wild animals litter long stretches of marshland and pose a major health problem.

(The final 15 paragraphs were deleted)

Story Of A Flood

One problem which plagues newsmen arises from fragmenting a long-span news event into daily segments. John W. Colt, then news editor of *The Kansas City Star*, realizing this wrote a chronological re-cap on one of the most damaging floods ever to inundate a metropolitan area. This flood, which struck in July, 1951, claimed 41 lives, made 200,000 homeless, and caused $1,000,000,000 in property damage. It is believed to be the most severe in the history of the United States.

Unfortunately, the story is so long (the story and two maps filled a newspaper page) it could not be printed in its entirety. Even so, enough appears here to show how Colt built his story gradually from a slow, folksy beginning to a throbbing climax, a true literary crescendo. Lavish background enriches the story. Further, Colt updated the story by urging that a solution be sought to the Kansas-Missouri recurrent floods.

By John W. Colt
News Editor of The Kansas City Star, July 22, 1951

The folks in Kansas began to believe in June that the month had been traded for April, judging by the rain.

There was a lot of talk about damage to the wheat and the harvest was delayed; little creeks and rivers were running bankfull by June 20.

Then the deluge hit in the last days of the month and in the first days of July.

Rain reports showed some places in the eastern half of the state as getting five to ten inches in 12-

hour periods. The Eastern Kansas rivers, the Big Blue, the Solomon, the Saline, the Smoky Hill, the Delaware, the Republican, began flooding the lowlands. All of these are in the basin of the Kaw, the largest river in Kansas, but wadable most of the year. The Big Blue meets the Kaw at Manhattan, 130 miles west of Kansas City, and there the two rivers collided, drowning out transcontinental highway No. 40 and backing up into several blocks of the business district of the college town.

Started All Over Again

The Fourth of July was bright and clear and there was hope the strange rains were over. The next day they started again, all over the Kaw watershed, steady drumming downpours, day and night.

Rain beat the ripened wheat into the ground. No one had ever seen anything like it.

There was talk about building an ark because in most places it actually had rained forty days and forty nights.

In those forty days some areas had received a year's normal rainfall.

Manhattan had a real flood; water up to the second floor of stores on the main street. Seventy city blocks flooded.

An army officer was electrocuted when he stumbled in the water and fell against a traffic light pole on a main street.

About 4,000 persons had water in their homes and a lot of them fled to College Hill, the high spot on the campus of Kansas State College.

A Kansas Trouble

Kansas City sympathized with Manhattan, but it was 130 miles away, and the flood seemed somewhat remote. Kansas was always having trouble with floods, droughts, tornadoes, or something. Anyway, some of the people in Manhattan had joined with the farmers in the valley above the town to block for years the building of a giant water-impounding reservoir on the Big Blue, which army engineers called on their blueprints Tuttle Creek dam, and said would hold enough floodwater to make the Kaw not so dangerous. . . .

Then the Kaw flood hit the state capital, Topeka,

sixty miles nearer Kansas City. It spread widely over lowlands, breaking or infiltrating strong, high dikes. Twenty thousand persons fled this flood.

And still it rained.

Lawrence, seat of the state university and only forty-eight miles west of Kansas City, was next on the Kaw's timetable of destruction. A smaller town, only 2,000 fled the flood. But it was called the worst since 1903, maybe since 1844.

Going Up and Up

The Kaw at Kansas City was rising fast. It comes in straight from the west, rolling in a great half circle between two great industrial districts in Kansas City, Kansas, those of Armourdale and Argentine, then makes a broad curve where it hits Missouri state line and flows almost directly north into the big Missouri river as it comes down south from Nebraska. The place where the Kaw curves laps the richest industrial district of Kansas City, Mo., known as the Central Industrial district. Along its great circle lie the giant packing plants, the soap plants, the acres and acres of stockyards, the flour mills, the grain elevators, where the wealth of the Middle West is stored and processed.

Just north of the confluence of the Missouri and the Kaw is a relatively new factory area, Fairfax, mostly devoted to heavy industry with the Phillips refinery and 53 million gallons of oil and gasoline in a tank farm; the giant General Motors assembly plant, which rivals Detroit; the new, 4-block long Sunshine Biscuit plant, and a hundred other manufacturing concerns. It has its own airport, with 8,000-foot runways, and the world maintenance base for Trans World Airline, a hangar a quarter mile square.

Five Great Districts

Just across the Missouri to the east is Kansas City's Municipal airport, five minutes from downtown hotels. And east and north of the airport is the North Kansas City industrial district, which rivals Fairfax. These five industrial areas are crosshatched by hundreds of miles of rail tracks as all transportation from the west and north funnels in.

That was the setting for disaster.

All this was protected by dikes 35½ feet high, equipped with floodgates at every creek flowing into the Kaw and the Missouri. They were proud dikes, rip-rapped with acres of stone on the river sides and topped by an 8-foot flood wall of reinforced concrete three feet thick on the Missouri banks of both rivers. They had been built through the years to cope with a flood five feet higher than the one which devastated the valleys of Kansas City in 1903.

Kansas City Not Worried—Yet

But even with the bad actions of the Kaw at Manhattan, Topeka and Lawrence, most Kansas Citians weren't too worried. The dikes had held back the flooding rivers more than forty years and many millions had gone into them. Of course the army engineers and various flood committees had been dinning the refrain that dikes could not be sufficient; that impounding the water behind big dams in the watershed was the only system which would work under all circumstances.

The Kansas farmer regarded this as mainly "city talk" and his voice was strong enough in Congress to impede a dam program in the Kansas basin. If the money was going to be spent he was for soil conservation type of flood control where the water was caught on the farms by terracing and ponds and little lakes.

It was farm against city and the city didn't want to make the farmer too mad because he was its best customer.

By the first of last week the Kaw and the Missouri both were bankfull at Kansas City. There had been a lot of rain up north in the Missouri basin, too. The rivers were bankfull but that was minor, since they hadn't yet started to crawl up the dikes. And then the crest started moving down the Kaw from Lawrence. By July 11 it had begun to go over the low farm levees fifteen miles west of Kansas City, Kansas. A small bridge or two washed out. Army engineers and hydrologists became truly alarmed.

Careful calculations showed the Kaw crest was carrying an astounding volume, 50 per cent more water than came down in the flood of 1903. The Kaw moved then at 260,000 square feet a second. It was moving now at more than 500,000 second feet. Even the big flood of all time in 1844 moved only 360,000 second feet.

Still it was argued that the vast flooding of the upper valley and the fact that the Missouri was many feet lower than in 1903 might allow the dikes to compress the flood into a nondestructive force when it hit Kansas City.

July 12 the vanguard of the flood hit the Kansas City, Kansas, chute. It rose six inches an hour until it was racing along two or three feet below the top of the dikes, up where no water ever had been before, and still rising. The piers of the nineteen bridges carrying rail and motor traffic across the Kaw began to take an awful battering from driftwood, from whole farmhouses which had been swept away above.

Hundreds of volunteer and paid workers were rushed to the levees to pile sandbags on weak spots. Rock trucks dumped tons of stone at points where cutting was observed.

The Kaw Finally Lets Go

The Kaw still rose. July 12 the battle of man against river was at its height. The worst weak spot seemed on the south bank, the Argentine side. Shortly before midnight the workers were forced to flee near the Old Southern bridge where the dike long had needed strengthening, a project for which a contract had been let. The Kaw was coming over and through the levee. It poured tons of water in a gush down over the dike into Argentine. Two thousand residents fled to the bluffs, some with the wall of water only a few hundred yards behind them. The vast Sinclair oil refinery, the Santa Fe installations, including a new hump yard, scores of diesel locomotives, countless freight cars, a 50-million-dollar investment by the Santa Fe alone, went under water.

The Whistles Wail

And if the river would top the Argentine dikes, was there any reason to believe it would stay out of Armourdale, across to the north and east? Officials decided there was none. At 10:20 p.m. wailing factory whistles, speeding police cars with sirens screaming, gave the prearranged signal to evacuate by midnight. Twelve thousand persons took what belongings they could in motor cars and trucks and drove for high ground to the north over streets and viaducts clogged with traffic.

Most of these persons were workers in the packing plants and soap factories, and they knew that their jobs would be gone, too, before dawn. Shelters were set up in churches, schools, all public buildings in the dry northern part of Kansas City, Kansas.

At 5:20 a.m. the tidal wave of the Kaw started over the Armourdale dikes at the West Kansas Avenue bridge. The dike did not break. There was just too much water. Soon the Kaw was pouring over all along the levee, a 4-mile stretch. It cascaded down the other side of the levee and soon was fifteen to thirty feet deep all over Armourdale—six square miles. The Kaw had gone up clear over the Kaw drainage district gauge, which measures only 40 feet. Another gauge indicated the height at 50.4 feet and this was translated to mean a height of 43.4 feet for the drainage district, or nearly eight feet over the dikes. . . .

Rescue boats set out to pick late stayers off roofs and out of trees. Skeleton crews had stayed in big plants. They welcomed the boats from roofs, fire escapes and building ledges. Hundreds were rescued by noon.

When it became light enough to see it, the Kaw stretched from Argentine bluff to Armourdale bluff, and only the tops of the taller houses, big trees, grain elevators and the upper stories of the industrial plants were visible.

The concrete flood wall running along the Missouri side of the broad curve of the Kaw still protected the central industrial district and its stockyards, with thousands of cattle, hogs and sheep in the pens; the Columbian Steel tank company, which boasts it builds tanks for the world (some of the employees used smaller ones to float to safety); 150 other plants and industries, and all the complexity of rail yards, switch tracks, docks and buildings which make up a great city's modern production center.

In it also was the Turkey Creek pumping station which supplied more than half the water for Kansas

City. There, too, was the sprawling American Royal Building where the stock exhibitions and horse shows yearly draw people from all the Southwest.

Mayor Gets Up Early

The Mayor of Kansas City, William E. Kemp, was up early that morning of Friday, July 13. The rain had stopped. He had been assured by Army engineers that the central industrial district was safe. An airline had arranged to take him, with the engineers, on an aerial survey of the Kaw. When they boarded the plane, the river still was below the concrete dike tops.

When they came back over the city, 45 minutes later, the central industrial district had been merged with the sea that was Armourdale and Argentine. The Kaw first slashed through a sandbag wall where the Santa Fe Railroad cut the concrete barrier on its normal level. Then the Kaw simply rolled over the top of the wall clear to its juncture with the Missouri. It sent a wall of water three feet high, at 15 miles an hour, to the big bluff on the east; old Quality Hill.

Workers who had formed skeleton maintenance crews in the industries fled to viaducts in motor cars and trucks.

There was no time to save anything.

The Turkey Creek pumping engines were snuffed out as the engineers took to boats at the last minute. The havoc was complete. Water stopped coming from faucets on the high spots all over Kansas City. But no person died.

Hogs as Victims

Six thousand hogs at the garbage disposal plant were the first victims of the flood, and died or were swept out into the river channel, many of them still swimming as they disappeared. Most of the cattle and sheep in the stockyards had been herded into the overhead chutes by which they are customarily moved from one part of the yard to another and were saved. Cowboys rode their horses through the deepening water to safety. . . .

That would seem to be enough disaster for Kansas City in one day, but it was far from the end. Stretching from the Kaw Valley into the heart of Kansas City is low lying Southwest boulevard, and the waters soon made it a canal along its western length and almost to the vicinity of Kansas City's big Union station, where seep water halted electric generators in the sub-basement.

A 6,000-gallon oil tank, partly filled with diesel fuel, had been torn loose somewhere in the vicinity and floated down the boulevard with the current. Only a few blocks from the downtown district it struck a fallen high tension wire and exploded, spewing burning oil on the waters.

It was just at this point that the bulk stations of Phillips Petroleum company and Socony-Vacuum Oil company are located for rapid city delivery. Both had hundreds of thousands of gallons of all types of fuel in steel tanks. And other similar installations are grouped there within a five-block area. The burning oil first fired the Phillips tanks and they went up with a roar which rocked downtown buildings.

The Socony-Vacuum office building and tanks joined in flames. Clouds of black smoke rose thousands of feet and the flood in a 4-block-square area was turned to a sea of fire.

It was congested with buildings and stores which were later engulfed. . . .

Oil Tanks Explode

Firemen, working in boats, pumped the flood waters against the flames, with little effect. An 8-block area, including lumber valued at 2 million dollars in the Schutte yard, finally was aflame. Dozens of oil tanks in the vicinity exploded like a chain reaction in the five days before the fire finally burned out Tuesday.

The tanks ranged in size from 10,000-gallon naphtha containers to 500,000-gallon fuel oil reservoirs.

The loss, which has not been calculated accurately yet, will run close to 10 million dollars.

More than twenty firemen and volunteer fighters were burned and injured.

So on that black Friday, the 13th, Kansas City faced its greatest flood and its greatest fire.

That wasn't all. Two main highway bridges span the Missouri at Kansas City. With the downstream flood these were the only ones still operating clear down to St. Louis. One is the Hannibal bridge, built in 1870 as the first rail bridge across the Missouri and revered as an antique which had marked the start of Kansas City's progress. It had been rebuilt many times, with a vehicular roadway added as a top deck. It is so low that one section had to be constructed to swing out at right angles for boats to pass. A quarter-mile downstream is the second span, the Armour-Swift-Burlington bridge, which carries the bulk of all traffic into Kansas City from the north.

Barges Smash Into Bridge

Tied up at Kaw Point, a half-mile upstream from the Hannibal, were four grain barges waiting their loads of Kansas wheat, delayed by the rains.

Late Friday when the big fire was at its worst the full force of both the Kaw and the Missouri tore these barges loose from their heavy hawser chains. Three of them were immense craft, 300 feet long, and the other about half their size. All four swung out into the Missouri, twisting and whirling like chips, and bore down on the Hannibal bridge.

The smaller barge got there first.

The bridge tender had seen all coming and threw the switch which opens the center span to let the first barge through, with nice calculation and timing. Nothing happened.

A fuse had burned out on the electric motor which swings the ponderous section. The small barge helped, though. It smashed against the center section, knocked it open to a 40-degree angle and went on through. A government towboat, chasing it, angled through a moment later.

Two big barges were only yards behind the towboat. By some inconceivable chance both arrived at the bridge opening at the exact moment and, like fleeing rats, seemed to dive for the hole to beat one another.

They came together with a crash which echoed back from the bluffs, and wedged fast, welded together against the bridge and in the partly opened section.

That was lucky, because if either had hit a pier directly there is little doubt the entire structure would have gone on downstream with them. The third barge lodged a moment later, head-on into the opened section. And they were stuck there, ending their menace to the A.-S.-B. bridge below. Workers hastened to chain them tight to the Hannibal.

Towboat Catches Small Barge

In the meantime the little barge had borne down on the A.-S.-B. If a pilot had been at its rudder he couldn't have done a better job of guiding it between the middle piers of that structure. The towboat caught the barge a half mile farther on, lassoed it like a wild steer and tied it firmly to the south bank, to end its threat to three other railroad bridges in the Kansas City reach and a half dozen farther down. It would have been inconceivable that it could have piloted itself safely through all those piers.

The Missouri and the Kaw early in the night began threatening to break into the Municipal Airport, the Fairfax district and into North Kansas City. The big airfield was evacuated, with air liners, freight carriers and all private ships flying the auxiliary field south of the city at Grandview. The 5,000 residents of North Kansas City were ordered by the mayor to leave at once. The Phillips refinery at Fairfax shut down, as did General Motors. Because of the low water pressure and the fire hazard, Mayor Kemp ordered all business and all nonessential industry in all of Kansas City not to open Saturday morning.

The evacuation of North Kansas City is a separate story in itself. The dike had actually been sheared away at one spot. Bulldozers were butting earth into the weak spot, but a Niagara might come through at any moment.

Residents took to their cars. Some tried to move all their furniture; some none. Every conceivable type of vehicle, from a 2-wheel trailer to transport trucks, picked up everything movable, from homes, from industries, from stores. Hundreds of new and used cars in the dealers lots, the full complement of truck lines, earth graders, steam rollers, house trailers, went up the big hill on No. 69. By the next morning all the highways leading into the high plateau above the valley of the Missouri were simply lanes between a great array of vehicles parked on the broad shoulders, in front yards, in filling stations, in new subdivisions, everywhere. Never had a city been evacuated more speedily, more completely. Residents went to stay with friends, in churches, in schools.

North Kansas City became a dead city, with only police, state patrolmen, naval reservists and soldiers guarding its borders, with orders to shoot looters. Once out no one could go back. That continued for the week-end, the strangest week-end the city ever had experienced.

A Night of Labor

The crest of the Missouri and the Kaw passed Kansas City at 3 a.m. Saturday morning, but the danger did not lessen. The swift current was cutting at the dikes, at the airport, at Fairfax and still menacing North Kansas City.

Thousands of men and hundreds of trucks, bulldozers and all manner of earth-moving equipment had sought to shore up all levees all Saturday night. At daylight it appeared they had won.

Early hours of Saturday passed without dire event except at Fairfax, where the Jersey creek floodgate collapsed and water gushed through it in small volume to spread slowly through the Phillips tank yard and over the runways of the airport, also now evacuated.

Water Infiltrates

Efforts were concentrated there in the battle anew. Sand boils from seepage under the dikes started appearing at many spots.

These were hemmed in with sandbags and when the water rose to the level of the river on the other side of the dike it stopped.

But the seepage and the water from the Jersey creek break had its effect. Water on both sides of the dike at the south end of the district finally made that section only a squishy mound of earth. It collapsed at 6 o'clock Saturday night and the flood roared in, the same old story of the dikes which didn't hold. Within minutes 200 million dollars worth of industries and four square miles were under 10 to 20 feet of yellow water.

At the far northwest end of Fairfax is the Quindaro light and water plant which supplies electricity and water to 130,000 persons in Kansas City, Kansas, and its suburban areas in nearby Johnson County. It is a municipal plant on ground somewhat higher than the balance of Fairfax, but still well below the dikes.

Authorities, willing to believe now the worst was coming everywhere, had anticipated the Fairfax dike break and started building a temporary levee 500 yards to the east to seal the plant off from the rest of Fairfax.

Then began a night-long dramatic battle of trying to build the levee faster than the water rose.

It was coming up almost a foot an hour and the workers, national guardsmen, volunteers and city employees, 500 with 200 dump trucks, two draglines and five caterpillar earth movers, labored frantically along the quarter-mile levee, broadening its base to 10 feet and sandbagging its inner face. The light plant's giant generators and pumps hummed on at capacity and the 2000-degree boilers glowed through the night, supplying the sleeping city. They could not be shut down even for a moment, such is the appetite of a great city for electric power and water.

A shutdown would have meant new disaster. The threat of a devastating explosion if the water broke through and hit the boilers was ignored.

The levee was only four feet high when the first of the floodwaters crawled to its base.

A Hill Goes Down

Giant searchlights from the roof of the plant and near-by hills aided the workers, bathing them in a glow stronger than sunshine as they virtually removed a near-by clay hill of several acres and deposited it on the levee.

Here too, sand boils appeared at a dozen places at once from seepage, and a broken sewer line gushed surface water into the enclosure.

Dump trucks stopped both with loads of powdered coal and slack taken from a mound of thousands of tons stored near by for the utility's fuel.

It was touch and go until 4 a.m., when the flood started gaining. By that time all areas of Fairfax were flooded and the water was coming against the dike with a definite cutting current.

Within 1 Foot

The dike was 10 feet high and the water 9. Ralph Duvall, manager of the plant, virtually gave up hope to save the dike. He ordered that a second dike be started 200 yards nearer the plant. More trucks and earth moving machinery had been obtained by frantic radio pleas. At 5 a.m. the water seemed to weary workers to be not rising so fast. They still were one to two feet ahead of it. And at 6 a.m. it appeared it was not rising at all.

The first hope came then that the battle would be won.

It had been considered that if this plant went out, most of the people would have had to be evacuated from Kansas City, Kans. People cannot live in a congested area under modern conditions without water or power for any long period, and no help could have been expected from Kansas City, Mo., and its dwindling water supply. Power plants there had estimated they could lend only 15,000 kilowatts, a minor fraction of the need.

Workers were heartened by the dawn. At 7 a.m. army engineers directing the fight surveyed the situation and said the plant had been saved. Radio pleas soon brought 2,000 new workers to the scene to relieve those who had gone through the night. A third levee was constructed inside the other two. But the first one held, and late Sunday the flood started receding with the drop of both the Kaw and the Missouri. This rescue of the municipal plants has been the one bright spot in the whole picture of Kansas City's disastrous week-end.

Rail Cars Emerge

On Monday both the Missouri and the Kaw went down almost as fast as they had risen. The freight cars and locomotives started emerging from the rail yards like sleeping sea monsters.

Cattle were rescued from the stockyards by cowboys driving them through only flank-deep water.

A good deal of frozen meat was removed from packing house coolers. Turkey Creek pumping station opened to workers who started shoveling silt away from machinery.

The score: Four industrial districts lost; North

Kansas City saved; the light plant saved; the Municipal airport still dry; no major bridges lost.

Three persons drowned. The bodies were not discovered until the flood subsided.

No disruption of electric power.

The Northeast Industrial district, virtually undamaged, ready for new construction.

About 90 per cent of Kansas City's residential district was untouched by the waters. It is on high ground.

None of the main downtown district suffered, and few outlying retail districts were inundated except those in Armourdale and Argentine and along Southwest boulevard.

So in some respects, Kansas City is lucky.

Kansas City started digging out, with the help of a native son, President Truman, Congress and apparently with the sympathy of the whole country. The great work of rehabilitation got under way. Unions offered labor and contractors machinery and supervision.

Flood Control Needed

A lesson had been learned. It is that dikes cannot hold a flood which they simply compress to greater heights; that it is an economic catastrophe for everyone alike to sacrifice the most valuable land of an area in trade for relatively cheap farm land in a river's basin which should have been used for a series of lakes and reservoirs to contain unusual rainfall and keep it from sweeping destruction on the heavily populated centers.

Kansas City civic leaders believe it will not be difficult to convince Congress and all the people that this must be done; that the Pick-Sloan plan is the only solution. It was at a cost of nearly a billion dollars in Kansas and Missouri; less than half of which would have built the reservoir and dam system and left enough over for soil conservation, too. It would have saved the homes of 100,000 people in the two states and the economic dislocation of at least five times that number.

Accidents & Man-made Disasters

MAN'S INTELLECT AND SKILL and sweat have indeed wrought miracles in our time—flights to outer space, cures of dread diseases, increasingly rapid travel, a national standard of living only royalty could aspire to, and many more.

Triumph And Tragedy

Unfortunately, sometimes his machines fail him. A dramatic reminder of the "Triumph and Tragedy" potential of man's devices took place March 1, 1962, in New York City.

The largest crowd in New York City history (4 million plus) submerged Astronaut John Glenn with their love and confetti (3,474 tons, another record). Less than an hour before the parade 95 passengers and crew of an American Airlines Boeing 707 jet liner died in the plane's plunge into Jamaica Bay. This, too, was a record—the largest toll for a single airplane crash in the United States. Newsmen staked out to cover the Glenn welcome had to switch signals to cover two of that city's all-time top stories, and cover them simultaneously.

Although reporters on another paper, the New York *World-Telegram and Sun*, won Pulitzer Prizes for their crash stories, a New York *Herald Tribune* writer spun a perfect preface for this chaper. The piece follows without comment as indeed a uniquely thoughtful prologue to a great newspaper's brilliant coverage.

[70]

New York Herald Tribune, March 2, 1962

Man reaches for the stars, but he stands upon the earth. And his fallibility and failings go hand in hand with his capability and achievements. Yesterday this city honored a space hero—even while stunned by a great air disaster. Today it still feels the thrill of pride in John Glenn—and it mourns the ninety-five who died at Idlewild.

It was supremely ironic that the two events should happen not only on the same day but almost at the same hour—that even as Glenn and his fellow astronauts were preparing for their triumphal procession through the city's heart, along its fringes an airline pilot was struggling desperately—and vainly—to keep his plane in the air.

Man's skill and science were enough to carry him safely 150 miles into space and three times around the earth. But at least in this one tragic instance they were not enough to carry him to safety and to life only a few hundred feet above the shallow waters of Jamaica Bay.

And so Col. Glenn received the homage of the city, although the city knew, and he knew, the dark shadows that lay over so many families and so many homes. "To everything there is a season," the Bible says, ". . . A time to weep, and a time to laugh; a time to mourn, and a time to dance." Yesterday was a moment for both: a moment to exult in man's greatness, and to acknowledge his insufficiency.

Progress, we know, is slow, and it often is bought at a bitter price. Col. Glenn warned yesterday, as he has before, that there will be space flights from which no one returns. We may be sure that there will also be other tragedies, from the mines below the earth to the skies above it. But we know, too, that man will persevere and persist and progress, for he knows no other way.

There Isn't Much Left

Airline crashes more easily accessible to reporters have killed more people than this one near Grand Canyon. However, Robert F. Alkire's story still stands unchallenged with the best of air crash stories. The Salt Lake *Tribune* won a Pulitzer Prize for its enterprising coverage, of which Alkire's story was a part.

This story features brief sentences, simple organization, and excellent word choices. Real punch comes from his using such fresh expressions as "black drape" (par. 4) and "the burn area drains down both sides" (par. 7).

His description is artful: "as though a giant had carefully mixed small bits of metal and black paint and dumped it neatly over the top of the huge rock" (par. 7), "rivers flow together in a muddle of twists and turns" (par. 10), "the raging Colorado is only a trickle, twisting through jagged walls of rock" (par. 11), and "several planes wheel like cautious buzzards" (par. 13).

Alkire's story has other rather obvious qualities, among them understatement, repeated play on the theme "there isn't much left," and portraying the futility of rescue efforts. Clearly he has created a model worthy of any writer's study.

By Robert F. Alkire
The Salt Lake Tribune, July 2, 1956

CEDAR CITY, Utah, July 1—I have just come from the scene of the world's worst commercial air disaster. There isn't much left.

Bits of torn metal and blackened fire-burned areas mark the only trace of two giant airliners—a DC-7 owned by United Airlines and a TWA Super-Constellation—that Saturday carried 128 persons to death.

The site of the crashes is about 22 miles northeast of Grand Canyon, Ariz. Men who live and work in this country call it "the most rugged in the world."

Near the confluences of the Little Colorado and Colorado Rivers in Grand Canyon there stands a 6,500-foot bluff—Chuar Butte. On a 700-foot knoll extending east from the butte there is a black drape. That possibly will be the final resting place of the 58 passengers and crewmen who rode the tumbling United Airlines DC-7 to destruction.

Metal Glints in Sun

A half mile south of the butte, in a narrow canyon, a bit of metal glints in the sun. And at this spot—designated as Temple Butte—another 70 persons riding a Trans World Airliner plunged to death.

Even a trained observer could be fooled by the lack of evidence at the site. No large chunks of aircraft. No broken, twisted seats. No bodies visible from a plane 220 feet above the scene.

Where the DC-7 thudded into the knoll, it looks as though a giant had carefully mixed small bits of metal and black paint and dumped it neatly over the top of the huge rock. The burn area drains down both sides of the knoll, indicating the DC-7 struck with such force on the very edge of the rock that about half of it was flung 50 feet or more up over the top.

In the region of the Constellation wreckage there are bigger chunks of metal, but again no signs of bodies or even the definite outlines of a fuselage in the burn patch. Even if a ground party were to reach the area, chances of climbing the vertical 700-foot knoll to the UAL liner are dim, indeed.

As you approach the area by air from the northwest, you understand the frustrating difficulty of locating even a huge airliner in the maze of side-canyons that stretch away from the mighty Colorado River and its containing Grand Canyon.

Rivers Form Maze

From 4,000 feet overhead, all canyons look hauntingly alike and rivers flow together in a muddle of twists and turns that make it difficult to separate the Colorado from its feeder streams. Faint paths of small animals wander aimlessly over the red sand among the low, green-hued sagebrush. Here, a man afoot must be careful of his path as death is only the next step away.

The sun has no mercy and nature no shade for 120-degree temperatures fire the sand, and the careless or foolish can die fast. As you come abreast of the canyon rim, the sand breaks away and 2,000 feet below the raging Colorado is only a trickle, twisting through jagged walls of rock.

Where is the Little Colorado that pinpoints the site of the crashes?

A dozen meandering 2,000-foot high canyons pour into the area, but only one is the smaller river. Still, it isn't necessary to look at the ground. Straight ahead in the mist above the chasm, several planes wheel like cautious buzzards. Now and then one dips from the pattern over the crash and zips past the black scar on the knoll, rising again to circle again—futilely.

Several of the circling aircraft are seaplanes, members of rescue services, but out of their element here, and others are private and military planes. They are not there to look for survivors for almost certainly there are none. But they serve to guide other craft into the area and to advise ground directors.

Crash Near Plateau

Perhaps the strangest thing about the crashes is that both planes are a mere mile or two from the east side of the canyon (the river flows north and south at the site).

Had the tumbling airliners fallen that distance further east, they would have struck a broad plateau and been spotted immediately. Ground parties and helicopters would have had no difficulty reaching them.

But in their locations amid the rugged canyon walls, even experienced pilots wonder whether a 'copter could reach the site.

Perhaps the most terrible thing about the scene is the lack of evidence. You wonder how two giant four-engine airliners with tremendous wing spans and carrying tons of metal and equipment could so obliterate themselves along with their human cargoes.

It is with a flood of relief that after several passes within 220 feet of the blackened knoll, you climb back above the river mist and into the sunlight, leaving 128 victims of the world's bloodiest commercial aviation disaster to what is in all probability their final rest.

Texas City Disaster

Whenever Americans talk about modern-day disasters sooner or later someone mentions the greatest mid-Century one of them all, Texas City. More people were killed (nearly 1,000) and injured (4,000) in this fire and explosion catastrophe than in any other post-World War II domestic disaster. Newsmen from throughout the United States descended on the scene.

The Dallas *Morning News* sent 10 reporters and photographers, among them Charles Burton and Ben Bradford. Their joint story was one of the best of several strong pieces written about the disaster. The Burton-Bradford story gains its strength not so much from specific phrasing as from the way in which they structured it. This is organized in the fact pattern wherein each fact in the news event appears in a single block of paragraphs in the order of diminishing reader interest.

First, the writers summarized three major facts in the top five paragraphs. Paragraphs one and two are devoted largely to casualties. Paragraph three treats with fires, and paragraphs four and five, explosions and threats of explosions.

Note how they introduced the next fact, the number of dead, with a brief, pointed sixth paragraph. Paragraph 11 introduces a two-paragraph section on the injured. Other sections are on explosions (par. 13–15); property losses (par. 16–20); survivors (par. 21–25); Grandcamp explosions, told twice in two chronological narratives (par. 26–35); Monsanto plant (par. 36–37); oil and chemical fires (par. 38–39); use of bulldozers (par. 40); thefts (par. 41); warnings and reactions (par. 43–47); general area of destruction (par. 48–49); tidal wave (par. 50); eyewitness accounts (par. 51–67); distance explosions felt (par. 68–81). Note in the fact section devoted to eyewitness accounts (par. 51–67) each person's statements are recorded separately. This reduces the chance of confusing readers.

The story is highly detailed, strengthened with considerable specific factual background information.

By Charles Burton and Ben Bradford
The Dallas Morning News, April 18, 1947

TEXAS CITY, Texas, April 17 (Thursday)—Explosions that ripped through this gulf seaport in chain-reaction fashion Wednesday morning left uncounted hundreds of dead and thousands of injured in their wake.

Estimates of the dead ranged up to 1,200. By nightfall, the Red Cross reported 500 bodies had been counted. Great dockside areas still had not been combed for victims because of recurring similar explosions, spreading fires and the danger of a monstrous new blast in the host of oil and chemical plants that occupy most of the city's areas.

At 1 a.m. Thursday fourteen fires were raging on the water front. Only one building was standing in a two-mile area. Damaged water mains kept firemen from doing more than prevent the blazes' spread.

Occasional explosions rumbled through the city after nightfall and spotlights were hurried to the scene of each to see if rescue workers or firemen had been trapped.

A 7,000-ton freighter, the High Flyer, loaded with 900 tons of ammonium nitrate, was burning fiercely at dockside early Thursday, the Associated Press reported. A new explosion was feared.

There was no way of counting the dead.

Mayor J. C. Trahan, lanky, 31-year-old overseas veteran, said at midafternoon 150 dead had been identified. Dr. Clarence Quinn, in charge of the city's improvised hospitals, said 300 to 350 bodies had been handled by late afternoon, and workers hardly had begun their task of probing the ruins of the great Monsanto Chemical Plant.

Morgue keepers at 12:30 a.m. had registered 239 bodies and reported others were still coming in, but more slowly. This figure did not include bodies taken to Galveston and Houston.

Sgt. Wiley Whatley of the Houston Police Department estimated the dead remaining in the blasted buildings at between 400 and 500.

He based his statement on the number of bodies in the city's makeshift morgue, converted from a school gymnasium, and the number who normally would have been at work.

Estimates of the injured ranged up to 3,000.

It will be days before the total casualty list will be completed.

The French ship Grandcamp, whose explosion at 9:12 a.m. set off the series of terrible blasts, was wrecked and no survivor of it could be found; the multi-million-dollar Monsanto plant was flattened so that an eyewitness said "It just doesn't exist"; great oil storage tanks burned through the day and into the night, and large sections of the city of 15,000 were shattered.

Townspeople Flee

Chlorine gas was loosed by the Monsanto explosion, and rescue workers donned army gas masks before rushing into the area.

Many townspeople fled their damaged homes in fear of fresh blasts.

Estimates of property loss were admittedly guesses, but a United Press compilation put the figure at possibly 75 million dollars.

Lt. D. B. Small, stationed at the navy base at Hitchcock, surveyed the town from the air and reported damage almost total over a four-square-mile area.

Every house and business establishment in the city apparently suffered damage, he said. Those within a quarter mile and up to a half mile were for the most part demolished beyond hope of reconstruction. Business houses in the downtown section, nearly a mile from the explosion, were shattered.

The city hall looked as though an artillery shell had hit it. Across the street, the roof was blown in on the city's largest theater.

Children in the city's schools, most of them in class at the time, were injured by glass fragments when window panes shattered.

Survivors in Daze

First outsiders to reach the scene found survivors wandering crazily. Said one relief worker: "The injured are everywhere, some of them staring blindly as you pass because they are still too dazed to think."

These persons got first calls of disaster workers. The dead were left until later, until some of the pitifully wounded could be led out of the water-front area.

Airplane shuttle service was set up to carry as many as possible to hospitals outside the disaster area. Facilities at Houston and Galveston were quickly swamped.

Many of the less severely injured, after being bandaged and taped, wandered glassy-eyed through the streets, looking for their kin. Others groped aimlessly through stores and homes, unable to say what they sought.

Wednesday night scores of weeping women, some with children, stood around the city hall, the chamber of commerce, or just in the street, waiting for word of their men. They might be tied up by rescue work in the gas-filled docks area. Or their bodies might be in the wreckage of the Monsanto plant. There was no way of knowing, but most of the families feared the worst.

The explosion was touched off by the Grandcamp, a former American Liberty ship taken over by the French. This was the generally accepted version of the tragedy:

Crewmen on the doomed vessel discovered a smoldering fire in its cargo of nitrates at sea at 4 a.m. Wednesday. The ship put into port and requested aid of the Texas City fire department.

Four fire companies responded and sought to stem the blaze with water and steam. Then efforts were made to move the vessel out into the open water of the bay.

Suddenly the ship blew up. First there was a minor explosion, then fifteen seconds later a blast of atomic fury that set off the explosive chain that leaped through the Monsanto plant and flattened it.

Witnesses from cities across the bay said smoke mushroomed as in pictures of the atomic bomb at Bikini, except that it was black.

Subsequent explosions scattered the disaster into the oil refining and storage area near by.

Scores of Curious Die

Scores of persons attracted to the dock area by the clanging fire engines were killed instantly. There was no trace of the forty men on the Grandcamp— named, ironically, for an invasion beach in Normandy—or of fifty-seven city firemen, three of whose blackened trucks stood twisted and torn as mute memorials to their heroism. Only eight members of the volunteer fire department were known to be alive; the fourth truck had vanished as if by magic.

A survivor, Dr. W. H. Lane, official of Monsanto, said: "The ship was docked about 500 yards from our main office. All of a sudden there was a frightful explosion as the ship disintegrated."

Pieces of the ship were scattered over a four-mile area.

"There followed a series of three or four other explosions, one right after the other."

Nearly every Monsanto worker was trapped. Screams of those inside were audible to firemen hours after the first explosion, but long before anyone could venture in the wrecked plant.

The plant, producer of styrene, an explosive ingredient of synthetic rubber, covered about thirty acres. It was just a burning shell.

Six major oil and chemical fires lit the Texas City sky after nightfall. Smoke, shooting up 5,000 feet, drifted to sea under a strong north wind. The black trail could be seen more than forty miles at sea, naval fliers reported, and was visible for thirty miles inland.

Two of Texas City's four large oil refineries, the 7,500-barrel Stone Oil plant and the 20,000-barrel Sid Richardson Company, were smoking ruins, their stills, pipes and tanks twisted and black. The oil tank farms of the Republic and Humble Oil Companies likewise were fire-wrecked.

Bulldozers were sent by the State Highway Department to clear debris and help hunt workers believed trapped or dead in the Monsanto plant. They also were clearing away the wreckage of the Texas City Terminal Company grain elevators, which burned.

Some automobile thefts were reported, but 1,500 peace officers were on hand and city officials said the situation was under control.

Storekeepers boarded up broken windows after the explosion, then opened coffee bars. Sandwiches, cakes and other food and drink were handed out to disaster workers. Red Cross and Salvation Army canteens and emergency stations were set up.

Public address systems scattered through the city

urged the homeless to board army and navy buses to Camp Wallace and other nearby military installations where food and shelter were made available.

Rumor Causes Panic

After nightfall the loud-speakers blared a warning that a ship loaded with nitroglycerin was ablaze in the harbor and likely to blow up at any minute. This started a panicky rush for the highways by residents and disaster workers alike until authorities branded it a false rumor.

"Everybody started screaming and trying to get away," said Sgt. Harry Goldberg of the Dallas County Sheriff's office. "When the roads jammed up many of them left their automobiles with the keys in them and went on foot. For miles and miles you could see autos trying to get away. Some of the people had babies in their arms.

"They told everybody at the airport to leave. They were going off and leaving the planes."

All highways were blockaded at dark to keep all but official workers out of the area.

The blast seemed to follow the Gulf, Colorado and Santa Fe Railroad spur line southwest from the dockside. Most of the town's big plants are in that section.

One oil tank, a thousand feet from the nearest blaze, was crumpled like a piece of tinfoil.

A tidal wave which sent a wall of water described as neck deep some 200 yards inland did little damage to property already scarred by the explosion itself. It washed a barge fifty feet up on the bay shore.

J. L. Eckland, Texas City warehouse worker, dripping from oily water spewed up by the explosion, said: "The ship blew up, and everything was black. When it got light again, there were dead people all around me."

Searches for Family

Death struck even from the air. Fred Brumley and John Norris of Pelly were flying over the water front in a private plane when the blasts began. Concussion made them lose control of the plane and they crashed to their deaths.

W. H. Sandberg, vice-president of the Texas City Terminal Railway Company, left the Grandcamp just five minutes before the explosion.

"The concussion blew out windows of every home in town," he said. "It blew in ceilings in business buildings. It cracked new buildings from end to end. Doors were blown from their hinges.

"As for the Monsanto plant—it just doesn't exist any more."

Juan Torres, 33, held a straight face for a moment, then began crying when he told of his search among the dead for his family.

He puttered aimlessly through the wreckage of his home, a quarter mile from the docks, and recounted his story.

"My father and my brother, they were working on the ship and the dock—I think. My sister-in-law, she went down to watch the boat burn. I can't find them now. They died—I think."

Torres excused himself. "I have some friends that need me. Good-by."

He blew his nose and shuffled up the debris-littered street. In his back yard, pitted with falling steel fragments from the explosion, a pen full of pigs rooted happily.

Volunteer Describes Tragedy

Phillip Flores, 21-year-old army veteran, escaped the big blast, then returned to the disaster scene to help remove the dead and injured.

"I was in the warehouse about twenty-five or fifty yards from the Monsanto plant," he said, "when I heard a puffing boom. It didn't do much. About fifteen seconds later the big one came and everything went bust.

"I dropped the flour I was carrying and fell on my belly. Then I crawled to a big stack of flour and stuck my head under the sacks. People screamed around me.

"Then I got out and ran until I thought my lungs would burst. At home and in town I looked for my people. I found out they were all right. Then they started calling for volunteers to help get out the dead and injured.

"I went with the volunteers. I almost wish I hadn't. In the place I worked arms and legs were scattered around the wreckage.

"People were screaming. Some of them wiggled in circles because they didn't have any legs and couldn't get up.

"One of them screamed very loud. His leg was gone. I couldn't see what he looked like. His face was gone."

The explosion rocked an area about 300 miles in diameter.

Mrs. J. C. Colwick, of Palestine, 160 miles north of Texas City, said her house shuddered twice as if there had been an earthquake. Slight earth tremors were felt at Grapeland, twenty miles south of Palestine.

To the east, Port Arthur and Orange, 100 miles distant, reported the blast was audible and rocked buildings. At Pelly, twenty-seven miles to the north, a man said the sound "hurt my eardrums."

Damage was heavy at Galveston, eight miles across Galveston Bay. Plate-glass windows in stores and home were broken, plaster fell from ceilings and the city rocked beneath the series of explosions. Citizens rushed into the streets in alarm, fearing an earthquake.

Room of Death

How can a reporter transport readers to the scene of a devastating fire, one which kills 87 children and three teachers? Robert Wiedrich solved the problem admirably in his story for the Chicago *Tribune* on a parochial school fire.

This "with," or supplementary, story reminds one of a television camera which pans scene after scene. Note, also:

1. The powerful word usage—"crumpled" (par. 1), "hacked" (par. 3), "hurled forward" (par. 11), "sloshed" (par. 13).

2. The brief, punchy sentences.

3. Personification—"the statue looked out over a room of death" (par. 9).

The story flows brilliantly, resulting in part from repetition: "fire, a fire" (par. 7); "a porcelain figure," "and the statue" (par. 8, 9). Easily the most forceful connective technique in this story comes in paragraphs 9 and 10: "The teacher was dead," "So was the pupil." Other connectives used to indicate a scene change include: "In a corner," (par. 2), "In another room" (par. 6), "The school's second floor" (par. 17), "Outside the school" (par. 23), "On Chicago avenue" (par. 24), "In Our Lady of the Angels church" (par. 25).

Even so, this analysis fails to point to the real strength of this story. Nor do such things as calling attention to his use of contrast, contrast of Christmas carols and no Christmas for this neighborhood (par. 24), or interesting phrasing, "interior walls ceased to exist" (par. 17). All of these help, but this story gains excellence primarily because of the carefully chosen specific detail which is presented simply and clearly.

Wiedrich did not have to include statistical data; the who, what, when, where, why; the fire-fighting information; and other details. These were reported in the main fire coverage story. Largely because of this he was able to portray more accurately the over-all fire scene than could any straight news account or several pictures.

By Robert Wiedrich
Chicago Tribune, Dec. 2, 1958

Six small forms, the bodies of 4th and 5th graders, lay crumpled against the wall.

In a corner, the charred body of a nun lay buried in debris of the roof which had fallen into the room.

A fireman hacked at the wreckage of a second floor classroom in the Our Lady of the Angels Elementary school. Tears streaked his smoke smeared face.

Rows of Desks

"O, God, I've got two of my own in school," he said.

"What if these were mine?"

In another room, the desks of 2d and 3d graders stood row on row. Each bore a water logged geography book. It was called "Our American Neighbors." Each was open to the chapter on lumbering.

This was the aftermath of fire, a fire so hot and so swift that several score young lives were taken in a matter of minutes as rescuers worked as fast as they could, but found that it was not fast enough.

A porcelain figure of the Virgin Mary stood on a book case. It had been a planter. The leaves of the plant, tho, were ashes.

And the statue looked out over a room of death. The water-soaked papers of a child working an arithmetic problem lay on a desk. The ink had run and the figures were blurred. The paper would never be graded. The teacher was dead.

Agony of Flame

So was the pupil. You could see where both had sought to flee the searing heat of the fire.

The nun's desk had been hurled forward as she struggled to reach her charges in the final agony of flame.

And the pupil's small body was by the desk, his features contorted.

A battalion chief sloshed thru the water that flowed on the concrete floor. He said he had been one of the first at the scene.

He wept as he told how firemen had tried to raise ladders to screaming children as they clung from second floor windows, pleading for the help which for many never came.

Four Found Dead

"We tried," he said. "God, how we tried. But we couldn't move fast enough. No one could live in that fire.

"I saw four of them leaning over a window sill, crying. We tried to reach them. Then suddenly they slumped, doubled over the sill. They were dead when we got to them."

The school's second floor was burned out, wall to wall. Sections of roof had collapsed. Interior walls ceased to exist.

A wool mitten, decorated with sequins, lay in the rubble.

Twenty more minutes and the children would have been out of school; 1,200 seconds and death would have been cheated.

The blaze struck at 2:40 p.m. Classes ended at 3 p.m.

Desks in Corridor

Firemen stumbled over the wooden desks that stood in a double line in the second floor corridor.

"The ones who jumped were lucky," said a division marshal. "They just broke arms and legs. I hope I never see something like this again."

Outside the school, parents stood. Priests knelt to give the last rites to canvas-covered forms which once had been children. Mothers wept and fathers tried to comfort, but cried, too.

On Chicago avenue, a block to the south, a loud speaker blared Christmas carols from the door of a record shop. But Christmas in this neighborhood would be grim.

In Our Lady of the Angels church, just east of the school, the lights were out. Fire had burned the power lines.

But in the pitch black church people knelt and prayed, the bitter smell of smoke in their nostrils. And on the steps a woman cried. A cold wind swirled the smoke from the still smouldering school about her.

A Ship's Final Agony

Captain Kurt Carlsen and his two-week war against the raging Atlantic was THE conversation topic in early January, 1952. The Associated Press chartered a tug and sent Alvin J. Steinkopf and Leonard Leddington to the scene. They flashed a running story to London via radio and cable.

As would be expected, the greatest drama appears in the first half of this story, devoted to the rescue and to the Enterprise's demise. Strong, specific, graphic verbs move the story along smoothly: "snatched" (par. 2), "leaped" (par. 3), "clambered" (par. 4), "was heaving" (par. 6), "battled" (par. 6), "thrashed" (par. 8), "had been scurrying" (par. 12), "fluttered" (par. 13), "was strewn" (par. 17), "was pitched out" (par. 17). Expressive phrasing and personification add: "solitary duel" (par. 7), "its final agony" (par. 8), "the motley assortment of boats" (par. 12), "the writhing vessel" (par. 12), "a heave to port" (par. 16), and the whole of paragraph 29.

Again, structure is easy to follow. A summary in the first two paragraphs gives readers the essential facts. A three-paragraph chronology of the rescue comes next. Then, the story gives a rather detailed and graphic account of the drama from the ship's first distress to rescue and sinking (par. 6–22). The final chronological telling of the drama, in which other important details are given, occupies the remainder of the story. Note in the final chronological account the writers began earlier, giving the point of origin and destination. This information is even more vital to a wreck of a common carrier; it helps tell an audience if this is the airplane, train, bus, etc., that friends or relatives may be aboard.

The Associated Press, Jan. 10, 1952

LONDON—the gallant American freighter Flying Enterprise sank in the stormy Atlantic Thursday after a mighty two-week duel with the sea.

Its heroic captain, Kurt Carlsen, and 1st Mate Kenneth Dancy of the tow tug Turmoil were snatched from the churning waters to safety.

Carlsen and Dancy leaped overboard when it became evident the 6,711-ton freighter was going down under the crashing waves.

The stand-by rescue fleet closed in. The tug Turmoil threw over a rope ladder and the two men clambered to safety.

They were in the water only about 4 minutes.

Carlsen refused to give up until the stricken freighter obviously was heaving her last. He had battled since the Christmas Day hurricane to save his ship.

His solitary duel with the Atlantic began Dec. 29 after he ordered all hands to abandon the ship, which carried a crew of 40 and 10 passengers. Dancy joined him last Saturday.

The big freighter thrashed about in its final agony for 40 minutes before it disappeared into the ocean.

For more than 24 hours the vessel had been virtually on its side.

End in Sight

At 3:08 p.m. (8:08 a.m. E.S.T.) Thursday it became obvious to the U. S. destroyer Keith, standing by, that the Enterprise was about to go down.

It and other nearby boats began the long-planned rescue operation at once.

The motley assortment of boats which had been scurrying about the freighter for days approached the writhing vessel as the Turmoil's lights flashed the signal "C-L-O-S-E."

The funnel of the Enterprise by this time was slapping the surface of the sea. The bow was considerably lower than the stern. A little American flag still fluttered over the rear part of the superstructure.

The wind was blowing fiercely, pitching the rescue tugs about like chips of wood.

Water poured into the funnel of the dying Enterprise.

The two men leaped overboard, even as the Enterprise gave a heave to port and began slowly to roll over on her side.

Part of her cargo—worth more than a million dollars—was strewn on the ocean. Soon other parts of the Enterprise began to crack, and more cargo was pitched out into the sea.

A Gallant Death

By 3:34 p.m., the Enterprise was fully on her side. It was a gallant death.

The rescue fleet saluted it. In the last few minutes the tugs sounded their sirens. Only the bow of the Enterprise was visible.

At 4 p.m. flares on the surface of the water near the ship were lighted, casting a weird light over the area as the Enterprise took her final lunge.

One minute later the Enterprise was below the sea.

The Enterprise, an Isbrandtsen Line vessel insured for $1.25 million, was en route from Hamburg, Germany, to New York when the Christmas hurricane caught her about 300 miles off England.

For days she was adrift with a crack in her hull. She sent an SOS Dec. 28. Then last Saturday the tug Turmoil began towing her toward shore.

Carlsen and Dancy had caught a heaving line after many desperate tries and made it fast, then fastened a towing line.

The Enterprise and her dauntless skipper almost won.

The crippled ship was only 12 hours towing distance from Falmouth (about 38 to 40 miles) when the 750-yard towline snapped early Wednesday morning under the buffeting of the heavy seas.

Beginning of End

It was the beginning of the end.

The elements were against the courageous skipper. Once again they brought up a storm to thwart him.

Repeated efforts to rig up a new towing line failed because of the wind and high seas.

Then later Wednesday the tilted ship started drifting and settling slightly deeper in the water. It twisted about 10 degrees farther over on its left side.

Thursday morning it lay listing 70 degrees and when the winds and heavy seas rolled it, the ship leaned as low as 80 degrees.

The rolling kept Carlsen off the deck most of Wednesday. He came out Thursday morning to look over the remnants of the broken towline, then went back with Dancy to rest, partly on the wall and partly on the floor of their lopsided perch high in the starboard deckhouse.

Still Carlsen would not give up.

Carlsen and Dancy ventured out to the starboard side of the funnel in mid-morning (Thursday) on the high side of the sharply slanting deck.

About 6 hours later they gave up their watch, mounted the funnel and leaped into the sea. That was at 3:26 p.m. Thursday.

Thirty-four minutes later the Enterprise plunged beneath the waves and one of the great epics of the sea was ended.

Kathy Is Dead

The name Kathy Fiscus holds a special place in the hearts of millions of Americans who lived through heroic efforts to save the 3½-year-old girl's life in April, 1949. She had fallen down an abandoned well while playing in an open field near San Marino, Calif. Radio networks broke frequently for on-the-spot bulletins. Television cameras gave live coverage. Newsmen streamed to the scene. Curious spectators turned the atmosphere into one of a grim carnival.

Probably more than any other reporter Miss Carolyn Anspacher of the San Francisco *Chronicle* captured the full ramifications of the news event. Call it the woman's touch. Regardless, this story's simple, understanding tone beautifully paints a correct picture of an event involving deep human emotions, not all admirably expressed.

Note how interesting, specific details are dovetailed into the general chronological narrative, so tightly written the most demanding editor would be hard put to blue pencil a single word.

Structurally, the story is told once in the first three paragraphs. Then Miss Anspacher gave a second, essentially chronological, telling (par. 4–13). She wisely began this narrative very near the climax of the news event. After this comes a third narrative (par. 14–end). A flashback (par. 36–37) gave her an opportunity to insert a final vivid scene of the finding of Kathy's body. This story is organized perfectly in the highly useful tell and re-tell pattern, one which lends itself readily to descriptions of action.

By Carolyn Anspacher
The San Francisco Chronicle, April 11, 1949

SAN MARINO, April 10—Kathy Fiscus is dead.

The blonde child, for two full days and nights the most spotlighted little girl in the world, was found crouched in death tonight deep in her well-pipe tomb.

Her body, still grotesquely twisted from the cramped confinement, was brought to the surface at 9:52 p.m.

Rescue workers reached her about three hours

earlier, wedged in the gradual bend of the well pipe into which she had fallen at 4:45 p.m. Friday.

Workers Silent

Dr. Robert McCulloch, one of the Fiscus family physicians who went down the rescue shaft, reported Kathy had died shortly after she stopped speaking to her mother that afternoon. Her last sound was at 6:30 o'clock Friday.

Dr. McCulloch said she apparently had drowned.

For hours after the body was reached, the child's fate had been shrouded in the silence of the rescue workers.

And then, at 8:50 o'clock, Dr. Paul Hanson, the doctor who brought Kathy into the world, stepped up to the loudspeaker, facing the crowd of some 3,000 spectators.

He hesitated a brief moment. The throng hushed. He began speaking. ". . . Kathy is dead . . ."

A groan rose from the crowd.

". . . We ask you to leave the scene. . . . If this had been your child, we are sure you would not want a crowd to remain at the scene of the tragedy."

Sordid Anticlimax

A few onlookers broke off from the fringe and walked off. But most of the multitude remained. The throng that for two days and nights had given silent sympathy now became a mob of the morbidly curious.

Long after the tiny, hunched body had been brought up and taken away, the souvenir seekers lingered, tramping the gouged area in a sordid anticlimax to an epic struggle of men and machines against the earth in quest of a child's life.

These last few hours—since the 3½-year-old child's dark dungeon was pierced—were fraught with breathless drama.

Tension mounted perceptibly in the crowd as the whine of the pipe-cutting saw came out of the loudspeaker. The broiling sun had now dropped below the hilly horizon.

And then came the first break in the long vigil. An improvised bosun's chair was lowered into the steel casing jutting above the mouth of the rescue shaft. That was at 5:50 o'clock.

To the anxious onlookers, that meant one thing—the cutters were in the old well pipe. The breeches buoy was to go down when the aperture was effected.

Word flashed up that Kathy was sighted. The crowd had already sensed that, and an eerie hush of expectancy settled over the people beyond the rope barricades.

Fast Developments

Was she dead or alive? Engineer Raymond Hill, top boss of the operations, did not say.

From then on developments came fast.

O. A. Kelly and Homer (Whitey) Blickensderfer, who cut their way to Kathy's trap, asked that the microphone be cut off. That left the crowd to guesswork.

The door of an ambulance waiting near by was opened. Physicians were alerted. Attendants stood by, ready with a stretcher.

Hill mounted the casing and talked with the two men below. No comment was voiced.

In a few minutes the big bucket went down. They pulled up Blickensderfer. He staggered from exhaustion, near collapse. His nose was bleeding.

His clothes were caked with muck, his face was drawn. He huddled with Hill. And soon he was packed off to a hospital.

Air Stopped

Ever since Kathy had tumbled to her doom, firemen in relays had sat near the well's mouth and patiently, incessantly turned the gramophone-like crank of an apparatus that sent air hissing into the hole. They now stopped—with no explanation.

Hulking men gathered at the well. A rope was lowered. Another hush fell. A generator still working suddenly hummed eerily loud.

Twilight fell fast. The Kleig lights banged on and lit the tense scene with a ghastly glare.

Two men stood over the well mouth, patiently waiting for a signal. Four others held the rope, poised to pull.

The crowd was now getting restive. Police began having difficulties with tense watchers along the barrier.

The men at the well mouth pulled slowly, steadily on the rope.

Hill said Kathy was still held tight in the 14-inch pipe. It'll take more digging, more help. A murmur of disappointment rippled over the crowd.

Kathy's parents, Mr. and Mrs. David Fiscus, who had retired to their near-by home earlier and were given a sedative, came out and climbed in a waiting police car.

They were dry-eyed, grim. Mrs. Fiscus still wore the blue dress and red sweater she had on Friday when Kathy vanished.

It was not until almost two hours later that the watchers learned Kathy was dead.

Covered By Water

And it was much later that Kelly, visibly shaken, told reporters how he came upon the body.

"I knew she was dead the minute I saw her. She was three feet below the level of the window. She was upright and covered with water."

Shortly before Kelly came up, the working crane's cable began rising and Dr. McCulloch appeared. In his arms he held Kathy's body, her pink party dress covered by a gray shroud.

After the body was taken away in a black car, the dog-tired men went back to their machines. Ahead lay one more night of toil—to fill the rescue shafts and the costly well pipe.

"When I leave here," said Hill, the rescue director, "no one will know there has been any activity around this field but plowing."

A Touch of Heroism

In our dreams, as in Keystone Cop movies, the seemingly interminable frustrations to heroic deeds abound. Elston Brooks of the Fort Worth *Star-Telegram* found such a "nightmare" in real life. He wisely let the story tell itself, simply, ungarnished. Therein lies the beauty of this human interest item, one which the author hopes will counteract some of the death and destruction reported in Part 3 and Part 4.

Too, this serves as a reminder that reporters should remain alert for the off-beat when covering police and fire beats.

By Elston Brooks
Fort Worth Star-Telegram, Nov. 13, 1954

C. F. Colwell of 1201 Boulevard really had no aspirations to be a hero.

But once he got started on a rescue mission Friday afternoon, he had more obstacles thrown in his way than a basic trainee trying for a week-end pass.

The 39-year-old painter was in a car with his brother, C. E. Colwell, outside the brother's apartment house at 202 Lamar when flames broke out in the dwelling.

"My brother is on crutches with a broken hip, so I volunteered to go inside and get his clothing," Colwell said Saturday.

Call Fire Department

People were just standing around in the smoke-filled hall; no one could get them to phone the fire department.

"So I dropped the stuff in my arms and phoned the firemen.

"Then I asked if everyone was out. They thought everyone was, but they weren't sure about Mrs. J. W. Griffin, up on the second floor."

Colwell decided not to guess and began bounding up the stairs.

A tenant rushing downstairs with a mattress knocked him sprawling to the foot of the stairs.

"After I got over that, it was too late to go upstairs so I went outside, and, with two other men, started calling for the woman to jump."

Braces for Catch

When the 74-year-old woman appeared at her window she was carrying a bottle of catchup and a jar of mayonnaise.

Colwell braced himself to catch Mrs. Griffin.

She dropped the catchup on his head.

"That got me off balance. I still wasn't braced when she jumped to me."

The impact sent him crashing to the ground.

But Mrs. Griffin was able to escape with only a

broken leg and minor burns. She was taken to Harris Hospital where her condition was reported as fair Saturday.

When firemen extinguished the blaze, Fire Marshal Killian said the building was a 50 per cent loss. He said the blaze started from a defective connection on a gas heater in the apartment of the manager, Miss Martha Hinkle.

The clothing belonging to Colwell's brother?

"Burned up," said Colwell Saturday. "I never got back to it."

PART 5

Man and the Law

MANY NEWSPAPER EDITORS assign beginning reporters to cover crime on the theory that reader appeals in this beat's news are obvious. Others, realizing crime reporting involves more than statistics, entrust crime coverage only to seasoned staffers. These men know to look below the surface for real causes so they can help alert their communities to possible solutions. For that which seems obvious on first glance may prove a symptom rather than the deeper lying and more basic cause.

Berserk Gunman Kills 12

Few reporters more ably fill this bill than the late Meyer Berger of The New York *Times*. Berger, who began his career as a copy boy at the age of 11, rose to the rank of excellence with only a grade school education.

The first paragraph of his Pulitizer Prize story summarizes the action and identifies Howard Unruh, the killer. The second paragraph answers the highly pertinent question: Is he mentally ill? The next two paragraphs tell of Unruh's injury. Then come details about "Why" Unruh felt persecuted (par. 5–7). His and family backgrounds, all vital, appear next (par. 8–9). The remainder of the story is chronological. Note, too, how Berger wove information from the police questioning into his narrative. The amount of specific factual detail is overwhelming.

The result—a highly readable, interpretative, comprehensive, simply related news story. What more can we ask of any reporter?

By Meyer Berger
The New York Times, Sept. 7, 1949

CAMDEN, N.J., Sept. 6—Howard B. Unruh, 28 years old, a mild, soft-spoken veteran of many armored artillery battles in Italy, France, Austria, Belgium and Germany, killed twelve persons with a war souvenir Luger pistol in his home block in East Camden this morning. He wounded four others.

Unruh, a slender, hollow-cheeked six-footer paradoxically devoted to scripture reading and to constant practice with firearms, had no previous history of mental illness but specialists indicated tonight that there was no doubt that he was a psychiatric case, and that he had secretly nursed a persecution complex for two years or more.

The veteran was shot in the left thigh by a local tavern keeper but he kept that fact secret, too, while policemen and Mitchell Cohen, Camden County prosecutor, questioned him at police headquarters for more than two hours immediately after tear gas bombs had forced him out of his bedroom to surrender.

Blood Betrays His Wound

The blood stain he left on the seat he occupied during the questioning betrayed his wound. When it was discovered he was taken to Cooper Hospital in Camden, a prisoner charged with murder.

He was as calm under questioning as he was during the twenty minutes that he was shooting men, women and children. Only occasionally excessive brightness of his eyes indicated that he was anything other than normal.

He told the prosecutor that he had been building up resentment against neighbors and neighborhood shopkeepers for a long time. "They have been making derogatory remarks about my character," he said. His resentment seemed most strongly concentrated against Mr. and Mrs. Maurice Cohen, who lived next door to him. They are among the dead.

Mr. Cohen was a druggist with a shop at 3202 River Road in East Camden. He and his wife had had frequent sharp exchanges over the Unruhs' use of a gate that separates their back yard from the Cohens'. Mrs. Cohen had also complained of young Unruh's keeping his bedroom radio turned high into the late night hours. None of the other victims had ever had trouble with him.

Unruh, a graduate of Woodrow Wilson High School here, had started a GI course in pharmacy at Temple University in Philadelphia some time after he was honorably discharged from the service in 1945, but had stayed with it only three months. In recent months he had been unemployed, and apparently was not even looking for work.

Mother Separated From Husband

His mother, Mrs. Rita Unruh, 50, is separated from her husband. She works as a packer in the Evanson Soap Company in Camden and hers was virtually the only family income. James Unruh, 25 years old, her younger son, is married and lives in Haddon Heights, N.J. He works for the Curtis Publishing Company.

On Monday night, Howard Unruh left the house alone. He spent the night at the Family Theatre on Market Street in Philadelphia to sit through several showings of the double feature motion picture there—"I Cheated the Law" and "The Lady Gambles." It was past 3 o'clock this morning when he got home.

Prosecutor Cohen said that Unruh told him later that before he fell asleep this morning he had made up his mind to shoot the persons who had "talked about me," that he had even figured out that 9:30 a.m. would be the time to begin because most of the stores in his block would be open at that hour.

His mother, leaving her ironing when he got up, prepared his breakfast in their drab little three-room apartment in the shabby gray two-story stucco house at the corner of River Road and Thirty-Second Street. After breakfast he loaded one clip of bullets into his Luger, slipped another clip into his pocket, and carried sixteen loose cartridges in addition. He also carried a tear-gas pen with six shells and a sharp six-inch knife.

He took one last look around his bedroom before he left the house. On the peeling walls he had crossed pistols, crossed German bayonets, pictures of armored artillery in action. Scattered about the chamber were machetes, a Roy Rogers pistol, ash trays made of German shells, clips of 30-30 cartridges for his use and a host of varied war souvenirs.

Mrs. Unruh had left the house several minutes before, to call on Mrs. Caroline Pinner, a friend in the next block. Mrs. Unruh had sensed, apparently, that her son's smoldering resentments were coming to a head. She had pleaded with Elias Pinner, her friend's husband, to put a little gate in the Unruhs' back yard so that Howard need not use the Cohen gate again. Mr. Pinner finished the gate early Monday evening after Howard had gone to Philadelphia.

At the Pinners' house at 9 o'clock this morning, Mrs. Unruh had murmered something a b o u t Howard's eyes; how strange they looked and how worried she was about him.

A few minutes later River Road echoed and re-echoed to pistol fire. Howard Unruh was on the rampage. His mother, who had left the Pinners' little white house only a few seconds before, turned back. She hurried through the door.

She cried, "Oh, Howard, oh, Howard, they're to blame for this." She rushed past Mrs. Pinner, a kindly gray-haired woman of 70. She said, "I've got to use the phone; may I use the phone?"

But before she had crossed the living room to reach for it she fell on the faded carpet in a dead faint. The Pinners lifted her onto a couch in the next room. Mrs. Pinner applied aromatic spirits to revive her.

Panic Grips Entire Block

While his mother writhed on the couch in her house dress and worn, old sweater, coming back to consciousness, Howard Unruh was walking from shop to shop in the "3200 block" with deadly calm, spurting Luger in hand. Children screamed as they tumbled over one another to get out of his way. Men and women dodged into open shops, the women shrill with panic, men hoarse with fear. No one could quite understand for a time what had been turned loose in the block.

Unruh first walked into John Pilarchik's shoe repair shop near the north end of his own side of the street. The cobbler, a 27-year-old man who lives in Pennsauken Township, looked up open-mouthed as Unruh came to within a yard of him. The cobbler started up from his bench but went down with a bullet in his stomach. A little boy who was in the shop ran behind the counter and crouched there in terror. Unruh walked out into the sunlit street.

"I shot them in the chest first," he told the prosecutor later, in meticulous detail, "and then I aimed for the head." His aim was devastating—and with reason. He had won marksmanship and sharp-shooters' ratings in the service, and he practiced with his Luger all the time on a target set up in the cellar of his home.

Unruh told the prosecutor afterward that he had Cohen the druggist, the neighborhood barber, the neighborhood cobbler and the neighborhood tailor on his mental list of persons who had "talked about him." He went methodically about wiping them out. Oddly enough, he did not start with the druggist, against whom he seemed to have the sharpest feel-ings, but left him almost for last.

Newlywed Wife Shot Dead

From the cobbler's he went into the little tailor shop at 3214 River Road. The tailor was out. Helga Zagrino, 28 years old, the tailor's wife, was there alone. The couple, incidentally, had been married only one month. She screamed when Unruh walked in with his Luger in hand. Some people across the street heard her. Then the gun blasted again and Mrs. Zagrino pitched over, dead. Unruh walked into the sunlight again.

All this was only a matter of seconds and still only a few persons had begun to understand what was afoot. Down the street at 3210 River Road is Clark Hoover's little country barber shop. In the center was a white-painted carousel-type horse for children customers. Orris Smith, a blond boy only 6 years old, was in it, with a bib around his neck, submitting to a shearing. His mother, Mrs. Catherine Smith, 42, sat on a chair against the wall and watched.

She looked up. Clark Hoover turned from his work, to see the six-footer, gaunt and tense, but silent, standing in the doorway with the Luger. Un-ruh's brown tropical worsted suit was barred with awning shadow. The sun lay bright in his crew-cut brown hair. He wore no hat. Mrs. Smith could not understand what was about to happen.

Unruh walked to "Brux"—that is Mrs. Smith's nickname for her little boy—and put the Luger to the child's chest. The shot echoed and reverberated in the little 12 by 12 shop. The little boy's head pitched toward the wound, his hair, half-cut, stained with red. Unruh said never a word. He put the Luger close to the shaking barber's hand. Before the horrified mother, Unruh leaned over and fired another shot into Hoover.

The veteran made no attempt to kill Mrs. Smith. He did not seem to hear her screams. He turned his back and stalked out, unhurried, a few doors north. Cominick Latela, who runs a little restaurant, had come to his shop window to learn what the shooting was about. He saw Unruh cross the street toward Frank Engel's tavern. Then he saw Mrs. Smith stagger out with her pitiful burden. Her boy's head lolled over the crook of her right arm.

Mrs. Smith screamed "My boy is dead. I know he's dead." She stared about her, looking in vain for aid. No one but Howard Unruh was in sight and he was concentrating on the tavern. Latela rushed out, but first he shouted to his wife, Dora, who was in the restaurant with their daughter, Eleanor, 6 years old. He hollered "I'm going out. Lock the door behind me." He ran for his car, and drove it down toward Mrs. Smith as she stood on the pavement with her son.

Latela took the child from her arms and placed him on the car's front seat. He pushed the mother into the rear seat, slammed the doors and headed for Cooper Hospital. Howard Unruh had not turned. Engel, the tavern keeper, had locked his own door. His customers, the bartender, and a porter made a concerted rush for the rear of the saloon. The bullets tore through the tavern door panelling. Engel rushed upstairs and got out his .38 caliber pistol, then rushed to the street window of his apartment.

Unruh was back in the center of the street. He fired a shot at an apartment window at 3208 River Road. Tommy Hamilton, 2 years old, fell back with a bullet in his head. Unruh went north again to Latela's place. He fired a shot at the door, and kicked in the lower glass panel. Mrs. Latela crouched behind the counter with her daughter. She heard the bullets, but neither she nor her child was touched.

Unruh walked back toward Thirty-second Street, reloading the Luger.

Now the little street—a small block with only five buildings on one side, three one-story stores on the other—was shrill with women's and children's panicky outcries. A group of six or seven little boys or girls fled past Unruh. They screamed, "Crazy man!" and unintelligible sentences. Unruh did not seem to hear, or see, them.

Autoist Goes to His Death

Alvin Day, a television repair man who lives in near-by Mantua, had heard the shooting, but driving into the street he was not aware of what had happened. Unruh walked up to the car window as Day rolled by, and fired once through the window, with deadly aim. The repair man fell against the steering wheel. The car seemed to wabble. The front wheels hit the opposite curb and stalled. Day was dead.

Frank Engel had thrown open his second-floor apartment window. He saw Unruh pause for a moment in a narrow alley between the cobbler's shop and a little two-story house. He aimed and fired. Unruh stopped for just a second. The bullet had hit, but he did not seem to mind, after the initial brief shock. He headed toward the corner drug store, and Engel did not fire again.

"I wish I had," he said, later. "I could have killed him then. I could have put a half-dozen shots into him. I don't know why I didn't do it."

Cohen, the druggist, a heavy man of 40, had run into the street shouting "What's going on here? What's going on here?" but at the sight of Unruh hurried back into his shop. James J. Hutton, 45, an insurance agent from Westmont, N.J., started out of the drug shop to see what the shooting was about. Like so many others he had figured at first that it was some car backfiring. He came face to face with Unruh.

Unruh said quietly, "Excuse me, sir," and started to push past him. Later Unruh told the police; "That man didn't act fast enough. He didn't get out of my way." He fired into Hutton's head and body. The insurance man pitched onto the sidewalk and lay still.

Cohen had run to his upstairs apartment and had

tried to warn Minnie Cohen, 63, his mother, and Rose, his wife, 38, to hide. His son Charles, 14, was in the apartment, too. Mrs. Cohen shoved the boy into a clothes closet, and leaped into another closet herself. She pulled the door to. The druggist, meanwhile, had leaped from the window onto a porch roof. Unruh, a gaunt figure at the window behind him, fired into the druggist's back. The druggist, still running, bounded off the roof and lay dead in Thirty-second Street.

Unruh fired into the closet where Mrs. Cohen was hidden. She fell dead behind the closed door, and he did not bother to open it. Mrs. Minnie Cohen tried to get to the telephone in an adjoining bedroom to call the police. Unruh fired shots into her head and body and she sprawled dead on the bed. Unruh walked down the stairs with the Luger reloaded and came out into the street again.

A couple had stopped at River Road, obeying a red light. The passengers obviously had no idea of what was loose in East Camden and no one had a chance to tell them. Unruh walked up to the car, and though it was filled with total strangers, fired deliberately at them, one by one, through the windshield. He killed the two women passengers, Mrs. Helen Matlack Wilson, 43, of Pennsauken, who was driving, and her mother, Mrs. Emma Matlack, 66. Mrs. Wilson's son John, 12, was badly wounded. A bullet pierced his neck, just below the jawbone.

Several Take Refuge in Grocery

Earl Horner, clerk in the American Stores Company, a grocery opposite the drugstore, had locked his front door after several passing men, women and children had tumbled breathlessly into the shop panting "crazy man * * * killing people. * * *" Unruh came up to the door and fired two shots through the wood panelling. Horner, his customers, the refugees from the veteran's merciless gunfire, crouched, trembling, behind the counter. None there was hurt.

"He tried the door before he shot in here," Horner related afterward. "He just stood there, stony-faced and grim, and rattled the knob, before he started to fire. Then he turned away."

Charlie Petersen, 18, son of a Camden fireman,

came driving down the street with two friends when Unruh turned from the grocery. The three boys got out to stare at Hutton's body lying unattended on the sidewalk. They did not know who had shot the insurance man, or why and, like the women in the car, had no warning that Howard Unruh was on the loose. The veteran brought his Luger to sight and fired several times. Young Petersen fell with bullets in his legs. His friends tore pell-mell down the street to safety.

Mrs. Helen Harris of 1250 North Twenty-eighth Street with her daughter, Helen, a 6-year-old blonde child, and a Mrs. Horowitz with her daughter, Linda, 5, turned into Thirty-second Street. They had heard the shooting from a distance but thought it was auto backfire.

Unruh passed them in Thirty-second Street and walked up the sagging four steps of a little yellow dwelling back of his own house. Mrs. Madeline Harrie, a woman in her late thirties, and two sons, Armand, 16, and Leroy, 15, were in the house. A third son, Wilson, 14, was barricaded in the grocery with other customers.

Unruh threw open the front door and, gun in hand, walked into the dark little parlor. He fired two shots at Mrs. Harrie. They went wild and entered the wall. A third shot caught her in the left arm. She screamed. Armand leaped at Unruh, to tackle him. The veteran used the Luger butt to drop the boy, then fired two shots into his arms. Upstairs Leroy heard the shooting and the screams. He hid under a bed.

By this time, answering a flood of hysterical telephone calls from various parts of East Camden, police radio cars swarmed into River Road with sirens wide open. Emergency crews brought machine guns, shotguns and tear gas bombs.

Sergeant Earl Wright, one of the first to leap to the sidewalk, saw Charles Cohen, the druggist's son. The boy was half out the second-floor apartment window, just above where his father lay dead. He was screaming "He's going to kill me. He's killing everybody." The boy was hysterical.

Wright bounded up the stairs to the druggist's apartment. He saw the dead woman on the bed, and tried to soothe the druggist's son. He brought him downstairs and turned him over to other policemen, then joined the men who had surrounded the two-story stucco house where Unruh lived. Unruh, meanwhile, had fired about thirty shots. He was out of ammunition. Leaving the Harrie house, he had also heard the police sirens. He had run through the back gate to his own rear bedroom.

Guns Trained on Window

Edward Jozlin, a motorcycle p o l i c e m a n, scrambled to the porch roof under Unruh's window. He tossed a tear gas grenade through a pane of glass. Other policemen, hoarsely calling on Unruh to surrender, took positions with their machine guns and shotguns. They trained them on Unruh's window.

Meanwhile, a curious interlude had taken place. Philip W. Buxton, an assistant city editor on the Camden Evening Courier had looked Unruh's name up in the telephone book. He called the number, Camden 4-2490W. It was just after 10 a.m. and Unruh had just returned to his room. To Mr. Buxton's astonishment, Unruh answered. He said hello in a calm, clear voice.

"This is Howard?" Mr. Buxton asked.

"Yes, this is Howard. What's the last name of the party you want?"

"Unruh."

The veteran asked what Mr. Buxton wanted.

"I'm a friend," the newspaper man said. "I want to know what they're doing to you down there."

Unruh thought a moment. He said, "They haven't done anything to me—yet. I'm doing plenty to them." His voice was still steady without a trace of hysteria.

Mr. Buxton asked how many persons Unruh had killed.

The veteran answered: "I don't know. I haven't counted. Looks like a pretty good score."

"Why are you killing people?"

"I don't know," came the frank answer. "I can't answer that yet. I'll have to talk to you later I'm too busy now."

The telephone banged down.

Unruh was busy. The tear gas was taking effect and police bullets were thudding at the walls around him. During a halt in the firing the police saw the white curtains move and the gaunt killer came into plain view.

"Okay," he shouted. "I give up. I'm coming down."

"Where's that gun?" a sergeant yelled.

"It's on my desk, up here in the room," Unruh called down quietly. "I'm coming down."

Thirty guns were trained on the shabby little back door. A few seconds later the door opened and Unruh stepped into the light, his hands up. Sergeant Wright came across the morning glory and aster beds in the yard and snapped handcuffs on Unruh's wrists.

"What's the matter with you," a policeman demanded hotly. "You a psycho?"

Unruh stared into the policeman's eyes—a level, steady stare. He said, "I'm no psycho. I have a good mind."

Word of the capture brought the whole East Camden populace pouring into the streets. Men and women screamed at Unruh, and cursed him in shrill accents and in hoarse anger. Someone cried "lynch him," but there was no movement. Sergeant Wright's men walked Unruh to a police car and started for headquarters.

Shouting and pushing men and women started after the car, but dropped back after a few paces. They stood in excited little groups discussing the shootings, and the character of Howard Unruh. Little by little the original anger, born of fear, that had moved the crowd, began to die.

Men conceded that he probably was not in his right mind. Those who knew Unruh kept repeating how close-mouthed he was, and how soft spoken. How he took his mother to church, and how he marked scripture passages, especially the prophecies.

"He was a quiet one, that guy," a man told a crowd in front of the tavern. "He was all the time figuring to do this thing. You gotta watch them quiet ones."

But all day River Road and the side streets talked of nothing else. The shock was great. Men and women kept saying: "We can't understand it. Just don't get it."

They Belong To Me

Reader interest in details about a person accused of committing heinous crimes is high, especially if the person has been caught after a protracted, intensive search. Press conferences often are held for the accused. But virtually never has such a story approached the impact attained by Jack Smith in this rare gem for the Los Angeles *Times*. Readers who begin his dramatic, highly descriptive, detailed story dare not leave it unfinished. For the tempo and excitement introduced in the opening sentence builds steadily to a climax novelists strive for in vain.

Smith organized it in a series of individual segments, all strung together neatly with a variety of transitional devices—question, repetition of a key word or phrase, contrast. This press conference organization plus present tense verbs heighten the immediacy of the event. Smith's use of quotations for the well-expressed, the meaty, and summary for the less rapidly moving also merit study. His analyses of Stephen Nash and overpowering description of him literally seat us at the press conference. All of these techniques plus a keen sense of timing contribute to this story's strength.

By Jack Smith
Los Angeles Times, Dec. 14, 1956

Stephen Nash figures lawyers won't do him any good—not a man who has killed 11 human beings because he gets a kick out of murder.

"Lawyers!" he says, and laughs his mocking laugh. "Fifteen Willie Fallons couldn't win this case!"

Nash leans forward on his wooden chair in the interview room of the County Jail. His raw, sagging face grows thoughtful.

"Jesus died over 2000 years ago. He's the only one who could help now."

He rocks back in his chair and laughs aloud.

"And I doubt if even He could have done it — in His heyday."

So Stephen Nash, 33, sums up his chances in this world.

But Nash is happy—for a wretched man.

He's got his murders. They can't take those away from him.

"They belong to me!" he says fiercely. "They're mine! I certainly earned them."

Not Afraid To Die

And he's not afraid to die for his prizes; his beauties; the dead whose bodies have lain on beaches and sidewalks and in deep waters from Sacramento to Los Angeles.

"I'm willing to pay the price society sets on them," he says. "It's like going into a store and buying merchandise, isn't it?"

Nash knows all about death, and he knows how he will die.

"Maybe I have not lived like a man," he says. "But I certainly will die like one. They've only got a couple of little pills up there under the seat in the chamber. You can only die once."

He talks rapidly, eagerly, with a macabre cheerfulness that puts his listeners ill at ease. He gestures like a ham actor with hairy, huge hands that have a faintly female flutter. His mouth is wide and rubbery over the toothless gums. His large dark eyes under the bushy brows are like evil windows opening into the black cavern of his mind.

He is a man, he says. A human being.

"I killed a cat or two when I was a kid," he remembers. "That's about all."

Then his face lights up with a better memory.

"Until Burns," he says, adding his chilling "Haw!"

Burns was his first. Burns made him realize what his life work was to be. Burns was William C. Burns, 23, whose body he cramped into a duffel bag and tossed into San Francisco Bay.

Who were the others?

"Let's see," says Nash, crimping his face into thought. He counts slowly on his fingers. "There was Burns. And Berg. And then Barnett . . ." He frowns. "The three B's, I call them. There were three B's and an E . . . that's that fellow Eche . . . and an R."

Regrets Killing Boy

Nash's face grows stern and his eyebrows fall.

"The kid," he says. "He was the R."

The kid was 10-year-old Larry Rice, a Venice schoolboy, who met Nash on the way home from school and died under a Santa Monica pier with a mass of stab wounds in his back.

"Don't ask me about the boy," Nash says. "I don't want to discuss it any further."

Was he conscious stricken about the boy?

"Yes, yes. When people talk about it I am. It was just an unfortunate mistake on my part."

There were six others, of course. But Nash isn't talking about them. Not unless he gets paid for it. He wants $500 for the whole lot.

"Everybody's looking for something for nothing," he says, growing surly.

"There are honest people who would rob a good killer in a hot minute. Their consciences don't bother them. I'm on a lower social level."

What's he going to do with the money?

"I don't know. I haven't thought much about it. I just like money. I always liked money."

Will he ever name his six nameless victims before he dies unless he's paid?

"Certainly not," he says scornfully. "I'm going to take them with me in the gas chamber. I figure it will do my soul some good.

No Women Victims

Didn't he ever kill a woman—or think about it?

Stephen Nash's face grows reflective, sad.

"Women," he says softly. "I know, the usual pattern followed by a frustrated person—like me—is to follow women and attack them." He thought about it a moment. "But I . . . just never did."

Nash said he tried to get women interested in him. "Plenty of times. But it didn't work. I gave it up. Easily."

What drove him to kill more and more after he got started?

He laughs—back on his favorite subject.

"Why, I don't know. You get one, and then you get 10. And then 20, 50. And then you say, 'All right, I'll try for 100!'"

He roars at his own humor. "It's like a quiz show, you know?"

Didn't he ever think of using a gun? Wouldn't it have been simpler?

"Naw," he says contemptuously. "A gun's too . . . impersonal. I like to talk to a man a half-hour. Find out what kind of a man I'm doing in. Some of them aren't worth taking. That Burns fellow. I told them about him for $30. That's all he was worth.

Choking's No Good

"I'll tell you another thing about killing," he says. "This choking is no good. You know the scenes in the movies where they choke somebody like this?"

His big hands come up to illustrate. "And all of a sudden they go like this?" He makes a choking sound in his throat. "And then they go all limp? Those movies are wrong. They don't go like this [choking sound] and they don't go limp. Haw! I can tell you they don't go limp."

It was choking that got him in trouble, he recalls. When he jumped a man named Higgins and couldn't kill him with a lead pipe and tried to "choke him out."

Nash apologized for that one.

"That was in my amateur days. I didn't know anything. I've learned plenty since. I did six months for that. He got away. He was one of the lucky ones." Nash spits out a leaf of tobacco to show his scorn. "That hard-headed Okie!"

He was nearly linked with the Burns murder over the Higgins assault, he recalls.

"There was blood all over the seat of the car. The police experts they went over it and said it was animal blood. Haw! It was animal blood all right . . . male animal!"

It was Burns's blood.

But that case proved to Nash that he'll never escape the gas chamber by pleading insanity.

"I'll be found sane. Don't worry about that. I beat those two psychiatrists in Oakland, didn't I? Two psychs went over me and they let me walk out scott free. Haw!"

Nash figures to put on quite a show in the courtroom. "Boy, I'll have a ball!" he says jovially. Then a cloud comes over his face. "Say, what about that contempt of court? The judge can fine you for that, can't he?"

He worries over this. Then an idea strikes him. He grins. "You don't have to pay, do you? They can't make you pay. You can do time for it. I'll have a ball!"

No Known Family

Is there a family to worry about him?

"I never had a family. My mother and father were just a guy and a girl who got together. I think they told me about it a couple of weeks after I was born. Or a couple of days. I was born in the Bronx, I guess.

"I don't know. Honestly, there's so little I know about myself."

The gleam returns to his baleful eyes.

"But I know about human beings. That's why I killed so many."

Nash thinks his victims died pretty well, for human beings. All except Higgins.

"He wouldn't have made a good death."

The rest of them?

"I was quite surprised. Most of them died very well. No crying, no screaming, no praying for mercy."

The kid, too?

"I'm not interested in talking about that. No more free information."

But death is always interesting, even his own.

He lifts his heavy jaw, draws on his stub of cigarette and gives it his deepest thought.

"Yes," he admits. "I expect two hard days. Maybe the third and fourth days before the chamber. My subconscious will take over. There will be little desire to live. I'm still human. But then my mind will take over, the day before and the day. I certainly will die like a man."

There was suddenly another voice in Nash's world.

"You'll die screaming," somebody said quietly.

Nash's open face snapped shut in anger. He bent forward and scowled at the man who had spoken. He dropped his cigarette butt and ground it out with a foot. He aimed a long, rawboned finger at his tormentor.

He spoke in a voice that, for the first time, had lost its banter and was charged with human emotion.

"Out in the street," he said, "you'd be dead now!"

Who Are The Guilty?

"When children kill who are the guilty?" An answer to this provocative question was sought in an eleven-part series written by Victor Cohn, the Minneapolis *Tribune* science reporter. The series ran in December, 1947. Cohn checked several score of cases from throughout the United States before finding adequate scientific data on the eight selected for this series. He worked on his research eight months during which he travelled widely and interviewed many psychiatrists, psychologists, and sociologists.

William P. Steven, managing editor of the *Tribune*, wrote "Since the publication of 'Who Are the Guilty,' there has been a quickened and increased interest in the scientific aspects of delinquency. These stories have social significance—they represent journalism as a means of enlightenment and a force for improvement."

The *Tribune* is to be congratulated for financing this study; few newspapers would have done it. Yet this alone does not automatically qualify a story for inclusion in such a book as this. What does make these stories of high quality is their (1) thoroughness, (2) understandable, yet scientifically correct language, (3) straightforward, easy-to-read organization, and (4) inclusion of needed details without resorting to sensationalism.

This article is the first in his series.

By Victor Cohn
Minneapolis Tribune, Dec. 8, 1947

A 12-year-old boy in Chicago recently murdered a little 7-year-old, one of his playmates.

We gasp at this tragedy, and many ask why newspapers must print these "sensational" stories.

But how many ask another question: "Why did the boy do it?"

Why do children, and adolescents, kill? How can we stop them?

● Why did Howard Lang stab Lonnie Fellick and crush in his skull?

● Why did William Heirens, 17, murder two women

and finally Suzanne Degnan, 6, dismembering Suzanne's body and scattering it in the Chicago sewers?
● Why did Oliver Terpening, 16, calmly pick up a rifle and murder a boy and his three sisters, Oliver's closest friends?
● Why did Albert Jones, 14, strangle a 15-year-old girl he liked, then shoot a housewife as she was getting him a cookie?

Two Murders a Day

The list could be much longer. In 1946, 808 boys and girls under 21 were arrested for homicide—12 out of every 100 American murderers! Of these youths, 256 were under 18. Sixty-nine were 15 and under.

In the first six months of 1947, 415 boys and girls under 21 killed—more than two murders a day!

Why? Who are the guilty?

For eight months I have been collecting case histories and asking that question of psychiatrists, psychologists and sociologists all over the country. From them I have received a thousand answers. Each story is a tangle of facts.

Nation Is Lagging

But all the specialists have agreed on one thing. The stories, however unpleasant, must be told, if Americans are to understand the desperate need for helping the thousands of unhappy children whose plight these murders dramatize.

For this nation is shamefully behind the times in its treatment of maladjusted children, of boy and girl delinquents—and of juvenile killers.

Just last March an Albany, N. Y., district attorney had to urge his state legislature to modernize the law so that he would not be compelled to send a "normal" 14-year-old boy to the electric chair for hanging an 8-year-old chum. (The law, so far, has not been changed.)

Dr. Ralph S. Banay, New York psychiatrist who has made an exhaustive study of children who kill, pleads in his book "Youth in Despair" (to be published in January by Coward-McCann):

"The only cause for optimism is the amount of space the press devotes to this and similar cases.

Soon, no literate person will be able to remain unaware of the importance and magnitude of the problem of juvenile delinquency, and the out-dated nature of existing laws."

Stories Aren't Pretty

The experts agree. The stories are not pretty. But this is an emergency.

We must face the facts.

Why, then—let us begin with one of the most revealing histories of all—did a 17-year-old "model" college boy become a triple killer?

The true story of William George Heirens was brought to light by three medical experts, after a long series of interviews conducted in the quiet of the chapel of the Cook county jail.

The experts, appointed by the court, were Dr. Harry R. Hoffman, Illinois state psychiatrist; Dr. Foster Kennedy, chief neurologist at New York City's Bellevue hospital, and Dr. William H. Haines, director of the Cook county criminal court behavior clinic. (Duluth-born Dr. Haines was graduated from the University of Minnesota medical school in 1932 and later spent a year at Rochester's Mayo clinic.)

Danger Signals Ignored

The story they unearthed began with abnormal sexual behavior when Heirens was only 9 years old. It continued with a series of bizarre episodes—outstanding, even in this unenlightened age, for the way parents, school, church and authorities ignored the danger signals.

William Heirens was a "solitary child, sensitive but difficult to know," reported the doctors. "Apparently no one ever had a close or confidential relationship with him. Certainly his parents did not."

At 9, this pitiful boy began stealing women's underclothing from clotheslines, cellars and unlocked houses. He would put the undergarments on and experience self-satisfaction.

At 11 or 12, he began to steal other things instead, not because he wanted them, but because "it seemed sort of foolish to break in and not take anything." Now he experienced his physical excitement merely at the act of crawling through an open window.

Heirens Gave Warnings

Psychiatry knows such behavior well and calls it "fetishism": sexual gratification by the sight or touch of some substitute object (another person's hair or foot or some piece of wearing apparel) or even by some substitute act.

Fetishism is no childish quirk, but a clear warning that treatment is needed. Young William gave society warnings aplenty.

For one thing, he confessed his fetishism to a priest. For another, when only 9, and still concentrating on women's clothing, he appeared before a children's court.

At 13, on the day he was to have graduated from grammar school, police caught him breaking into a storeroom. He spent a year at a private school for delinquent boys, but two months after his release was again arrested for burglary. His parents begged and the court granted probation, so William might attend a private prep school.

Accepted at College

He was an honor student and faithful in fulfilling his religious duties. At 16, after placement tests, the liberal University of Chicago accepted him as a sophomore, dispensing with the fourth year of high school and first year of college.

But William's deep maladjustment continued.

Now the youth (190 pounds, 6 feet tall and "strong as an ox") roamed the Chicago lake front at night, stealing into perhaps 300 homes and apartments within less than 10 months—with the same perverted purpose as in his childhood thefts.

A tragic struggle raged within his mind.

In 1942, after twice seeing the movie "Dr. Jekyll and Mr. Hyde," he had invented an imaginary "George." It was "George," not William, who was evil. As William studied in his Chicago dormitory room, "George" would tempt him.

Urge Drove Him Out

"Usually when I had to get out," Heirens said, "I would ask him (George) where he was going. We would talk back and forth . . . I would argue in every way possible with him, but he always wanted to get out.

"When I tried to resist him, I would get a head-ache," Heirens confessed. "It seemed like my head was a balloon filled with water."

Trying painfully hard, Heirens three or four times locked his clothes in a closet. But the urge drove him out clad only in bathrobe and slippers, forced him through his window into sub-zero weather, along an icy sixth-floor gutter and down a fire escape to go on more weird burglary sprees.

Often he merely entered a home and then, fully satisfied, departed without stealing anything. When he did steal, he remained uncaught, because he never tried to sell the loot.

He intended no murders. He committed three.

Each time, he testified, "it was the noise that set me off."

In June, 1945, he entered the apartment of Mrs. Josephine Ross, a divorcee. She awakened, screamed, and he stabbed her to death.

Scrawled Message

In December, 1945, he entered the apartment of Frances Brown. A dog barked, and Miss Brown—a stenographer honorably discharged from the WAVES three months earlier—ran out of the bathroom in her nightgown. She screamed, and he shot her, then stabbed her until she was dead.

He dragged her body back into the bathroom, found her lipstick and scrawled an agonized message on the wall: "For heaven's sake, catch me before I kill more. I cannot control myself."

Twenty-eight days later he strangled the blonde, blue-eyed Degnan child. Again he had been surprised as a victim awoke during his prowling.

Forgot Mutilation

William told the doctors that he remembered murdering Suzanne, but could not recall mutilating her body. Here, there was partial amnesia.

Trying to remember, Heirens said, was like gazing at a floor with holes in it. "I've tried to look through the holes to see what is down there. There are just not enough holes to find out."

After the Degnan affair, he went to an all-night restaurant, had coffee and doughnuts, then at 6 a.m. returned to his dormitory to study. Five months later he was caught by police during another burglary.

The doctors found Heirens physically normal in almost every respect. But when they inserted a sharp needle into his fingertip, almost to the base of the fingernail, the boy felt no pain. Nor did he feel sharp pin pricks at many sensitive parts of the body.

This was hysteria—"imaginary reality."

Conscience Was Clear

So the specialists said: "This striking reduction of power to appreciate painful stimulation as such, together with its remarkable deepening as the result of suggestion, is to us clear proof of the patient's hysterical personality."

And the invention of the evil George revealed "a power for hysterical fantasy to be expected in a hysterical individual passing through long-sustained emotional conflict."

Putting the blame on George enabled William to live with untroubled conscience—and continue prowling.

The boy had "an immense egocentricity," despite his failure to rule himself. He pasted pictures of Hitler, Goering and Goebbels in his scrapbooks, and he wrote:

"I wonder why I can't run the world. . . . Wouldn't it be great to have that much power? Men sacrifice their lives for it. There must be an easier and faster way to gain control."

Aware of Acts

William Heirens, the experts concluded, suffered from no psychosis (the most extreme form of mental disease) or retarded intelligence. He could understand "the proceedings against him," conduct his defense in a "rational and reasonable manner" and had "always been aware of the nature and purpose of his acts."

However, the report concluded: "He has a deep sexual perversion, and is as emotionally insensitive within as he is incapable of feeling pain without. He is unstable and hysterically unpredictable."

Why?

There is no easy answer, but inadequate sex education must bear much of the blame. Dr. Foster Kennedy has said, "If Heirens had received a proper sex education, he probably would have been normal."

When William was 10 or 11, he saw some sex antics among small boys. Upset, he told his mother (whom Dr. Kennedy described to the New York Academy of Medicine as "a prim, buttoned-up woman, a good housekeeper, chic and smart, and a strict Catholic").

She told William only: "All sex is dirty. If you touch anyone, you get a disease." Other than that, no sex instruction was given by William's parents.

Normalcy Repugnant

Heirens' examiners became convinced that the boy actually regarded normal sex experience as far more repugnant than murder.

At the university, he finally had begun to have a few dates. On eight occasions, he said, he tried haltingly to embrace girls. Each time he immediately burst into tears and was "upset and unable to sleep."

No such remorse followed any of his burglaries or killings.

Legally, Heirens was declared "sane." He pleaded guilty to the three murders, was sentenced to life imprisonment and sent to Joliet penitentiary. Prison psychiatrists soon judged him unbalanced, and he was transferred to the psychiatric division of the Illinois state prison at Menard.

Dr. William Haines told me, "Heirens was in fact mentally ill."

Why didn't society find that out sooner—say when he was 9 years old?

Dr. Ralph Banay contends: "Had the boy then been turned over at once to a qualified psychiatrist for examination, it is safe to predict that the subsequent murders would not have been committed."

Why did William Heirens kill?

Instead, why not ask: "Who tried to stop him?"

Who are the guilty—William Heirens and the other child killers? Or their parents, their clergymen, their children's court judges, their teachers—you and I?

It Vas No My Mule

Texans were literally up in arms in opposition to a state Supreme Court ruling in March, 1950, so much so that they contributed to repay the loser—an immigrant farmer—the damages assessed. Because, you see, "It vas no my mule," which caused an automobile wreck, William Hagedorn proved. Yet he was found guilty . . . because he failed to appear in court to defend himself—a victim of a strange language and stranger court procedure.

Dawson Duncan of The Dallas *Morning News* staff, among others, covered the trial through the Texas civil court system. This story, based on payment of damages, is one of those rare times when dialect adds. It adds by communicating the disbelieving bewilderness of this old German farmer. Duncan wisely summarized for readers actions which had been reported previously, even though this event had received wide coverage and editorial comment in The *News*.

Note the simple, step-by-step chronology beginning in paragraph five and running to the end. Simplicity adds greatly to this story's effectiveness.

By Dawson Duncan
The Dallas Morning News, March 29, 1950

LOCKHART, Texas—The law took Farmer William Hagedorn's $2,632.20 bank account Tuesday.

Every penny he had in the First Lockhart National Bank—his cash savings of half a century in frugal living and farming near here—went to pay damages for an auto wreck caused by a mule he did not own.

The humble, 77-year-old German farmer couldn't understand it. Over and over, he repeated, "It vas no my mule."

Just the same, six of the nine justices of the Supreme Court ruled he had to pay more than $3,000 in damages to the W. C. Alexanders of Austin.

Atty. Fleetwood Richards called Hagedorn into his office Tuesday. In simple language he told Hagedorn this was the end of the court fight. He had done everything he could to save him. What the Supreme Court said now was the law in this case.

He told Hagedorn that William Yelderman, attorney for the Alexanders, had agreed to take the $2,632.20 in full payment of the judgment and court costs. With two years of interest and court costs, the total now would be over $3,600.

Farmer Still Can 'No Unnerstand'

By agreeing to the offer, Richards told Hagedorn he could be completely free of the balance of the judgment.

Haltingly, the man who can't read or write English said:

"I do no unnerstand.

"Ve vun here. Then ve vun in court at Austin. Then ve lose in another court in Austin. I do no unnerstand. It vas no my mule."

"Yes," agreed Richards. But the last time they lost in Austin it was in the Supreme Court and that made it the law so far as Hagedorn was concerned.

Then Richards told him District Judge John R. Fuchs soon would be in the courthouse to enter the final order. Judge Fuchs could explain it to him in the German language he well understands.

Hagedorn sat silently as tears welled in his faded eyes and his labor-roughened hands trembled.

"Better I go get my wife," he decided.

Judge Fuchs was willing to wait a couple of hours. He is terribly upset about it, too.

But he had done all he could. He reversed an earlier ruling which he made in absence of Hagedorn after he had been led to believe Hagedorn admitted owning the mule. Then he denied damages.

The Court of Civil Appeals at Austin agreed with him. But a majority of the Supreme Court did not. It ruled Judge Fuchs' first order must stand and Hagedorn must pay $3,126.84 damages.

Goes Back Home for His Wife

Hagedorn went to his little farm home between Uhland and Niederwald and got his wife, Paulina. Because of illness, she had difficulty in walking.

Slowly the aged couple trudged up the iron steps to the second floor of the Caldwell County courthouse.

There Judge Fuchs slowly told them what they must pay and what the offer of a final settlement of the judgment meant. Once it was in English, so attorneys would know. Then again in German, so the Hagedorns could fully understand.

He told them it meant the case was settled for all time—that they could keep their little farm and once more start a bank account that would be theirs. It meant they would have to pay only the bank account of $2,632.20.

The Hagedorns tried hard to keep back their tears. She asked a question in German.

"It means that you can keep that little farm, free of debt," answered Judge Fuchs.

Hagedorn also asked a question in German.

"You have a clear conscience," answered the judge.

"We all know you have done no wrong. I know it is an injustice. And now many thousands of Texans also know it was an injustice.

"There are many who want to correct this injustice by giving you money to pay what has been taken away from you."

Hagedorn interrupted again.

People Do Not Want Injustice Done

"No, you must take the money the people want to give you. I hope—I can not say that it will—but I hope it will be as much as you have lost. It is because the people of Texas do not want an injustice done to you."

He told them of a $25 check Richards had received from a Wichita Falls lawyer who thought there should be enough lawyers in Texas wanting to right a wrong to make up the $2,632.20.

"There will be others, I know," he added.

"You have been hurt. But this case will be a lesson for others. In that way it may be you will have helped many others."

Hagedorn realized then there was no more hope to keep his money. He nodded silently.

Judge Fuchs started to go from the office into the courtroom. He saw Mrs. Hagedorn struggle to arise from her chair.

Instead, he called for the clerk to bring the records to him.

Carefully he read the judgment and release of any further claims against the Hagedorns. He approved and signed in the court records terms of the "full and final adjudication."

Yelderman then went across the street to get the money from the First Lockhart National Bank—the bank that also had tried in court, but unsuccessfully, to keep from paying out Hagedorn's account.

Hagedorn and his wife started back to their little farm, wondering how they will ever again save up what they had planned to be their old age pension.

———————————————

REPORTING
AT ITS BEST

PART 6 ━━━━━━━━━ ★★★★★★

WAR, HOT AND COLD

AMERICANS celebrated Japan's capitulation, Aug. 14, 1945, assuming this would herald a return to world-wide peace. But this dream disintegrated in less than a year, to be replaced by what has come to be known as cold war. The question might well be asked: How hot must a cold war flare before it becomes war? Scarcely a month has passed without fighting somewhere—Greece, China, Southeast Asia, Korea, Hungary, Suez, India, Pakistan, Tibet, Latin America, Africa. It is as if the very globe we live on is honeycombed with holocaust, erupting spasmodically through geographically diverse fissures. Is it any wonder then that seven of the nine stories in this chapter are of war?

Japan Signs, Second World War Is Ended

Where better to start than with Homer Bigart's imaginative story on the signing of Japan's surrender. It appeared in the New York *Herald Tribune*. This and other articles won for Bigart the Pulitzer Prize for international reporting.

The story is pointedly brief—Why pad it? Its greatest power comes from clever phrasing, especially in the lead. His subtle reminders of the grimness of the occasion, the suffering of Americans, and our reaching the brink of defeat give added depth and purpose.

By Homer Bigart
New York Herald Tribune, Sept. 3, 1945

ABOARD U.S.S. MISSOURI, TOKYO BAY, Sept. 2—Japan, paying for her desperate throw of the dice at Pearl Harbor, passed from the ranks of the major powers at 9:05 a.m. today when Foreign Minister Mamoru Shigemitsu signed the document of unconditional surrender.

If the memories of the bestialities of the Japanese prison camps were not so fresh in mind, one might have felt sorry for Shigemitsu as he hobbled on his wooden leg toward the green baize-covered table where the papers lay waiting.

He leaned heavily on his cane and had difficulty seating himself. The cane, which he rested against the table, dropped to the deck of the battleship as he signed.

No word passed between him and General Douglas MacArthur who motioned curtly to the table when he had finished his opening remarks.

Lieutenant-General Jonathan M. Wainwright, who surrendered Corregidor, haggard from his long imprisonment, and Lieutenant-General A. E. Percival, who surrendered Singapore on another black day of the war, stood at MacArthur's side as the Allied Supreme Commander signed for all the powers warring against Japan.

Their presence was a sobering reminder of how desperately close to defeat our nation had fallen during the early months of 1942.

The Japanese delegation of eleven looked appropriately trim and sad. Shigemitsu was wearing morning clothes—frock coat, striped pants, silk hat, and yellow gloves. None of the party exchanged a single word of salute while on board, except the foreign minister's aide, who had to be shown where to place the Japanese texts of the surrender document.

Shigemitsu, however, doffed his silk hat as he reached the top of the starboard gangway and stepped aboard the broad deck of the Missouri.

9 Trapped GI's Stand Off Waves Of Reds In 10-Hour Onslaught

Less than five years after the Japanese surrender American soldiers were killing and being killed in the Korean "police action." This was an embarrassingly tragic war in that United Nations forces, largely supplied by the United States, were all but driven into the sea during the early weeks of the conflict. Then, in late November, when total victory seemed assured, endless waves of Chinese Communist troops overran United Nations positions in the icy mountains at the northern border of North Korea, slaughtering thousands of Americans and wounding thousands more. The brutal Korean winter was no less an enemy as troops fought off hordes of Chinese and virtually impassable roads to reach safety. Again, the twin questions arose: Could our troops avoid annihilation? Would they be driven off the peninsula?

Not one United States newsman was in Korea when hostilities broke out. So with the build-up of arms came the amassing of war correspondents. Marguerite Higgins established herself during the war and such veterans as Keyes Beech, Chicago *Daily News;* Jack MacBeth, Associated Press; and Gene Symonds, United Press, resumed their war correspondence roles.

Miss Higgins asked and gave no quarter while establishing herself as the first real front lines woman correspondent. Her copy was spiced with graphic description, often gathered under fire. This piece for the New York *Herald Tribune* is fairly representative. Note her use of summary and quotes to relate this relatively minor battle. Comparing this skirmish to Indian fighting (par. 2) illustrates her imaginative approach to reporting.

By Marguerite Higgins
New York Herald Tribune, Aug. 17, 1950

WITH U.S. 34th INFANTRY REGIMENT, On Central Front in Korea—The circular grain-filled mill was completely surrounded, and there were only nine men left in Charlie Company (C Company) who could still shoot. Forty wounded were stacked in the middle of the room.

It went straight back to Indian-fighting covered-wagon warfare, only the gimmick here was that the Korean enemy had superior fire power.

"And yet, by God, we somehow held them off for ten hours until our tank broke through and got us. It was the roughest thing I've heard of in this war."

This was Lt. Charles Payne, of Neosho, Mo., speaking. He is the only officer still around to tell the tale, perhaps the most dramatic of the war. Lt. Payne has a good basis for comparison, for he has been continuously in action since the first day of American participation in this war, when I saw him lead a bazooka team into action.

The Communist onslaught against the trapped American company was only one remarkable incident of the current American attempt to wipe out the enemy bridgehead against the Naktong River here.

"The main reason we stood them off, I think, was because we had given up all hope of getting out," Lt. Payne said. "Once we had accepted death as inevitable, everybody calmed down. It even became kind of exciting instead of just plain terrifying. We would ration out ammunition—we took it from the dead, the dying and the wounded—and go from window to window, waiting to fire till each man was sure he could really hit something."

The last-ditch stand of Charlie Company in the grain mill on the Naktong River road developed out of a counter-attack in which it was sent to rescue another hard-pressed unit.

"The enemy let us go right down the road past their positions, then closed in on us from all sides," Lt. Payne said. "Most of us took shelter under a bridge about 100 yards from the mill. We had lots of wounded down there. Finally, they started shooting under the bridge. They had machine guns, automatic weapons, rifles, everything on us. I told the walking wounded to make a dash for the mill, and the rest of us ran with them, trying to give cover as best we could. The guy running next to me got it just as we reached the mill."

The mill had thin walls, but big bags of grain afforded Charlie Company shelter from the bullets peppering the building. The remnants of the company reaching the mill had one Browning automatic rifle, carbines and M-1s.

"We stacked the wounded in the middle, two and three deep," Lt. Payne continued. "It was pretty awful as the day wore on because we ran out of water and first-aid kits.

"A few died. There was one guy kept begging me to shoot him all day. After the tank came we got him down to the aid station and they were trying to get a helicopter to take him back because he would never have survived the ambulance ride. I don't know what ever happened to him.

"In the mill they kept hitting the oil cans and the oil in the machinery. It was pretty terrible because the hot liquid kept dropping down on the wounded there in the middle of the room."

Lt. Payne, the battalion executive officer, assigned the men to windows with ammunition to use only when they were sure of a killing.

"In the first minutes it was pretty panicky in there. A couple of guys made a break for it across the rice paddies, and got it. Then we knew there was no alternative, so we were stuck. We decided to go down fighting. Pretty soon the guys were saying, 'Look at that one step into the firing,' and just try to get as many of them as we could dust off, and stuff like that. I knew they had steadied and everything was O.K."

The Koreans kept coming at the building in waves of a dozen or more, but accurate fire threw them back.

"There was a brief period when we thought they had given up," Lt. Payne recounted. "We saw them marching away from us in formation. I told the guys not even to breathe. But the wounded kept groaning. That chilled you, because you thought it might divert them back to us. But later we found that they had just gone around to come at us another way."

Charlie Company took refuge in the mill at 8 a.m. At 6:30 p.m., when help came, a substantial number of wounded had died from their old wounds, and there were new wounds inflicted by enemy guns and grenades.

"We could see the tank coming towards us, opening up on machine gun positions, with blasts tossing Reds into the air, and boy, were we happy," Lt. Payne said.

"Lt. Albert Alfonso of Honolulu, and his company were with the tank, and they came through, firing from the hip. The Reds kept firing, but we got everybody out and back down the road."

Lt. Payne, a very lucky guy, is the only staff officer of his battalion still at the front and still pressing his luck. The rest were killed or wounded.

Not At Tarawa Or Iwo Did Men Suffer So

Chicago *Daily News* editors had the choice of two graphic stories of the First Marine Division's fighting withdrawal from the Changjin Reservoir—one by their own Keyes Beech and one by Jack MacBeth of The Associated Press. They ran both. These were two of the most vividly descriptive, moving, dramatic stories to come out of the Korean War. It is difficult to choose between them, so let's look at both, realizing both Beech and MacBeth reported largely what they lived through.

Beech's lead, often quoted and misquoted, tells clearly what happened. Beech, the veteran war correspondent, drew on his experience for paragraphs six and seven. He wrote sympathetically of the Marines, a branch he has come to love, and so has great compassion and admiration for them, their suffering, and their eventual break to freedom over seemingly impossible odds. These soldiers become people, friends under the deft pen of Beech. The incidents and quotes selected are unchallengeable.

By Keyes Beech
Chicago Daily News (Foreign Service), Dec. 11, 1950

YONPO AIRSTRIP, Korea—"Remember," drawled Col. Lewis B. "Chesty" Puller, "whatever you write, that this was no retreat.

"All that happened was we found more Chinese behind us than in front of us. So we about-faced and attacked."

I said "so-long" to Puller after three snowbound days with the 1st Marine Division, 4,000 feet above sea level in the sub-zero weather of Changjin reservoir. I climbed aboard a waiting C-47 at Koto airstrip and looked around.

Sixteen shivering marine casualties—noses and eyes dripping from cold—huddled in their bucket seats. They were the last of more than 2,500 marine casualties to be evacuated by the U. S. Air Force under conditions considered flatly impossible.

Whatever this campaign was—retreat, withdrawal or defeat—one thing can be said with certainty.

Not in the Marine Corps' long and bloody history has there been anything like it.

And if you'll pardon a personal recollection, not at Tarawa or Iwo Jima, where casualties were much greater, did I see men suffer as much.

Cold Is Major Threat

The wonder isn't that they fought their way out against overwhelming odds but that they were able to survive the cold and fight at all.

So far as the marines themselves are concerned, they ask that two things be recorded:

1. They didn't break. They came out of Changjin reservoir as an organized unit with most of their equipment.

2. They brought out all their wounded. They brought out many of their dead. And most of those they didn't bring out they buried.

It was not always easy to separate dead from wounded among the frozen figures that lay strapped to radiators of jeeps and trucks.

I know because I watched them come in from Yudam to Hagaru, 18 miles of icy hell, five days ago.

That same day I stood in the darkened corner of a wind-whipped tent and listened to a Marine officer brief his men for the march to Koto the following day. I have known him for a long time but in the semi-darkness, with my face half-covered by my parka, he didn't recognize me. When he did the meeting broke up. When we were alone, he cried. After that he was all right.

I hope he won't mind my reporting he cried, because he's a very large Marine and a very tough guy.

He cried because he had to have some sort of

emotional release; because all his men were heroes and wonderful people; because the next day he was going to have to submit them to another phase in the trial by blood and ice.

Besides, he wasn't the only one who cried.

In the marines' 12-day, 40-mile trek from Yudam to the "bottom of the hill" strange and terrible things happened.

Chinese Boil From Every Canyon

Thousands of Chinese troops—the marines identified at least six divisions totaling 60,000 men—boiled from every canyon and rained fire from every ridge.

Sometimes they came close enough to throw grenades into trucks, jeeps and ambulances.

Whistles sounded and Chinese ran up to throw grenades into marine foxholes. Another whistle and the Chinese ran back.

Then mortar shells began to fall. The 3rd Battalion of the 5th Marine Regiment was reduced to less than two companies, but still was ordered to "attack regardless of cost."

"We had to do it," said Lt. Col. Joe Stewart, Montgomery, Ala. "It was the only way out."

Fox Company, 7th Regiment, was isolated for three or four days—nobody seems to remember dates or days—but held at terrible cost.

One company killed so many Chinese the marines used their frozen bodies as a parapet. But for every Chinese they killed there were 5, 10 or 20 to take his place.

"What-'n-hell's the use in killing them," said one marine. "They breed faster'n we can knock 'em off."

The Chinese had blown bridges and culverts behind the Americans. The marines rebuilt them or established bypasses under fire.

No part of a division escaped, including headquarters sections composed of file clerks, cooks and bakers. Bullets plowed through a Korean house in Hagaru occupied by Gen. O. H. P. Smith.

Always the infantry had to take high ground on each side of the road to protect the train of vehicles that sometimes stretched 10 miles.

When the Chinese attacked a train the artillerymen unhooked their guns from their vehicles and fired muzzle bursts from between trucks at the on-rushing foe.

This was effective, but rather rough on marine machine gunners who had set up their guns on the railroad tracks 15 or 20 yards in front of the artillery.

If there was an occasional respite from the enemy there was none from the cold. It numbed fingers, froze feet, sifted through layers of clothing and crept into the marrow of your bones.

Feet Sweat, Then Freeze

Feet sweated by day and froze in their socks by night.

Men peeled off their socks—and the soles of their feet with them.

Among the men of the 5th Marines, Lt. Cmdr. Chester M. Lessenden, Jr., 32, Lawrence, Kan., a Navy doctor, became a hero.

"Lessenden is the most saintly, Godlike man I've ever known," said Stewart.

"He never seemed to sleep. He was always on his feet. He never said it can't be done. And yet he was suffering from frostbite worse than most of the men he treated."

(Lessenden is a graduate of the University of Kansas, where his wife teaches speech. They have two daughters.)

In their struggle to keep from freezing, the marines wrapped their feet in gunnysacks or pieces of old cloth scrounged from the countryside.

When they could they built fires, but this wasn't often because fire gave away their positions.

When they camped at Koto before the final break-through to the sea they made tents of varicolored parachutes used by the Air Force to drop supplies. The red, white and green chute tents looked like Indian wigwams.

Some covered themselves with Japanese quilts dropped from the air.

But they were the warmest when they were fighting. Combat was almost welcome because they forgot about the cold.

The cold did strange things to their equipment. Because of sub-zero temperatures artillery rounds landed as much as 2,000 yards short. Machine guns froze up. Men tugged frantically at their frozen bolts.

The M-1 rifle generally held up, but the marines cursed the lighter carbine.

Communications gear broke down because equipment, like men, can stand only so much. Canteens burst as water froze inside them.

Despite all these things, the Marines who walked down from Changjin reservoir still could laugh.

"It was impossible for us to get out because we were surrounded, encircled, and cut off," said one lieutenant. "But we never got the word so we came on out. That's us—we never get the word."

Escape Through Icy Hell

What is said of Beech's graphic description fits also Mac-Beth's article. He used a summary lead, one which tells the story accurately and forcefully. His first four paragraphs re-create the action vividly through salty, Marine-Corps-like language: "a gory nightmare of death" (par. 1), "did it on guts" (par. 3), "one of the fightingest retreats in military history" (par. 3).

Then he began the account chronologically (par. 6), tracing step by step the fight from encirclement. Rich language, brief sentences, interesting quotations, all contribute to the impact of MacBeth's story.

By Jack MacBeth
The Associated Press, Dec. 11, 1950

WITH MARINES WITHDRAWING F R O M CHANGJIN RESERVOIR, Korea—(AP)—American Marines walked out of 12 days of freezing hell Sunday, full of fight after a gory nightmare of death in Korea's icy mountains.

The U.S. Marine Division was rolling slowly into the northeastern Korea plains of Hamhung. The men's eyes and bearded faces, their tattered parkas and the strangely careless way they carried their rifles, showed the strain.

These thousands of Leathernecks did it on guts. They turned their encirclement into one of the fightingest retreats in military history. It was the longest pullback in Marine records—50 tortuous miles.

They broke out of a death trap sprung by many thousands of Red Chinese and Koreans and converted what looked like almost certain disaster into a moral triumph if not a military victory.

I watched the retreat.

The story began in the fleabitten Korean village of Yudam, on the western edge of the Changjin reservoir.

Pressure Was Overwhelming

Three Red Chinese divisions and one Chinese regiment attacked two Marine regiments in a surprise offensive the night of Nov. 28.

The pressure was overwhelming. The Marines struck right back.

When orders were given to pull back, the Leathernecks responded with an offensive.

For five hectic, heroic days they matched guts and wits against Chinese mass tactics. Neither was enough to win. They had to pull out.

Five days after leaving Yudam, the Marines reached Hagaru, at the south end of the reservoir. There they joined another small group which was encircled by strong enemy forces.

Elements of a third Marine regiment were under attack at Koto, 10 road miles to the south.

At daybreak, Dec. 7, the Hagaru Marines jumped off southward towards Koto.

For 24 hours, they fought one of the bloodiest battles of the Korean war.

I was in Koto when they came in. It was a gruesome sight—wounded men with their blood frozen to their skins; their clothes stiff with ice; grotesque dead men lying across trailers, stretchers; live men stumbling along, grumbling from frostbite, using their rifles as crutches.

Four thousand men were evacuated by air from Hagaru and Koto up to two days ago. More have been flown out since.

Most of these were Marines, the others were remnants of two battalions of the Army's 7th Infantry

Division, which was cut off and sliced up on the east side of the reservoir at the same time the Leathernecks were catching hell on the west.

The dead count is high. Two days ago I watched nearly 200 bodies nosed into a single grave by a bulldozer. There was no time for more elaborate arrangements.

For the record, the U.S. 1st Marine Division, one of the country's finest, has suffered heavily. The Communist enemy knows this.

Chinese Casualties Much Higher

The Leathernecks inflicted casualties on the enemy many times those suffered. The weather also took a heavy toll of Chinese.

Tension greeted the order for all the Marines to break from Koto.

One senior officer wept.

A grizzled Marine blurted: "These kids are too good to have this happen to them."

Saturday at sunrise patrols struck out from Koto toward Hamhung.

Intelligence reports had said the enemy was in this area in strength. There were fears that another bloodbath was in store similar to that on the Hagaru-Koto road earlier.

But the patrols reached their objectives on schedule. One suffered moderate casualties; the other made it almost without incident. Immediately after these groups had left, the vehicular columns began to move. Equipment considered more of a burden than its actual value was destroyed.

By noon the column was stretched about 2 miles south of Koto.

Dismal little Koto lies on a plateau 3,300 feet above sea level. For two miles south, the narrow road, if anything, goes up. Then it twists down a narrow gorge 12 miles to a valley below. Saturday and Sunday it was covered with ice. The temperature was 25 degrees below zero.

For four hours, the column stood motionless.

Build Bridge Under Fire

A bridge a mile below the crest had been blown by the Reds.

Before the engineers could work on it, a company

of Marines had to drive off a pocket of Chinese guarding it. This was done. Fifteen Chinese were killed and 50 captured. Others fled.

Lt. Floyd Ward of Evansville, Ind., commanded the bridging operation.

"It was a tough one," he said. "We didn't have enough of a span to close the gap so we had to build up the abutment. We completed the job in less than four hours."

Then the column started to roll, but road conditions made progress slow. By nightfall Saturday, some one hundred vehicles had moved across the new bridge.

The entire operation depended on the effectiveness of this bridge. There was no possibility of a bypass. On one side was a rugged cliff, on the other was a chasm.

About 9 p.m. artillery dropped several rounds in the bridge vicinity. One shell hit a truck.

As the enemy had not used artillery in this area before, and the fire apparently was coming from the bottom of a hill where a friendly battery was known to be in position, observers concluded it was friendly fire.

Throughout the night there was sniping from the hills overlooking the winding road.

Shortly after midnight the column came to a halt. It didn't move appreciably for four hours. Two miles south of the bridge, at a hairpin turn, two trucks skidded and blocked the road. About 100 husky Marines shoved them out of the way.

There was only starlight and brief flashes of brilliance as shells hit the towering hills all around us.

Dare Not Sleep

Four Marines on the truck I was riding huddled in blankets. All chewed gum and spoke occasionally in soft tones. They knew they dared not sleep. Each had a gun. A machine gun was mounted on the back of the truck, but it was not needed Saturday night.

These kids mainly had two thoughts uppermost in their minds: their families and their determination to whip the enemy.

"I'm still carrying a small hunk of steel in my

ankle," said one. "When I get home that will make me think of this damned place. Then again I'll feel like killing someone."

The column, stretching bumper to bumper all the way up the road, moved in fits and starts.

Just before daylight the mountain grade became less severe and the turns less harrowing. We were nearing the bottom.

For some reason I thought at this point of the dramatic 1st Cavalry Division sweep which I had accompanied across the country toward Seoul back in victory-flush September.

The contrast of this now-successful retreat quickly dispelled such pleasant reminiscences.

One of the Marines on the truck had a Korean pup.

Dog Cheers Weary Men

The dog had been whining through most of the night. As the full light of day appeared, the pup got up, stretched a bit and wagged his tail.

It was 7:30 a.m.

The pup's cheerfulness appeared to have been caught from his Leatherneck companions for whom nearly two weeks of concentrated hell had just ended. The Marines rubbed their sleepless red eyes and grinned.

There was no formal linkup with the 2d Division forces that had thrust up from the south.

The Marine column had proceeded in total darkness past individual members of the southern force without stopping.

After daylight, leading elements of the Marines continued southward from the juncture point in the vicinity of Chinhung, too weary to care about any formalities.

Christmas In A Foxhole

War is not all fighting. The tenseness, watchful alertness during periods of inactivity are tortuous. Add to this a deeply religious holiday, say Christmas, and you have the ingredients for high reader interest. This is doubly so when Gene Symonds, United Press, adds contrast—Christmas eve at home and in a foxhole (par. 2–3), the first Christmas and this one (par. 4).

His inspired story tells what Christmas is like at a bleak Korean outpost. Dramatic repetition of "quiet" with the novelist's use of "and" rather than punctuation (par. 1) sets the tone for this piece. He literally lets us taste the spine-chilling tenseness (par. 3). And to Symonds the ground doesn't merely freeze, it "tightens up" (par. 9). Note, finally, how he returned to the birth of Christ theme in the final paragraph.

By Gene Symonds
United Press, Dec. 24, 1950

SOMEWHERE NORTH OF SEOUL—It's a quiet Christmas eve up here in the foxholes—quiet and frightening and bitter cold.

There are no Christmas trees, no presents, no laughing friends shouting, "Merry Christmas," no tousled-haired kids to creep downstairs before dawn to see what Santa Claus brought them.

Christmas eve here is a machine gun sitting on the edge of your foxhole with the bolt back ready to go. It's a pale, full moon casting grotesque shadows among the fierce, rugged mountain peaks around you. It's your buddy crouching in the bottom of a freezing dugout with a blanket around his shoulders to smoke a cigaret.

It might have been a night like this in Bethlehem 1950 years ago when Christ was born—the night clear, cold, calm.

Out there, across those mountain peaks a few miles away, are the Communists. They have been building up a long time and tonight would be a nice time for them to strike.

Back from the front a short way in command tents and dugouts there are small fires, some companionship and perhaps a bottle or two that someone managed to hold on to.

Talk of Home

The talk, what there is of it, is all of home: "I wonder what the folks will be doing tonight?" and "I wonder what Mary got the kids for Christmas?" and "I hope to hell I am home for Christmas next year."

Some of the tents have radios and we can listen to Christmas programs from the armed forces radio station in Seoul. It helps a little hearing familiar voices like Jack Benny and Charlie McCarthy: yes, it helps a little, but not much.

There's a thin layer of snow on everything and you can feel the ground tighten up as it freezes solid after a brief period of relatively warm weather.

In Seoul there will be a midnight mass for United Nations troops but there will be no midnight services for Koreans, because of the curfew. Those Koreans who have managed to hang on to their radios will listen along with the soldiers to services broadcast from Tokyo.

Driving back from the front the cold bites deeper into your flesh and you feel sorry for the lonely MP's guarding bridges and roads. Some of them are permitted to have fires if they are far enough back from the front. They spend Christmas eve trying to keep warm.

There are not many refugees on the roads tonight. They have stopped wherever they could for the night in homes still standing after two successive waves of fighting, in barns and in stables.

It is not unlikely that a Korean babe will be born along the road in some shabby building this Christmas eve, 1950, in Korea.

A Protest That Became A War

The Hungarian revolution broke on a politically weary America in late October, 1956. We were first astonished at young Hungarians' courage, jubilant over their apparent victory, but finally appalled at Soviet brutality. The demonstrations which led to open warfare sprang from violent rioting in neighboring Posnan, Poland, a month earlier. Once it started, hatreds for top Communist officials Rakosi and Gero engulfed the masses, driving them to attempt the impossible.

These brave deeds will live long in the minds of other lovers of freedom, made even more lucid by some of the most expert reporting to come out of any war. John MacCormac of The New York *Times* topped his story with a brilliant summary which offers challenge as one of the greatest leads of all time. The remainder of his story clearly pictures the political as well as armed conflict and accurately reports this as a fight to replace hated leaders with the more moderate and nationalistically oriented Imre Nagy. Note, too, the tremendous detail in this story and MacCormac's determination to report clearly, specifically what was transpiring.

By John MacCormac
The New York Times, Oct. 27, 1956

BUDAPEST, Hungary—What began here Tuesday as a demonstration turned that same night into a revolt and yesterday became a war that was still raging today.

It is war by Soviet troops and Hungarian political policemen against the mass of the Hungarian people. The war is being waged on behalf of the Soviet Union and in support of the Hungarian Communist Government, which would fall in ten minutes if it were not for the presence of Soviet tanks in Budapest.

The Soviet troops were called in by the Hungarian Government while it still was dominated by Erno Gero, who had succeeded Matyas Rakosi as First Secretary of the Hungarian Working People's (Communist) party. Imre Nagy, for whose appointment as Premier the insurgent masses had been calling, did not take office until after the invitation to the Soviet troops had been sent, although by doing so he countenanced it.

Mr. Gero's removal from power did not occur until Mikhail I. Suslov, a member of the Soviet Presidium, and Anastas I. Mikoyan, a Soviet First Deputy Premier, who had successively visited Hungary when the fall of M. Rakosi was imminent, arrived in Budapest yesterday for a brief visit.

As late as last night the insurgents still were calling for a democratic government headed by Mr. Nagy, but one that would accede to demands that no Communist regime anywhere had yet accepted. But they were saying that Mr. Nagy already had demonstrated he was no Gomulka. This was a reference to Wladyslaw Gomulka, who has assumed control in Poland.

The trouble seems to be that Hungary has no Communist who like M. Gomulka would have courage to defy the Soviet leaders. The only alternative mentioned during the last few days has been Bela Kovaces, former leader of the Smallholders party who was imprisoned by the Russians when he tried to defy them in 1948. But his advent would mean the end of communism in Hungary and no one believes the Soviet leaders would allow that.

On this fourth day of the revolt, it shows no sign of subsiding. Last night the firing was heavier than ever.

This correspondent counted forty-seven Soviet tanks as they passed along the Danube in the direction of Secpel Island—which contains the greatest aggregation of industry in Hungary. There was fighting last night in the hills of Buda across the river, although Buda previously had been quiet.

And yet it looked Wednesday as if the intervention of Soviet troops, who had been called in at 4:30 o'clock that morning, had quelled the revolt. The Soviet forces had eighty tanks, artillery, armored cars and other equipment of a variety normally possessed only by a complete Soviet mechanized division. The insurgent Hungarian students and workers at no time had more than small arms furnished by sympathizing soldiers of the Hungarian Army.

Massacre Revives Revolt

What revived the revolt was a massacre. It happened in front of the Hungarian Parliament building, when hundreds of peaceful students and workers were mowed down by Hungarian political policemen and Soviet tanks.

Since only a few minutes earlier Soviet tank crews had been fraternizing with insurgents, it is possible that the massacre was a tragic mistake. The most credible version is that the political policemen opened fire on the demonstrators and panicked the Soviet tank crews into the belief that they were being attacked.

But in any case when the firing subsided Parliament Square was littered with dead and dying men and women. The total number of casualties has been estimated at 170. This correspondent can testify that he saw a dozen bodies.

Far from deterring the demonstration, the firing embittered and inflamed the Hungarian people. A few minutes later and only a few blocks from the scene of the massacre, the surviving demonstrators reassembled in Szabadsag (the word means liberty) Square. When trucks filled with Hungarian soldiers drove up and warned the demonstrators that they were armed, the leader of the demonstrators brandished a Hungarian flag and replied: "We are armed only with this, but it is enough."

On a balcony above appeared an elderly Hungarian clad in pajamas and a dressing gown and clasping a huge flag. He threw it down to the demonstrators.

Another man mounted a ladder to tear down the Soviet emblem from the "Liberty" monument in "Liberty" square. It was erected in 1945 by the Russians with forced Hungarian labor.

A crowd assembled before the United States legation in the square and shouted: "The workers are being murdered, we want help."

Finally, Spencer Barnes, Charge d'Affairs, told them that their case was one for decision by his Government and the United Nations, not for the local staff. The British Minister had received a deputation and given it the same message.

Among those watching this demonstration was a furtive figure clad in a leather coat. Suddenly someone identified him rightly, or wrongly, as a member of the hated Avo, the Hungarian political police. Like tigers the crowd turned on him, began to beat him and hustled him into a courtyard. A few minutes later they emerged rubbing their hands with satisfaction. The leather-coated figure was seen no more.

Ouster of Gero Demanded

During all these activities and while Soviet tanks continued to race through near-by streets firing their fusillades, the crowd never ceased shouting: "Down with Gero!" Less than an hour later the radio announced that Mr. Gero had been replaced by Janos Kadar, former Interior Minister and second secretary of the party. Mr. Kadar had been imprisoned by M. Rakosi during the anti-Titoist movement of 1949 when Laszlo Rajk, former Foreign Minister, was executed. Since his release six months ago, Mr. Kadar has reported that his fingernails were torn out by order of Mihaly Farkas, who is now in jail awaiting trial for the death of Mr. Rajk and other alleged Titoists.

Mr. Kadar is a Gentile while Mr. Gero is Jewish. For this and other reasons Mr. Kadar is unlikely to be as unpopular as his predecessor.

Whether Mr. Kadar and Premier Nagy can stabilize the Hungarian situation, however, is uncertain. At 3:30 o'clock yesterday afternoon they announced over the radio that they would open negotiations with Moscow to normalize Soviet-Hungarian relations.

They said the normalization would be sought on a basis of Hungarian independence involving the withdrawal of Soviet troops from the country and that "Soviet forces now here to restore order" would return to their base in Hungary the moment order was restored. They appealed to those with weapons to surrender them and promised that they would be dealt with in a spirit of forgiveness and not subjected to martial law.

Earlier in the morning a communique couched in very different language was issued stating that "our Government was not prepared for the dastardly attacks by counter-revolutionary elements and had to ask for help of Russian troops stationed in Hungary in accordance with the Warsaw agreement" (The East European defense alliance).

At 4 p.m. yesterday afternoon pamphlets were distributed signed by "Hungarian workers and university students." They read "We summon all Hungarians to a general strike. As long as the Government fails to grant our demands and until the murderers are called to account, we shall answer the Government with a general strike. Long live the the new Government under the leadership of Imre Nagy."

At 6 p.m. that evening a one-sheet newspaper was issued from the printing plant of the Hungarian Army. It had been occupied by the political police but apparently reoccupied by the Army. It was an Army officer who threw hundreds of copies from an upper window to a crowd waiting for them below. The sheet repeated the sixteen demands that had been formulated by Tuesday's peaceful demonstrators, which the Government had refused to print or broadcast.

Rebels Issue Statement

They were preceded by a statement saying:

"We swear over the bodies of our martyrs that we shall see freedom and independence finally triumph. In this time of crisis the leaders of the party and the Government have been concerned only with the prolongation of their power. What kind of leadership is it which has taken only a few hesitating steps under the pressure of the masses. This oligarchy has cost us enough victims in the last ten years. Now they have called in the Soviet Army to repress the Hungarian revolution.

"We demand:

"1. A provisional national government, including leaders of insurgent youth, which will carry out our sixteen points.

"2. The immediate rescission of martial law. There will be no further armed combat.

"3. The immediate denunciation of the Warsaw agreement. Soviet troops must peacefully depart from Hungary.

"4. Those responsible for the bloodbath must be put before a court. Prisoners must be released. There must be an immediate political amnesty.

"5. The creation of a Hungarian socialism on a really democratic basis.

"6. The Hungarian Army must take over the responsibility for assuring order. The Avo (political police) must be disarmed, otherwise the danger of bloodshed will persist.

"7. We shall continue the demonstrations until vic-
    tory but will remain calm. We condemn
    anarchy, destruction and looting.
"8. Citizens Imre Nagy and Janos Kadar are mem-
    bers of the Revolutionary Hungarian Govern-
    ment."

The appeal was signed "the new Provisional
Revolutionary Hungarian Government and National
Defense Committee."

The Soviet troops were called into Budapest obviously because the majority of the Hungarian Army
and ordinary police sympathized with the insurgents. Otherwise the army would have been amply
adequate to control un-armed demonstrators. It was
from the army that the demonstrators received their
first weapons and were instructed in their use by
soldiers who had surrendered them. Later it is said
they raided the Danubia arms factory.

It seems almost certain that the demonstrations
would have remained peaceful had not the political
police fired the first shot before the Budapest radio
station. The situation still might have been saved if
Mr. Gero had been dropped earlier from his position
as Communist leader and Soviet troops had not been
called in to Budapest. But the tactics of the Soviet
troops inflamed passions it seems unlikely any
Government can appease.

A succession of Soviet tanks, armored cars and
infantry bombarded for hours a whole block of
buildings around Engels Square beside the British
legation, in one of which one lone Hungarian sniper
had hidden himself. Two tanks and a fieldpiece kept
up a steady fire while three others dashed up and
down the street. At the end of all this could be heard
a single but heroic "pop" as the lone sniper fired
back from his hidden retreat. And in the middle of
it a civilian calmly strolled across the line of fire
with his briefcase under his arm.

The massacre before the Parliament occurred in
a mysterious circumstance for which no explanation
has been forthcoming.

Known is the fact that the crews of three Soviet
tanks began to fraternize with the insurgents
shortly before noon in front of the Astoria Hotel.
They shouted that they did not want to fire on un-
armed Hungarian workers.

They let a score of the demonstrators climb on their tanks and drove them to Parliament Square. This correspondent saw the Soviet soldiers there laughing and waving to the crowd of hundreds that had collected. But only a minute later from a few blocks in the distance he heard a violent cannonade and saw at the end of the street another Soviet tank firing in the direction of the crowd.

By the time he could make his way back against the crowd of fleeing demonstrators, the square and grass beside it were littered with dead and wounded men and women, while scores of survivors were hugging the ground or seeking shelter behind statues and hedges waiting for a chance to escape.

Some of the survivors said the Soviet tanks had begun firing on each other. But the more credible story was that a group of political policemen drawn up at one end of the square had begun to shoot at the demonstrators and that the Russians, believing they were the target, had themselves opened fire.

Soviet Soldier Wounded

That the Soviet forces suffered at least one casualty was demonstrated Wednesday morning when a Soviet soldier, bleeding from an abdominal bullet wound, was carried into the dining room of the Duna Hotel for treatment. He was bandaged by a Western physician.

A few hours later a Soviet armored car was set on fire near Engels Square. A worker told this correspondent that some Soviet tanks had been attacked with "Molotov cocktails," made according to an old Russian recipe out of wine bottles filled with gasoline.

During the three days in which all these events have occurred Budapest has been wrapped in a fog so heavy that one could not see across the Danube. This correspondent has been wrapped in a fog of frustration because from the early hours of Wednesday morning all communication with the outside world was cut off and for a time the frontiers were sealed. Until yesterday there also was a curfew.

The revolt began as a series of demonstrations that remained peaceful until about 10:30 o'clock Tuesday evening. The trouble began in front of the Budapest radio station when a delegation that had entered it to request the broadcasting of its "sixteen points" was arrested by political policemen who were guarding the building.

The crowd demanded their release and tried to storm the doors. At first the policemen tried to drive the demonstrators back with tear gas. Then they opened fire, killing one demonstrator and wounding several others.

When this correspondent arrived at midnight the radio station had been stormed. Its lower floors had been occupied by the demonstrators, while the political police held the upper ones. A group of students had mounted a balcony in front of the building, hung out Hungarian flags and Hungary's pre-Communist national emblem.

A military command car that had been set on fire burned with dense smoke and a rubbery stench. The air in the narrow street in front of the station reeked of tear gas which was reinforced by an occasional bomb hurled from the upper floors by the political policemen.

Trucks filled with Hungarian soldiers stood by, but their occupants were taking no action.

Shortly before midnight seven heavy Hungarian tanks rumbled into the area. Some of the demonstrators fled. But the leading tank displayed the national flag. Its crew cheered the demonstrators and numbers of them mounted it to shake hands with the soldiers. One youth shouted: "Come on, the army is with us!" and the crowd surged forward again to invest the building.

Soldiers Give Crowd Arms

It was obvious that the army was refusing to make common cause with the political police. An hour later several insurgents were observed with tommy guns in their hands. They said they had obtained them from the soldiers.

Meanwhile, the crowd was beginning to grow more violent. It threw up barricades at street intersections. These were flimsy affairs made of park benches but they were guarded by youths with tommy guns.

At one intersection the crowd overturned the automobile of a state official. It seemed for a moment as if an American car would share that fate, but the crowd grew good humored when it realized that the car was being driven by a Western newspaper man.

At 1:30 a.m. Wednesday the crowd stormed the plant of Szabad Nep, principal Communist newspaper. They brought with them the body of a dead demonstrator wrapped in a national flag.

The newspaper had just issued a one-page extra edition condemning the political police force for having opened fire on the demonstrators at the radio station.

Meanwhile, other insurgents stormed a Soviet bookstore, threw books into the street, and set fire to them. The headquarters of the Soviet-Hungarian Friendship Society was wrecked.

A tour of the city last night revealed that on many of the principal streets overhead trolley wires were down and rails had been removed to form barricades. One thoroughfare was blocked by two huge buses that had been overturned. The Hungarian National Museum was in flames.

Food has now become short. In the Duna Hotel last night no bread was available and only the simplest dishes were being served. Shops were open only briefly and long queues struggled to enter them.

Since there are no newspapers and radio broadcasts are discredited, the city is swept by the wildest rumors. These speak of thousands of dead and of the summary execution of 150 youthful insurgents in a sports arena at Tevve Utca, which is under martial law.

That the number of wounded is high is indicated by the fact that trucks, and even buses, have been pressed into service as ambulances.

City Of Death

United Press scored twin victories in covering the Hungarian revolution in the persons of Russell Jones and Anthony Cavendish. Jones, among the first American reporters to arrive and the last to leave, fashioned repeated penetrating appraisals. He received a Pulitzer Prize for his efforts.

Cavendish used a machine gun-like, staccato sentence structure in this article to pitch his story at a lofty dramatic level. So vigorous is his language, pungent odors literally waft from the copy. Our aural senses, too, receive shock treatment (par. 6) from the "crump" of artillery, "crack" of rifle, "boom" of tank guns, and "staccato rattle" of tommy guns.

Note his use of foreshadowing to lead into paragraphs 8, 9, and 10. A less skilled writer would have continued to use this indefinite beginning technique, but Cavendish knew when to quit. Terse accounts of skirmishes enliven the story.

Even so, Cavendish strove to achieve accuracy in the face of temptingly exaggerated claims, see paragraphs 26 and 27.

By Anthony Cavendish
United Press, Nov. 12, 1956

(United Press correspondent Anthony Cavendish flew from Warsaw to Budapest Oct. 29. He now has arrived in Vienna after being captured and held by the Russians more than 50 hours in the Hungarian town of Guber.)

VIENNA, Austria—The smell of death hangs over Budapest.

Hunger and disease stalk the living.

More than 200,000 Soviet troops—equal to 15 full Red army divisions—hold shattered Hungary in their grip.

Yet last ditch rebels fight on against the Red invaders.

When I left Budapest Thursday to bring out the story of the city's martyrdom, the bodies of freedom fighters and dead Russians still lay in its streets.

The crump of Russian artillery fire shook the ruins. Smoke rose from still burning buildings. Every now and then the crack of a rebel guerila's rifle shot rang out, followed by the boom of Russian tank guns and the staccato rattle of Soviet tommy-gunners.

The Fight Goes On

In alleyways, in darkened streets and from the glassless windows of shattered buildings, the fight goes on.

It is the steel-sided tank against the sniper bullet.

It is desperate youngsters who spring up as fast as others are cut down.

It is the flaming bottle of gasoline against armor and big guns.

It is perilous to be a Red army infantryman in that kind of battle without quarter.

The mastermind behind the Red army's efforts to crush free Hungary is generally believed to be Marshal Gregori Zhukov himself, conqueror of Berlin, hero of the Soviet Union, Soviet defense minister.

Westerners estimate that crack armored units make up 80 per cent of the Red army troops throughout Hungary.

The Soviets launched their attack at 4:50 a.m. Sunday, Nov. 4. A thunderous artillery barrage crashed into the old city around the former royal castle on the west side of the Danube.

Within an hour the Russians occupied all main centers and the bridges across the Danube.

Russians Massacre 300

A Soviet officer marched up to the main door of the Kilian barracks and demanded entry. A rebel sentry opened the door and shot him dead on the spot.

Red army tanks converged on the yellow stone building, already pock-marked from the earlier fighting. The tanks opened point-blank fire on it.

Within an hour it was blazing and more than 300 of the 700 original defenders were either dead or dying.

Directly in the line of fire was a children's clinic with more than 200 sick youngsters in it.

Doctors and nurses sent out desperate pleas to spare the building. But the Red army gunners were ruthlessly deaf to the appeals.

In an hour the building was a shambles, piled deep with the mangled bodies of children and other patients.

How many were killed there never was known for sure. But certain it is that few escaped.

And still, in the midst of battle raging all around them, old women wrapped in black shawls scurried through the ruins and smoke seeking a cabbage or a loaf of bread to feed their starving families.

The young men were all out fighting.

Or their bodies lay mangled in the streets. Soviet tanks drove callously over them.

Western observers put the Hungarian casualties in the first four days of the battle at around 5,000 Hungarians and perhaps 500 Russians. But when the city morgue was called to remove a body last Wednesday a harassed official replied that he already had 12,000 bodies stacked there.

That may or may not have been so. Most likely it was vastly exaggerated.

Death Toll Will Never Be Known

But the world probably never will know the true toll of death in Budapest—let alone the rest of Hungary—in that week that staggered the world.

The Russians blasted away a whole house to kill a single sniper.

They pulverized the Korvin national theater. They put the historic former royal palace through a cannon meat-grinder.

Even the Duna and Astoria hotels came under shell fire.

To add to the terror of the Hungarian population, many of the Soviet troops were Mongols, slit-eyed fighters from the steppes of innermost Asia, turned loose for the second time in 11 years on European cities.

Hungarian rebels tore up paving blocks and ripped down streetcar wires and piled them into barricades.

The tanks flattened the barricades and the men behind them, roared down on street lamps and signs and kept on their way.

Thursday morning I left Budapest by car in an attempt to bring the first story of the battle to the West. But I was held up by Russian troops in a western Hungarian city for 50 hours.

And it was not until Sunday night that I reached the free world in Vienna—lights, traffic, no thud of shells and no Russians.

———————————

Proletarians Fight 'Benefactors'

It remained for Russell Jones to put the Hungarian revolt into perspective for millions of Western readers. Only one who had dodged bullets with the revolutionaries, holed up in a factory with rebellious workers, talked with men of all walks of life could have drawn and supported these conclusions.

Jones's story moves rapidly, kaleidoscopically. For there is much detail to summarize in the brief space available. This and the believability of his subjects and their causes lend credence to this well-written story.

Note, too, his direct address "(you) Believe" (par. 2), his inverted sentence "Wherever came the spark . . ." (par. 6), and his strong next to last paragraph, especially the openings of both sentences. These are the fruits of a practiced hand. Jones received a Pulitzer Prize for his Hungarian revolution coverage.

By Russell Jones
United Press, Dec. 10, 1956

LONDON—The greatest shock to the Hungarian Communists and their Russian masters must have been the type of people who fought the hardest.

Believe none of the stories that this was a misguided uprising fomented to restore the great estate owners of the Horthy regency or the industrial magnates. I saw with my own eyes who was fighting and heard with my ears why they fought.

The first armed resistance came from students of the schools and universities, the youth who had been so carefully selected as the party elite of the future.

The fiercest fighters were the workers, the proletarians in whose name Communism had ruled. Even the Hungarian army, purged and repurged a dozen times, joined the battle for freedom or sat on the sidelines.

Revolt Leaders Were Communists

The two big names that came out of the revolt were Communist—Imry Nagy, a lifelong party member, and Lieutenant Colonel Pal Maleter, who had deserted to the Russians in World War II and returned as a Red partisan.

Wherever came the spark, it found its tinder among the common people.

The areas of destruction, the buildings most desperately defended and the dead themselves are the most eloquent proof of this. It was the workers' tenements that Soviet siege guns smashed, factory buildings that became forts and the tired shabby men with broken shoes and horny hands of the laborer who died by the thousands. The women with their hair bound with kerchiefs and the cheap and tawdry dresses of working people.

A seventeen-year-old girl, twice wounded at Corvin Theatre, told me she fought because "it isn't right that my father with four children to feed should get only 900 florints ($80) a month. "

Workers Protect 'Their' Factories

The chairman of the Workers' Council at the Csepel Iron and Steel plant with 38,000 workers, biggest in the country, said, "These are our factories. We will fight to the death to hold them. But we will continue plant maintenance because we want to work here again."

In Dorog, one of the coal centers, miners continued to work despite the general strike. But not to produce coal. They didn't want *their* mines ruined by flooding.

The same attitude is true in the country. The farmers want to get out of the collectives but they do not want the restoration of the landlords. They think everyone should have the right to own and till his own land. Something like 100 acres a family would be fair, they think.

It was for these simple, basic things that the Hungarian people fought. These and the right to speak and think freely, to elect men of their own choice, and to raise their children in their own way.

They will go on fighting for them.

U.S. Secret Weapon—Jazz

The successful prosecution of wars, cold ones included, requires strange artillery. One of America's most successful weapons is a squat trumpet player known to his millions of devotees as "Satchmo."

Imagination, all too often lacking, lifts this story by Felix Belair, Jr., of The New York *Times* into the realm of excellence. What a superb lead! And yet how accurate!

Belair analyzed intelligently the impact of jazz as a symbol of individuality, one of its major international appeals (par. 12, 15–16). Influenced by stories such as this our government has exported jazz more energetically, both via Voice of America and international tours of such musicians and their orchestras as Armstrong, Benny Goodman, Art Tatum, etc. Many other serious students of foreign policy agree with Belair's view that jazz is probably our most valuable propaganda weapon.

By Felix Belair, Jr.
The New York Times, Nov. 6, 1955

GENEVA—America's secret weapon is a blue note in a minor key. Right now its most effective ambassador is Louis (Satchmo) Armstrong. A telling propaganda line is the hopped-up tempo of a Dixieland band heard on the Voice of America in far-off Tangier.

This is not a pipedream from a backroom jam session. It is the studied conclusion of a handful of thoughtful Americans from Moscow to Madrid.

Somewhere in the official files of one of Washington's myriad agencies all this has been spelled out. Because nothing has been done about it, more than one observant American traveling the Continent has remarked: "We don't know our own strength."

Cash customers were turned away in droves tonight because Victoria Hall here could not accommodate the crowd that wanted to hear "Ole Satchmo" do tricks with his trumpet. The disappointed customers were not Swiss "hep cats" but sober adults willing to pay almost $4 to hear musical individuality.

All Europe now seems to find American jazz as necessary as the seasons. Yet Europeans don't bounce to the syncopated rhythm of Stan Kenton or Duke Ellington and their bands or the still popular recordings of Benny Goodman's quartet. They can swing and sway with Sammy Kaye, but for the most part they find in jazz a subject for serious study.

Long-hair Approach to Jazz

Theirs is what most Americans would call a "long-hair approach." They like to contemplate it, dissect it, take it apart to see what makes it what it is.

They like to ponder the strength of its individuality and speculate on the qualities that differentiate it from the folk music of any other country. Somewhere along the line they get curious about the kind of people that first contrived it.

This is not to suggest that Europe has turned its back on the symphony and classical compositions. Far from it. Wilhelm Backhaus was a sellout here last week with Beethoven's Piano Concerto in C Minor. But not even Walter Gieseking could have caused the recent Hamburg rioting by those turned away when they pulled in the Standing Room Only sign.

It was the same in Paris a few days later when Sidney Bechet and his soprano saxophone drew 15,000 Frenchmen to demand equality of opportunity to share 3,000 seats. Not to be deprived of their chance to demonstrate enthusiasm for his individual artistry, the unseated majority "wrecked the joint," just as the Germans did at Hamburg.

The popularity of jazz and the market for it is a phenomenon that strikes Americans returning to the Continent after a long absence. Men actually have risked their lives to smuggle recordings of it behind the Iron Curtain and by methods that the profit motive cannot explain.

A German Swiss of Zurich came closest to the explanation the other day after he had heard Hoagy Carmichael's "Stardust" from the keyboard of Art Tatum.

"Jazz is not just an art," he said. "It is a way of life."

Whatever the essence of the matter, the remark helps explain why the police states give up the attempt to outlaw jazz as the product of a decadent capitalist nation. In the satellite countries particularly, authorities learned the hard way that it was only the promise of a ragtime band later on that kept the radios tuned to their Communist preachments.

Something of the same strength of musical Americana caused uninhibited Moscow children to ask visiting American newsmen a year ago what they knew of Bing Crosby and Frank Sinatra.

More ponderous explanations of the attraction of American jazz are available from those in Europe who have given it a lot of thought. One is that the contest between musical discipline and individual expression it entails comes close to symbolizing the conditions under which people of the atomic age live.

Jazz Specialists on Radio

Whatever the exactions of musical discipline, there can be little question of the appreciation throughout Europe of the individuality of expression involved. Thus, it is not surprising to switch on a radio and hear a jazz band doing a syncopated adaptation of the Cesar Franck symphony or a piece of sacred music heard as written only at the Christmas season.

Tiny Switzerland boasts about a hundred amateur jazz bands, and about sixty of these specialize in the Dixieland variety. The radio station of every good-sized city has its "jazz specialist."

The biggest movie house in Zurich, like all others, was closed last Sunday, but it was packed before noon by the promise of a seven-piece Negro orchestra whose repertoire included "Muskrat Ramble," "High Society," "When the Saints Go Marching In" and "Royal Garden Blues."

Up the street from the movie house is a record shop. The window display mixes such names as Toscanini, Horowitz and Heifetz with Art Tatum, Sauter-Finnegan and Lionel Hampton. On a counter near-by can be obtained an album with ten monographic studies of Louis Armstrong—the trumpeter, the singer, the person. His genealogy, discography, and so on.

A separate record album contains the "Evolution of Duke Ellington" from his first to his latest recordings, with running commentary on the changes in his music as his own personality and that of his musicians evolved over the years.

"Jazz International," a program of the Armed Forces network, and "Night Train," another network feature from Western Germany, are as familiar throughout the Continent as the Ed Sullivan show to American televiewers. Probably the greatest American cultural triumph of modern times was the traveling show of "Porgy and Bess," the American folk opera, which now goes to Moscow.

An Unexpected Question

What many thoughtful Europeans cannot understand is why the United States Government, with all the money it spends for so-called propaganda to promote democracy, does not use more of it to subsidize the continental travels of jazz bands and the best exponents of the music.

The average European tour of a musician like Louis Armstrong and his band is about six weeks. On a profit and loss basis he can play only to the biggest audiences. Small houses mean deficits that not even devotees like 'Satchmo' can long endure.

With a small Government subsidy, he might play the smaller intermediate towns and his tour stretched to six months by train instead of six weeks by bus.

American jazz has now become a universal language. It knows no national boundaries, but everybody knows where it comes from and where to look for more. Individual Americans will continue to pack them in and the reasons for this are clear.

The New York Philharmonic-Symphony, London's Symphony and the Boston Pops are no strangers to any European capital. They are appreciated for their versatility as much as for their faithful renditions of the classics associated with European composers over the centuries.

But there is not a wide difference between the best symphony orchestras of the United States and Europe —not where the masses of people are concerned.

But nobody plays jazz like an American.

That is why Europeans are puzzled when a famous exponent of the art goes unnoticed by the official representatives of American life in Europe, whether embassies or legations or consulates.

Sometimes a private American citizen comes to the rescue with a cocktail party or simply a visit backstage.

But like the still-remembered visit to Vienna of Dick Button, the Olympic figure-skating champion, such unofficial recognition comes only after the rave notices in the newspapers. It is still recalled hereabout that Button was not even given United States commissary privileges or permitted to stay at the Bristol there, then the official American hotel.

REPORTING
AT ITS BEST

PART 7

Politics and Government

EVERY FOUR YEARS politics challenges the World Series, Hollywood's most buxom blond, and the latest TV sensation for public attention. Reporters frenziedly tail candidates, seeking a fresh angle to top a story based on the twelfth repetition of essentially the same tired speech.

Seen Our Adlai?

Richard L. Strout turned his attention from a candidate's statements to the journalistic chase. It was sort of embarrassing, you see, because he had lost his man, Adlai Stevenson. So he wrote his editor on The *Christian Science Monitor* a letter.

This story illustrates how a perceptive writer can adopt a style foreign to news writing when the event lends itself to that style. Describing his quarry, as Strout did (par. 3) is delightful. It blends into the writer's seemingly tireless search.

Strout maintained the letter format throughout this story without letting the technique impinge upon his news report. In fact it enhances his report by entertaining as well as informing.

Structurally, the letter is written chronologically. It gives the narrative highlight (par. 4, 5, 6), then returns to the letter device (par. 7) to introduce a longer chronology. Characteristically, this "telling" begins earlier and ends later in time sequence.

The piece, sparked by Strout's fine timing and excellent humor, is delightful, great fun. Yet it is an informative, balanced news report.

By Richard L. Strout
The Christian Science Monitor, Oct. 5, 1956

Not with Stevenson Party, Pittsburgh Airport, 1 a.m.

Dear Boss:

Have you seen anything of a man named Adlai E. Stevenson?

I am supposed to be covering him, but he has got away from me. In the past three days he has been campaigning in three states, and I have often been in the same state with him.

He is a man with a prominent nose, a rather dumpy figure, and a big, bright smile. He is an agreeable fellow to have around, because he makes entertaining comments. But he isn't around very much so far as newsmen go.

The last time I saw him was in the gym of Davis and Elkins College of Elkins, W. Va., with a beauty queen and a lot of other people. He was making a nonpolitical speech on conservation, and nobody could figure out quite why. He seemed to be at a loss, too. After that he got away. I and some 90 other members of the press, photographers, and staff have followed him across West Virginia in three buses, but we never did catch up, because you see, Boss, he was flying. We think he was flying for New York.

He was supposed to address a rally at 116th Street and Third Avenue in New York at 8:30 a.m., and another in Harlem 20 minutes later.

Could you tell me if he made it? We didn't.

This is going to be hard to explain, Boss, but I will try. I guess I had better go back a bit and take a deep breath.

Well, you remember, we all started out merrily across New Jersey in a motorcade. It was only last Thursday, but it seems months ago. Crowds were disappointing, but at least we were always within a mile or two of the candidate and occasionally right up with him.

That was true the first night at Jersey City, where Mayor John V. Kenny, inheritor of the Hague "I-Am-the-Law" machine, who appears to have stepped out of "The Last Hurrah," put on a rally with red fire

torpedoes, and bands. The sky was clear. I want
you to fix your attention on that, please.

'I've Seen Everything Now'

Well, this Kenny show was something to see. He
wears a pearl stickpin, and is not the kind of gentleman I would want to run against, Boss, for anything.
There is a certain glint in his eye. He is quite articulate, too. He addressed his followers from the platform of Public School No. 12 like a tribal leader.

He said Hudson County has the best "rough-and-
tumble political workers in the country," and warned
precinct captains that he wanted no nonsense come
Election Day. He was interested in results, not explanations, and he expected them to "deliver."

"Well," observed Mr. Stevenson when he was introduced, "I think I've seen everything now."

It was next day that somebody stole our train.

This is really going to be hard to explain. I will
take another deep breath.

Practically anything can happen on a presidential
campaign trip, and does to reporters with Mr. Stevenson.

I don't mean the Stevenson mimeograph machine
that won't print the letter "O" and the letter "D."
And I don't mean the Republican baby that always
seemed to cry at the outdoor rallies. What I mean
is that stealing a train is another matter.

You see, we boarded this train that Tuesday night
in Jersey City, and, oh it was good to get back onto
an old-fashioned campaign train again after all this
airplane hedge-hopping and motorcading.

Well, it took us out into the Poconos somewhere
that first night, and stopped and gave us a wonderful sleep; and when I woke up next morning there
was a field and a bush all aflame just outside the
window of Car 8, Roomette I. The sky was blue, too.
Fix your attention on that.

Our mistake was to leave the train that morning
to motorcade into Sunbury, Pa., while the engineer
switched it around somehow by another route. Sunbury is a lovely old-fashioned town, and Adlai spoke
in front of the courthouse, built in 1865, all covered
with Eisenhower banners. But when we walked to

the old-fashioned station, where the tracks ran right down Main street, with shops on either side, there was no train.

What Happened to 15-Car Train?

The neighbors all closed in on Adlai, and the affair got folksy. But, somehow, after half an hour or so of that on a tight schedule, you get to wondering. What had happened to a 15-car special train—the one with the private car at the end that used to carry Woodrow Wilson?

Adlai kept up a brave smile, but it is awkward to stand trying to look composed on a public platform when you are an important man. When the engineer showed up, he said he had been "delayed." He even denied that the train had been stolen.

Well, that night, Oct. 3, was the first time we lost our man. He got away. He decided to make a quick detour to Pittsburgh by plane to make a special coast-to-coast broadcast. Maybe you heard it, Boss. I didn't.

You see, we stayed on the train and somehow had to from Johnston, Pa., to Elkins, W. Va., that night. So while he was speaking we were traveling. All the reporters who were supposed to be covering him were off somewhere in the mountains.

The train's television couldn't get him. The radio couldn't get him save at the end (and never when we went under bridges.)

Oh, you have no idea at all, Boss, what it is to try to cover Mr. Stevenson!

This is getting to be longer than I expected, but next morning in West Virginia it was raining. Did I tell you to fix your attention on the weather?

Well, the first thing I knew, he had got away from us.

He was on a special plane for Pittsburgh. He was trying to reach New York in time for those speeches. No more planes for anybody. Have you ever been in Elkins? Nice town, hard to get out of.

In practically no time at all (if you don't count a couple of hours of repining and teeth gnashing), the 90 of us were following Mr. Stevenson to Pittsburgh at a 20-mile-an-hour clip in three old busses.

The foliage was lovely. We didn't look at it.

The wire service men were the most unhappy.

They are not supposed to let a candidate out of sight.

We had a Western Union man on board, but no place for columnists and assorted journalists to throw off copy.

"You got raincoats for your carrier pigeons, Dave?" we asked. (When anything goes wrong you blame Western Union.) "You going to send smoke signals?"

Too Wet For Smoke Signals

"Can't send up smoke signals," replied Dave Rush judiciously. "Leaves are too wet."

Well, that's the story.

The big "Stevenson-Kefauver press" busses wallowing through the night, behind a police car, suddenly pouring out all their passengers at mountain filling stations, leaving empty vending machines behind them and, on board, eating candy bars, popcorn, and gumdrops, at a quarter-in-the-slot place, washed down with milk from containers which somebody providentially discovered.

Have you seen a man named Adlai E. Stevenson?

Here I am at the Pittsburgh Airport, and they are turning off the lights. They may or may not get me onto that next flight to Washington.

As I said before, almost anything can happen on a campaign trip. As I sit writing this, I have a feeling that more of them happen to the Stevenson campaign trips than to most.

Respectfully,
R. L. S.

President Fires MacArthur

President Harry S. Truman loosed a storm of criticism and less vociferous praise when he relieved Gen. Douglas MacArthur of his commands April 11, 1951. Shortly after this the general returned to the United States where he received a hero's welcome and an invitation to address a joint session of Congress. At that time he made his "Old soldiers never die, they just fade away" speech.

Reporters who received the President's announcement in his office at 1 a.m. April 11 must have been stunned by the severity of this action, judging from The (New York) *Daily News* lead story by Jack Doherty and Jerry Greene.

This story treats with the subject understandingly yet objectively. Both the administration's and Gen. MacArthur's views are reported, giving the story balance. In addition this story is organized well. It gives a summary of the action, spelled out in 1, 2, 3 order, and the text of the President's announcement (par. 11–18). The remainder of the story adds significant details logically.

By Jack Doherty and Jerry Greene
The (New York) Daily News, April 11, 1951

Gen. MacArthur was relieved of all his commands by President Truman at 1 a.m. today.

The announcement at the White House climaxed a sharp disagreement over foreign policy that has stirred bitter debate in Europe as well as in Congress. MacArthur has contended the Communist issue must be met in Asia, and has said so publicly, to the embarrassment of diplomatic channels. His adversaries have urged more troops for Europe to check the Red menace.

Truman's unexpected order relieved the 71-year-old MacArthur as (1) supreme commander of the Allied powers, (2) commander in chief of the United Nations command, (3) commander in chief of the Far East and (4) commanding general of the U.S. Army in the Far East.

Truman messaged MacArthur:

"You will turn over your commands, effective at once, to Lt. Gen. Matthew B. Ridgway. You are authorized to have issued such orders as are necessary to complete desired travel to such place as you select."

Truman's announcement came as a bombshell. Correspondents were notified shortly after midnight there would be an announcement at the White House executive office. There was no indication of its text, but in view of the furor raging here and abroad over MacArthur, the press corps, which hurried to the scene long before the announcement, felt certain it concerned the General.

More than fifty correspondents, photographers, radio announcers and movie men began descending on the executive office building soon after they were notified of the announcement.

Biding their time in the press room only 50 feet from the President's office, reporters and cameramen swapped conjectures. Radio men were busy rigging up microphones, while the movie cameramen arranged their lights.

Then, promptly at 1 o'clock, the tension broke. Short summoned the men into Truman's office.

'With Deep Regret . . .' He Fires Mac

Then came Truman's announcement:

"With deep regret I have concluded that Gen. of the Army Douglas MacArthur is unable to give his wholehearted support to the policies of the United States Government and of the United Nations in matters pertaining to his official duties.

"In view of the specific responsibilities imposed upon me by the Constitution of the United States and the added responsibility which has been entrusted to me by the United Nations, I have decided that I must make a change of command in the Far East.

"I have, therefore, relieved Gen. MacArthur of his commands and have designated Lt. Gen. Matthew B. Ridgway as his successor.

"Full and vigorous debate on matters of national policy is a vital element in the constitutional system of our free democracy.

"It is fundamental, however, that military commanders must be governed by the policies and directives issued to them in the manner provided by our laws and Constitution.

"In time of crisis, this consideration is particularly compelling.

"Gen. MacArthur's place in history as one of our greatest commanders is fully established. The nation owes him a debt of gratitude for the distinguished and exceptional service which he has rendered his country in posts of great responsibility.

"For that reason I repeat my regret at the necessity for the action I feel compelled to take in his case."

Truman also announced that he had named Lt.

Gen. James A. Van Fleet as commander of the 8th Army to succeed Ridgway. Van Fleet reorganized the Greek army in its fight against Communists during the civil war there. He is en route by air from Fort Meade, Md., to Tokyo.

After Truman's announcement, press secretary Short told the press corps:

"Several recent instances have indicated a question as to whether Gen. MacArthur is in full sympathy with this Government's policy."

Short released several documents detailing correspondence since December between MacArthur and the Joint Chiefs of Staff, in which they told him repeatedly he was not to make any statements pertaining to policy matters without clearance with Washington.

Stinging Rebuke Was in the Making

Truman's ouster of MacArthur came after a day in which it was reported that the President had given the Defense Department a green light to administer a stinging rebuke to the General.

A high Administration source said yesterday that Truman had decided for the time being to take no part in the controversy, but to let Defense Secretary George Marshall and Gen. J. Lawton Collins, Army Chief of Staff, take action instead.

They reportedly were to rebuke MacArthur. There was some conjecture as to whether it was to be conveyed through Army Secretary Frank Pace Jr., who has been in Tokyo conferring with the Far Eastern commander.

One incident in the MacArthur controversy which stirred interest yesterday was the White House cancellation of a Presidential appointment with Erle Cocke Jr., national commander of the American Legion.

Cocke Outspoken

The Legion commander, who returned Monday from a trip through Europe and Asia, had a date to see Truman yesterday.

Short said the President called off the meeting because Cocke had discussed publicly and in advance what he planned to tell the President.

Cocke had told reporters in New York that he approved MacArthur's proposal to use Chiang Kai-shek's troops against Chinese Communists.

For a tired military commander, remote from his homeland and able to present his case only at second hand through missives and dispatches sent to friends and interrogators, Gen. MacArthur has made clear his difficulties with the State Department and the Chief Executive.

The fundamentals of his thinking, in his writings and speeches, are approximately as follows:

1. The Korean conflict, in which the nation has suffered more than 60,000 casualties, is aimless and without any political, economic, or geographic objective. Nevertheless, he says, Washington insists that it be continued indefinitely.

2. American troops fighting in Korea against Russian-trained North Koreans, and Chinese, trained and led by Communists, have been hampered by orders to refrain from bombing Manchurian supply depot air fields whence enemy fighters fly to attack American planes, and ports where enemy material is accumulated. These orders originated with the American State Department, reputedly because of fear of enraging Russia.

Chiang's Troops 'Neutralized'

3. State Department orders have "neutralized" Chiang Kai-shek's Nationalist Chinese forces in Formosa. MacArthur has urged that these troops, probably the best-trained army of Chinese ever gathered, be utilized to create a second front on the Chinese mainland, to stagger the Communist Chinese Government, and to force withdrawal of many Chinese troops from Korean fronts, relieving pressure on the Americans.

4. MacArthur repeatedly has warned of his belief that politicians at home are failing to envision the importance of halting Communist aggression in Asia and, as in World War II, are giving priority to rearming and preparing Europe to resist Russia. MacArthur says that unless Communism is barred from Asia there is no hope of holding Europe and insists that the vital battle will be in Asia rather than in Europe.

5. Under the present continued "limited objective" and "limited offensive" program which is the

only one that has had White House and United Nations approval in Korea, MacArthur has publicly stated that "no victory but merely a stalemate" can result.

Excoriated Reds

On March 7, at Suwon, Korea, MacArthur in an interview during one of many of his flying visits to the front from Japan, said:

"No longer is there even a shallow pretense of concern for the welfare of the Korean nation and people, now being so ruthlessly and senselessly sacrificed.

"Through endless bloodshed, it is apparently hoped (by the Communist foes) to enforce either international banditry or blackmail.

"Vital decisions have yet to be made—decisions far beyond the scope of the authority vested in me as the military commander, decisions which are neither solely political nor solely military, but which must provide on the highest international levels an answer to the obscurities which now becloud the unsolved problems raised by Red China's undeclared war in Korea."

'War Without Objective'

Later, in an interview with a British correspondent, on April 5, in Tokyo, MacArthur said:

"The United Nations forces in Korea are circumscribed by a web of artificial conditions. For the first time in my military career I find myself involved in a war without a definite objective.

"It is not the soldier who has encroached on the realm of the politician (referring to Washington and London objections to his statements and suggestions that a peace be arranged with the Chinese), but the politician who has encroached on that of the soldier."

MacArthur's differences with Washington and Truman first came into the open Aug. 28, 1950, when he sent a letter to the Veterans of Foreign Wars convention in Chicago. In it the General said Formosa was a key island in the American western defense line.

This was at complete variance to a policy statement issued just previously by Secretary of State

Acheson. The latter said that America's military defense line in the Pacific ran from the Aleutians to the Philippines, and included Japan and Okinawa, but skipped Korea and Formosa.

Truman intervened and ordered MacArthur to withdraw the VFW letter. However, the missive was made public in the Chicago *Tribune* after it was discovered that a Washington, D.C., magazine had published it in issues already in the mails.

Furor Over Chiang

The next open break between MacArthur and Washington occurred early in February when Tokyo dispatches indicated he had recommended use of Nationalist Chinese troops against Red Chinese forces in "Korea and elsewhere." In the furor in Washington which followed this disclosure, Truman denied that such recommendations had been received. And insisted that Formosa and Chiang's armies there remain neutral.

On March 24, MacArthur, apparently without previous consultation with Washington, issued a statement in which he said he was "ready to confer in the field with the commander in chief of the enemy forces in the earnest effort to find any military means whereby realization of the political objectives of the United Nations in Korea . . . might be accomplished without further bloodshed."

Then came UN charges that MacArthur had "wholly exceeded his authority as a military commander" by getting into the realm of political policies.

It was reliably reported that MacArthur was ordered to confine all statements to the military field and to clear any messages to the enemy with the Pentagon and the White House before releasing them.

Then came a letter written by the General in reply to an inquiry by House Republican Leader Martin (Mass.) which was read in Congress April 6. In it MacArthur sharply criticized preparations for war in Europe while neglecting the war against Communism in Asia.

The Copperdust Shadow Over Montana

Newspapers seldom print criticisms of other newspapers. But this first of six articles in a series by Thor Severson of The Denver *Post* is an exception. The *Post* devoted a full page to this highly detailed article and a map and picture illustrating it.

Severson called a spade a spade, yet this is not merely a vituperative piece. He buttressed the story with specific data on the Anaconda Copper Mining Co. and Montana Power Co. and their control over seven daily Montana newspapers—an excellent example of reporting in depth. (Anaconda sold these newspapers to private interests in 1959.)

The writing, too, merits commendation. Combining such a mass of factual details into an interesting, well integrated article requires considerable skill. In less experienced hands this could have become a disjointed jumble of loosely related mishmash. Note the smoothness of his transitions, the care with which phrases are turned.

By Thor Severson
The Denver Post, April 6, 1952

BUTTE, Mont.—Montana lives under the captive shadow of one of the world's most fabulous corporation giants—a giant so powerful it virtually ghost-writes this state's legislative program and wields enough dictatorial power to all but still the voice of the state's free press.

A twentieth-century fantasy?

No. Nor a flashback to the Treasure state's roaring past—to the day when Butte's copper kings bought votes and power like so much fish in the market, and owned the press lock, Linotype and headline.

This is Montana, 1952.

King Copper ruled in the yesteryear, he rules today. The only difference: The method.

In the lusty, free-wheeling day of Clark, Daly and Heinze, early-day Butte copper tycoons, the rule was with bared fist, rigged courts and bribed votes.

The rule today is with gloved hand and courtly manner—a rule of influence subtly exercised on all levels of Montana life and government, and a rule often propagandized by the "company" press.

But whether by bared fist or gloved hand, the result is the same. King Copper has Montana in his pocket. His hold is still strong, his grip unshakable.

Of Fabulous Wealth

The corporation behind this control? Actually, there are two—Anaconda Copper Mining company, the world's largest nonferrous mining industry, and its copperdust twin, Montana Power.

Both are fabulously wealthy, both powerfully influential. Their Montana interests are so closely interrelated they are almost identical. It is a sort of Damon-Pythias relationship. So close are the ties. In fact, they are known from the grasslands in eastern Montana to the state's mountainous west as "the company."

Some speak of "the company" in awed tones, with a reverence akin to worship. Some with fear. Some with burning humor. Some with hatred. Some with indifference.

But all Montana, whatever the level of life, senses the directing hand of "the company" behind the destiny of the state. To some, even, the company is Montana.

Anaconda, the fatter of the twins, has subsidiary holdings in fifteen states and large holdings in Chile, Mexico and Canada. It has assets totaling more than $700 million. It virtually owns the city of Butte, holds vast properties in Montana lumber, and owns three domestic railroads and a foreign railroad, as well as a steamship line—to serve its farflung operations.

And more than an incidental fact—Anaconda owns virtually all the fabulously-rich mining properties in Butte, and five of Montana's six most influential newspapers.

Montana Power, the leaner of the twins but fat in its own right, is a company which grew out of the clever buy-and-sell stock manipulations of John D. Ryan, company founder and onetime president of both Anaconda and Montana Power.

The liaison between these two agglutinative corporations, it becomes obvious, goes a long way back. Wherever you find Anaconda, you find Montana Power walking a step behind in the shadows.

It has a virtual monopoly on power and gas distribution in Montana, boasts more than 10,000 miles of transmission lines, almost 1,000 miles of gas mains.

Its operating revenue alone in 1950 in electrical and gas services totaled more than $26 million. It owns and operates twelve hydroelectric and gas plants, six on the Missouri River. And while it is "independent" today, it was for years an affiliate with American Power and Light, the behemoth of the utility world.

Study of Influence

But this is no indictment against powerful holdings, no argument with free enterprise, no simpering wolf cry against accumulative corporation wealth.

It is a study, rather, of "company" influence upon Montana life.

The revealing significance of this A.C.M.-M.P. liaison of control over the destiny of the Treasure state lies in the company ownership by Anaconda of five powerful Montana newspapers, three of which publish on both sides of the clock.

And it is found, also, in the influential hand Anaconda and Montana Power exercise over the state's legislature, directly and indirectly on Helena's capitol hill.

The chain of company newspapers, for purposes of geographical study, extends from Missoula on the far west to Billings in the east. Their circulation territories are so interlocking they sometimes spill over into each other's territory of operation—giving the company domination over the news border to border.

The papers: The Billings *Gazette*, the Helena *Independent-Record*, the Livingston *Enterprise*, the *Montana Standard* and *Butte Post* in Butte, the Missoula *Sentinel* and the *Missoulian* in Missoula.

There is criticism against this "company" ownership of the press, of course. Some is based on fact, some on imagination. Much of it is bald. Some is unsupported. Much of it can be supported.

The "company" press, itself, is known by many names. It has been called the "captive press," the "feudal press," a "slave press," an "apologist press . . ."

And the product of the "company press" is read

in many ways. Some read it with a screening eye, others with suspicion. Some with complete belief, others with indifference.

Not New in Montana

Actually company ownership of newspapers is not new in Montana. It was born in the buy-votes, buy-power era which mushroomed in Butte's battle of the copper kings. It was accepted in that day. But like a hangnail, it is irritating to modern-day Montana.

And it represents something darker . . .

The ownership and control of a "company press" the like of Anaconda's—disregarding the fair or unfair treatment of news for the moment—makes Montana the last outpost of a captive press in America.

There was a time in the day of Carnegie and Rockefeller when corporation ownership of the press was common. And, as was said, accepted. But that era, like the gas light, belongs to the past. It has given way to almost total independent ownership of the press. Everywhere but in Montana, that is. There, the lord-and-vassal state of news production still exists, even flourishes.

Again, dealing with a company press in "theory" only, corporation ownership of the press poses an eternal threat to the "free" press guaranteed in the most fundamental declarations of our democratic independence.

The company, at will, has in its power to "kill" any story it wishes, to impose a dangerous censorship. Independents may print the story. Yes. But so far as the chain papers of a corporation press are concerned, the story could die in the wastebasket, a casualty of the shears, at the whim of the company.

Or the company press can "ignore" a major "policy" story by either underwriting it or giving it a "policy" slant, or by burying the story on a "catch-all" page. Or by failing to print the story at all.

Or it can, as well, throw a screening blanket of darkness over public issues by ignoring them editorially, by writing around them, by dealing in calculated scattergun bursts. The result: Control, or attempt at control, of public thought.

That is the power, the latent backroom power, of a "company" press.

Sin of 'Omission'

But what of the A.C.M. chain. Its history is rife with so-called "company" journalism. The sin is more of "omission" than "commission" today, however. You see very few "policy" stories planted in today's A.C.M. press, but you can search in vain for a story that may be carried in, say, the independent press.

And its editorial policy?

You hear it echoed in casual interviews with businessmen, educators, men of the professions—that Montana's company papers deal in a sort of editorial Afghanistanism.

Montana's few independent publishers in the daily field, and they are few, very few indeed, delight in A.C.M.'s peevish and selective type of editorial policy, however.

It gives the few independents an open field to till editorially. And it makes their editorial voice even stronger, for the reading public likes a bold editorial—whether it agrees with the conclusion or not.

The A.C.M. papers deal often in international and, yes, national issues. But seldom is a state issue of controversy explored editorially, especially issues on taxation or corporate law.

The policy seems to be a policy of escapism. As one professional man put it: "They write editorially about everything except what you want explored . . ." It is, very often, an editorial routine of flowers-in-spring, havoc-in-China, life-among-the-Eskimos. The menu served up editorially, normally, is meatless. It is prepared for the vegetarian palate.

Take a few examples of so-called "policy" handling of the news by the Anaconda press. There is, for example, a major political battle being waged in Montana over whether silicosis, the racking lung disease so common among miners, should be brought under coverage of the Treasure state's workmen's compensation law.

It is not a new issue. It has been fought in virtually every session of the Montana legislature for decades—with, of course, the Anaconda Copper Mining company lined strongly in the ranks of the opposition.

But this time, instead of beginning anew the battle in the assembly, supporters of the measure have taken the proposal to the voters in the form of an initiative for vote next November.

Basically, supporters seek to remove industrial diseases, the like of silicosis, from the welfare rolls, arguing counties are being forced under the present law to shoulder an unjust burden.

In turn, they seek to charge compensation for silicotics against the "industry responsible"—which, quite plainly, means the mining industry.

A Major Story

The Helena *Independent-Record,* one of the five Montana newspapers owned by the A.C.M., broke the story in its Feb. 28 edition. It was a major story from the Montana viewpoint. For it affected vitally the state and county tax programs, and every victim of an industrial health disease in Montana.

Yet it was buried in the *Independent-Record*'s financial page, a five paragraph story with the feeble headline: "Initiative Planned to Change Parts of Present Statute. . . ."

No mention of silicosis was made. Three of the paragraphs were given to reporting the initiative was primarily a union-sponsored measure and to an explanation of the legal machinery for placing the initiative on the November ballot.

The last two paragraphs quoted an industry spokesman as labeling the initiative "patently socialistic" and traced the sponsorship of the initiative to former Representative Jerry J. O'Connel, long a target of "fellow-traveler" charges. It ended there—abruptly.

No voice was given to the measure's supporters. It was, in all, an underwritten, underplayed report on a major Montana issue, one which every voter may have to cast a ballot on in the fall.

The next morning, however, the Great Falls *Tribune,* Montana's major independent, considered the Associated Press wire story important enough to give it a three-column prominent play, and to carry a "follow" story giving spokesmen for and against the initiative a full, balanced exchange.

Available to All

The stories, written and dispatched by the A.P.'s Helena bureau and available to all Montana members, carefully explained the initiative, then gave opponents and proponents an equal exchange of opinion.

Moreover, the wire stories printed by the *Tribune* were ignored by A.C.M.'s morning publications. And the following Sunday, the *Independent-Record* and *Montana Standard*—both A.C.M. papers, ignored another A.P. story on the same issue.

The story reported an invitation, under a Butte dateline, of the Butte Miners union to an industries attorney to appear before the Butte union, and explain his criticism of the initiative.

The invitation, as carried by the A.P., read in part:

"We resent any inference that we are (circulating the petition) under pressure or under guidance of any political party. We are working for the interest of the workers suffering from silicosis, and we resent statements such as the one attributed to you . . .

"By no stretch of the imagination can we imagine an attorney making such a charge as 'patently socialistic' against a plan that would take the burden of cost of silicosis from the backs of the people and put it on the backs of corporations. . ."

Again, where the story was ignored by the A.C.M., it was carried by the Great Falls *Tribune*, an independent, although Great Falls was far from the scene of action.

Not 'Dated' Example

The comparison is singled out merely because of the time element. It is not a "dated" example. It, therefore, could reflect today's editorial policy of the A.C.M. press where a common state issue conflicts with a company issue. If not, it is at the least an isolated example of "suppression."

But to another case. . . .

Last February, the Montana safety conference met in Helena. Its meetings were staffed by a Helena *Independent-Record* reporter; his running stories were carried by the *Independent-Record*.

However, there was one "omission" in the *Independent-Record* report on conference actions—at least in detail. This was a resolution which:

1—Recognized occupational diseases and infections were continuing to take "far too great a toll in terms of health, earning ability and in some cases life itself from the workers in Montana."

2—Resolved to press for legislation and greater funds to carry out work to combat occupational diseases and infections.

The obvious reference, again, was to silicosis. The report, as was said, was not carried by the *Independent-Record,* and inasmuch as the conference was not staffed by the Associated Press, it did not reach any of the Montana dailies—A.C.M. or independents.

A Key Issue

Going back a bit further, to the 1947 state legislature, there was still another action on silicosis— a key issue at A.C.M. mining and legislative programs.

On Feb. 6, Representative John Emmons, a Deer Lodge Democrat, announced he would introduce a bill in the assembly declaring silicosis an "industrial accident" which would bring it under the workmen's compensation act.

His announcement was used by the Associated Press for one of its legislative "leads" that day. The Great Falls *Tribune* carried the story on page one the following morning, next to its top story. It was ignored by the A.C.M.'s corresponding morning paper in Butte. Yet, both had the same A.P. file. And the Helena *Independent-Record,* which covers the assembly with staff writers, ignored the story, too.

In a wide swing through Montana, one of the A.C.M. editors was asked about A.C.M. policy on legislative coverage. He told this reporter: "You'll notice all of our papers, except Helena, carry wire service reports on the legislature."

That is true. The A.C.M. press does carry wire reports on the legislature. All five of the company papers, in both morning and evening-side publications, carry a lot of "copy."

"That should make it pretty obvious we're not trying to slant news out of the legislature, shouldn't it?" he asked. But let a veteran Montana lawmaker, Representative Leo Graybill of Great Falls, answer:

"The A.C.M. follows a rather obvious program of legislative coverage. It prints fully the report on the cat and dog bill, and on most of the routine legislation. But where a tax or labor or compensation bill is involved, the report is screened.

"The story might be buried deep in the paper. It might not be carried at all. Or the facts may be cut to the bone. That happens most often. It seems to me that news page position—whether it appears on page one, or deep inside—counts for something in an objective newspaper.

"No. The company doesn't give an objective report on the legislature. And we all recognize the fact. They have one man at the press table with full credentials of a press man. But he doesn't write a word. All he does is keep track of the roll call votes, and telephones Butte the results.

"We all kind of laugh about it—the way the A.C.M. press covers the legislature. Especially the way the legislature is covered by the Helena *Independent.*"

Charge it up to an editor's individual judgment of news. Accept the company's position it is publishing a totally objective chain of newspapers.

Suspicion Invited

One fact is inescapable, however: The mere ownership of the press by an industry invites suspicion. A company inherits this suspicion the moment it wields both the tools of industry and the pen.

Moreover, the situation in Montana is unique in American life. There, Anaconda is not only the world's premier producer in the nonferrous metals industry. It also is the state's largest publisher.

Like Buttes' ore-rich metal mines, the frothing smelter plants in Anaconda and Great Falls, and a score of other subsidiaries in Montana, A.C.M. owns the big chunk of Montana's press.

She occupies a dual role—as an industrialist whose business is to mine and smelt ores, and as a publisher. The pen and the pick are so intermingled, it is difficult to tell where one begins and the other leaves off.

True, it is not a situation without precedent. It

has been said, there was a day when the corporation press was as much a part of American life as the hot dog is today.

But it is an antediluvian practice. Nowhere in America today is there a parallel. Elsewhere, industry long ago restored the press it kept in shackles to "free" enterprise, for the cry was loud and insistent against a captive press. And industry has learned since to live under the searching and often bold scrutiny of that free press.

A Good Investment

Why is A.C.M. in the publishing business?

T. B. Weir, a director of the subsidiary Fairmont corporation which has direct control over the A.C.M. press, said, "We're in the business because it's a good investment. That's our only interest."

Many doubt that. They say the ownership is an instrument—actual or potential, and both—of suppression.

Some years ago, one of Montana's independent editors became irritated with the company's obvious policy at that time of invoking a "news blackout" on anything Senator James Murray did in the U.S. Senate.

That was in 1943. But the observation still is recalled in Montana.

The editor, Miles Ramsey of the *Western News*, referred to a statement circulated by Murray that the corporation press was kept to serve special vested interests—specifically, A.C.M.'s and Montana Power's.

Editorially, he agreed with Murray that the company press had treated Murray "shabbily" and argued that the activities of a U.S. senator from the state in which a newspaper is published are "bound to be news whether the management of the paper is in accord with the senator's viewpoints or not."

Then, in a blistering indictment of a corporation press in general, the *Western News* said: "Certainly the control of the press by any special privilege-seeking group is not in the best interests of the public.

"I doubt if anyone will argue that point.

"But it seems to me that it is at least questionable if such control in the long run is to the best interest of the corporation itself. Gradually a suspicion is bound to seep into the public mind that such control must be exercised for a purpose of dubious worth to the public. . . .

"What the corporation might conceivably gain through control of news, which is likely to result in control of public opinion, could easily cost the corporation more in loss of public esteem. . . ."

Many Indifferent

That's one man's opinion on a company press. But in words perhaps not so well chosen, so scholarly spoken, other Montanans mirror the same reaction. There are many who are indifferent. Of course. But the searching reader chafes under the scissor blades of a company press. If he can find no wrong, the theory, itself, is irritating, for the reputation of a captive industrial press in America is short of goodness and light.

Another question . . .

Just how big is Anaconda?

The average Montanan has a vague mental picture of this giant who lives in the Montana house. He thinks of it in terms of an owner of Butte's mines, and the smelterer of Butte's copper. But the picture ends there in the average mind.

Actually, the full scope and sweep of Anaconda's holdings is staggering. It is both one of the world's major producers and consumers of copper.

It mines it, smelts it, refines it, then fabricates and sells it. It soaks up copper from diggings all over the globe, and boils it out in a gigantic, bubbling gusher.

But it is also a major producer of other ores: Silver, zinc, gold, lead. It produces 95 per cent of this nation's output in manganese, the defense-critical ore in such short supply.

Directly or through its subsidiaries or associated companies, it controls the annual production, for example, of more than 1 billion pounds of copper, 500 million pounds of zinc, 150 million pounds of lead, and more than 5 per cent of the world's production in silver.

Nor does its interests stop there. It owns more than 500,000 acres of Montana lumber lands, consumes approximately 40 million board feet of lumber in its operations alone. And on the retail end, it sells other additional millions of board feet through its controlled lumber yards throughout the state.

It operates three domestic railroads, all to service its own holdings. It owns all or the majority of stock in about fifteen domestic companies, and has major copper, molybdenite, gold and silver properties in a half-dozen foreign countries.

That's only a thumbnail sketch of its size.

Our Costly Dilemma

How to help the truly needy without falling victim to a few lazy, scheming spongers perplexes welfare agencies everywhere. The Buffalo *Evening News* sent reporter Ed May to serve as a caseworker for six months with the Erie County (N.Y.) Department of Social Welfare. His 14-part series, which treats with various aspects of "Our Costly Dilemma," won for him a Pulitzer Prize.

May's series touched on other social evils, among them the high cost of slum dwelling with its exorbitant profits to landlords. This article, approached from the standpoint of those receiving welfare assistance, places some of the blame for high welfare costs where it belongs, on rent gougers.

The story cites costs meaningfully, referring to specific cases to document the thesis. A reader gains the impression May missed nothing, not even the locks on mailboxes to prevent anyone from stealing welfare checks. Although understandable concern that public money be spent wisely might lead one to stack the deck against those receiving welfare assistance, May maintained an essentially balanced presentation. He treated his subject with sympathy.

The story moves steadily, speedily from the provocative lead to the final four-word paragraph.

By Ed May
Buffalo Evening News, June 20, 1960

Population: 36,301. This is the second largest city in Erie County.

It has no mayor, no tax rate and no boundary lines. Its name is Welfare City.

Its residents are scattered from the crowded tenements of Buffalo to an occasional ramshackle farmhouse in the outlying towns. And in its center—the tattered pattern of slums—it has its own special characteristics.

Welfare City's colors are gray and rust. The once white houses and yellow houses have succumbed to the brushings of countless rainstorms.

There are the locks on the mailboxes—so no one can steal the welfare check . . . light bulbs burning feebly in shadow-filled hallways. . . . The smell of fish (they're inexpensive) cooking on a stove.

"Landlord's Paradise," is what some caseworkers call it.

Rents Average $49.86

But in Welfare City, like in any other, there are the neat-as-a-pin places too, where a fussy housewife will greet a caseworker with an accusing glare if he should forget to remove his overshoes.

Today to keep a collective roof over Welfare City costs the taxpayers $7,000,000 a year. The rent bill ranks among the top of welfare's expense list.

In 1958, an Erie County Welfare Department survey showed it was paying $5,800,000 rent a year. Today, officials concede, with a higher caseload and higher rentals, that figure is much larger.

In my own caseload while I served as a caseworker in the Erie County Welfare Department the average rent was $49.86 a month without utilities. If heat, cooking and light are included, the figure rises to $63.80.

Lease Carefully Worded

"Some of these places aren't worth half the price we're paying for them," more than one welfare official has said.

As an example, take the case of John B., a steelworker and father of seven children. He is receiving supplementary help from the Welfare Department so he can make ends meet.

If it were not for his exorbitant rent he wouldn't be on welfare.

John earns an average of $80 a week. About 10% of it goes to pay for a 4-year-old furniture bill. What he's paying for already is worn out.

He lives in a seven-room, weather-worn flat in the Fruit Belt and his carefully worded lease says:

"Witnesseth that the landlord leases to the tenant and the tenant hereby hires and takes from the landlord . . . at the annual rent of one thousand and eighty dollars ($1080)."

One of Prime Dilemmas

For his $90 a month John gets the floors, the walls and the ceilings. Heat, and the gas stove to furnish it, are his responsibility. In the winter his shelter bill is about $130 a month.

If the flat were under rent control, reports the Temporary State Housing Rent Commission, the maximum monthly fair rental figure would be $34.50.

The two-apartment building is assessed at $3090. In two years the owner's gross rent receipts will exceed the assessed valuation.

Less than a mile away, a welfare client, occupying a similar seven-room flat, pays $22.50 a month.

This contrast is one of welfare's prime dilemmas. Only a few months ago Commissioner Paul F. Burke lashed out at slum landlords who are gouging your tax dollars away.

In the high welfare areas, tenement rents often are charged by the week. Anywhere from $20 to $30 is not uncommon.

Two Kinds of Arithmetic

This leads to tenant arithmetic and landlord arithmetic. The two are different.

In one of my cases, the client, paying $22 a week, was convinced it was $88 a month since you multiply by four. The actual figure (landlord arithmetic) was $95.33 since there are 4⅓ weeks in a month.

In a few cases, the unscrupulous have duped the uninformed because they have no understanding of the laws. Take, as an example, Mrs. Harriet F., one of my clients who was on welfare because she injured her foot.

Difference of Opinion

Mrs. F. said she owned the house she was living in and showed bundles of what she considered payment receipts that had been made to the "former" owner. A resource check produced this from the "former" owner's attorney:

"It appears this estate has been and still is paying the taxes on this property. It further appears that Mrs. F. has never paid any rental or other consideration for the use of this property."

In other words, Mrs. F. is paying rent, not making monthly payments toward the purchase of her house as she thinks. But as far as the owner's attorney is concerned, he knows nothing about rent or property payments.

Tangle of Violations

On the other side of the picture, some landlords who pride themselves on a "square deal" have refused welfare tenants.

"Too hard to collect the rent. Too much damage to the property," is their complaint.

City and county officials dealing with housing, as well as the banks, know the big-time slum operators by name. A half-dozen, they estimate, own hundreds of buildings alone.

These officials also know the sorry tangle of housing violations that thread their way through Buffalo. About 15,000 multiple dwellings now violate various fire, health and building laws. Since 1956, fewer than 700 have qualified for a certificate of occupancy.

Some Sent to Jail

One County Health Department spokesman termed "numerous" the houses which lack even minimum bathroom facilities of a toilet, wash basin and tub or shower.

Serious minimum housing law violations, he said, "run into the thousands" for lack of time and personnel to inspect the dwellings.

In New York City, on the other hand, a Special

Sessions Housing Court has fined a steady parade of landlords. Some, who were chalking up fines as "a business expense," were sent to jail.

The County Health Department's court record here looks like this:

In 1959 it took 438 cases to City Court. Because of various adjournments allowed by the courts this required 1110 appearances.

Sixteen persons paid fines.

PART 8

REPORTING
AT ITS BEST

PEOPLE

PROBABLY the greatest of all reader appeals is people—interesting people, prominent people—what they do, what they think, and what happens to them. Little wonder then that man reaches his writing zenith in stories about the famous, the near famous, the colorful.

Bapu Is Finished

The soft-spoken, ascetic Indian spiritual and political leader Mohandas Gandhi captured the imaginations of men everywhere, including many of the reporters who covered his life and death. He often fasted to near collapse in his crusades for Indian independence, human rights, and the dignity of man. And when he spoke his countrymen, even his enemies, listened.

Newly independent India, she gained her independence Aug. 15, 1947, was racked with bloody strife among the Hindus, Moslems, and Sikhs. Full scale war between largely Hindu India and Moslem Pakistan threatened. Hindus living in Pakistan fled south and Moslems in India moved to Pakistan amid bloody rioting. Apparently only Gandhi could forestall open and extended warfare. At this point an assassin felled him. Had the killer been Moslem, war undoubtedly would have come. Fortunately for the course of history the man who shot Gandhi was a Hindu.

James Michaels of United Press covered the assassination

[*184*]

and burial, writing stories of sheer genius. This story has been cited elsewhere as one of the great all-time news stories. Where does its strength lie? Largely in the simple, reverentially understanding treatment, in the inspired word selection, in the beautiful contrast. Let's dissect it for a well-deserved minute inspection.

The story is organized essentially in a tell and re-tell chronological pattern under a summary lead. The lead treats with two features—the assassination and Indians' reactions to the assassination. The story body elaborates on these in the order they appear in the lead: the assassination (par. 3–12) and people's reactions (par. 13–19). Hence, the lead gives a brief outline for the story. Two essentially chronological accounts of the assassination appear (par. 5–8 and 9–12). A large segment of the body devoted to reactions is chronologically organized (par. 21–24, for example), again because these reactions are physically expressed.

This story's major strength, however, comes from lucid use of appropriate, fresh, descriptive language. These verbs move the story at a steady pace: "plunged" (par. 1); "pumped" (par. 3); "emaciated" (par. 4); "crumpled" (par. 7), only frail Gandhi would crumple as paper; "was borne" (par. 11); "gasped and surged" (par. 17); "blazed" (par. 17); "fused" (par. 18); "whirled" (par. 19). Most of all the phrasing describes in language appropriate to Gandhi and India: "frail body, emaciated by years of fasting and asceticism" (par. 4); "homespun, sacklike dhoti and leaning heavily on a staff of stout wood" (par. 6); "shots sounded like a string of firecrackers" (par. 10), Michaels lets us hear the shots so we know they were fired from a small-caliber revolver; "It was a moment before Gandhi's devotees realized what had happened" (par. 10), how much better to permit readers to see the crowd react than tell them the crowd was surprised or stunned or some such; "a panic-stricken Moslem woman . . . 'God help us all!'" (par. 13), selecting one person to speak helps communicate clearly, if that person is so selected that she represents accurately others' feelings; and the whole of paragraphs 15 and 17. "Converging" (par. 15) is a brilliant word choice in a story replete with touches of greatness. In paragraphs 15 and 17 Michaels added sound with such phrasing as "stood weeping silently or moaning and wailing" (par. 15) and "The people gasped and surged forward" (par. 17). Contrast fortifies paragraph 17's description: "brilliant spotlight . . . wrinkled brown face . . . white sheet . . . blood-stained loincloth."

Simplicity adds greatly, too. Simplicity of sentence and paragraph structure and of specific expressions. Note how the granddaughter broke the news of his death, "Bapu (father) is finished" (par. 11). Other phrasing simply, brilliantly adds luster: "He spoke no word before he died" (par. 8); "Over all India the word spread like wildfire" (par. 13), Michaels began this paragraph with the scene to tell readers he is switching to another story topic; "The news set the people on the march" (par. 14).

Important explanation appears where needed: why an assassin would have this opportunity to kill Gandhi (par. 5), how the assassin was able to conceal the gun (par. 9), the three warring religious sects of India (par. 18), and Gandhi's influence over the masses (par. 19). Background, too, is inserted throughout.

One could profitably study this inspired composition for hours; its strengths are legion.

By James Michaels
United Press, Jan. 30, 1948

NEW DELHI—Mohandas K. Gandhi was assassinated today by a Hindu extremist whose act plunged India into sorrow and fear.

Rioting broke out immediately in Bombay.

The seventy-eight-year-old leader whose people had christened him the Great Soul of India died at 5:45 (7:45 a.m. EST) with his head cradled in the lap of his sixteen-year-old granddaughter, Mani.

Just half an hour before, a Hindu fanatic, Ram Naturam, had pumped three bullets from a revolver into Gandhi's frail body, emaciated by years of fasting and asceticism.

Gandhi was shot in the luxurious gardens of Birla House in the presence of one thousand of his followers, whom he was leading to the little summer pagoda where it was his habit to make his evening devotions.

Gandhi Crumpled Instantly

Dressed as always in his homespun, sacklike dhoti, and leaning heavily on a staff of stout wood, Gandhi was only a few feet from the pagoda when the shots were fired.

Gandhi crumpled instantly, putting his hand to his forehead in the Hindu gesture of forgiveness to his assassin. Three bullets penetrated his body at a close range, one in the upper right thigh, one in the abdomen, and one in the chest.

He spoke no word before he died. A moment before he was shot he said—some witnesses believed he was speaking to the assassin—"You are late."

The assassin had been standing beside the garden path, his hands folded, palms together, before him in the Hindu gesture of greeting. But between his palms he had concealed a small-caliber revolver. After pumping three bullets into Gandhi at a range of a few feet, he fired a fourth shot in an attempt at suicide, but the bullet merely creased his scalp.

Crowd Attacks Assassin

The shots sounded like a string of firecrackers and it was a moment before Gandhi's devotees realized what had happened. Then they turned on the assassin savagely and would have torn him to bits had not police guards intervened with rifles and drawn bayonets. The assassin was hustled to safekeeping.

Gandhi quickly was borne back to Birla House and placed on a couch with his head in his granddaughter's lap. Within a few moments she spoke to the stricken throng, among them Pandit Jawaharlal Nehru, premier of India: "Bapu (father) is finished."

Then Mani rose and sat crosslegged beside the body of the man whose life was forfeit for the cause of peace and humanity. She began to chant the two-thousand-year-old verses of the Bhagavad-Gita, the Hindu scripture.

Over all India the word spread like wildfire. Minutes after the flash was received in Bombay rioting broke out, with Hindu extremists attacking Moslems.

A panic-stricken Moslem woman echoed the thoughts of thousands with a cry: "God help us all!"

Crowds Converge on Birla House

In Delhi itself, in the quick-gathering gloom of the night, the news set the people on the march.

They walked slowly down the avenues and out of the squalid bazaars, converging on Birla House. There by the thousands they stood weeping silently or moaning and wailing. Some sought to scale the high walls and catch one last glimpse of the Mahatma. Strong troop contingents strove to keep order.

Tonight in response to the insistent demand of the people, his body was shown to them.

The balcony window of the house opened and the body was borne outside. The people gasped and surged forward as it was placed in a chair, facing them. A brilliant spotlight blazed on the wrinkled, brown face. The eyes were closed, the face peaceful in repose. A white sheet covered the bloodstained loincloth.

Within Birla House there was grief and mourning which at least for the moment fused the dissident sects of India—the Hindus, the Moslems, and the Sikhs—into a community of sorrow.

But there were grave fears, heightened by the savage outbreaks in Bombay, that without her saint to hold passions in check, all India might be whirled into strife.

A Modern Fairy Tale

One of Queen Elizabeth's ports of call during her mid-1959 visit to North America was Chicago. Newsmen via all the mass media recorded this historic occasion. But probably none captured the true spirit of her visit as imaginatively as did Dorothea Kahn Jaffe. To her this was a real-life fairy tale.

She wrote this beautifully simple, subdued human interest story for The *Christian Science Monitor*. The qualities that make this story memorable are its effective use throughout of the appropriate fairy tale theme, simple descriptive language, easy-to-read chronology. She selected each word with the greatest care. Her verbs, while not blatant, move the story along at an easy, measured pace. Note, for example, the dearth of weak "to be" verbs.

By Dorothea Kahn Jaffe
The Christian Science Monitor, July 7, 1959

Once upon a time there was a great city on the shore of an inland sea. This city had done marvelous things. It had built land in that sea to make a park for all the people. The park was lined with beautiful trees bordered with promenades and within the garden was a fountain that tossed its water high up toward the blue sky. Many mighty men came to visit this city from far countries.

But one thing the city lacked. It had never had a visit from the Queen of the land known as "The Mother Country," the nation from which its own nation had sprung. Then one day came the word the queen is coming.

And it was true.

On a bright summer morning when the breeze blew from the lake and the air of that city sparkled in the sunshine, there was a great coming together of the people beside the fountain in the lakeside park.

Everyone was looking out toward the waters where many ships were anchored. "She's coming! She's coming!" the people cried.

A small boat came speeding toward the shore.

A tall handsome Prince stood at the edge of the boat and held out his hand to his lady.

Then a cry went up from the people. For at last they saw with their own eyes the lovely figure of the Queen. She sprang lightly from the boat to a petunia barge and from the barge she stepped upon a blue carpet that led toward the city.

All looked upon her and smiled. For she was young and beautiful and she walked with a graceful step.

Soon she was speaking words of friendliness to the people of the city. And all the people were satisfied, for they said to each other and their children, "Now we have had a visit from the Queen."

Overjoyed Million Hail President In New Delhi

Sociologists study crowds—the way they behave and why they react as they do. Newsmen, too, at times study crowds, usually reporting largely how they react. To both types of observers crowds are fascinatingly interesting phenomena.

Two stories follow that treat with crowds as they reacted to a military-political and a political leader. Their copy is richly descriptive.

The first recounts the Indian reception accorded President Dwight D. Eisenhower during his visit to Asia in 1959. The second is an interpretative analysis of Soviet Premier Nikita Khrushchev's tour of the United States, also in 1959.

President Eisenhower, despite a heart attack, a mild stroke, and an operation for ileitis, visited Asia in December, 1959. His welcome, especially in India, was one of the loudest, longest, and most enthusiastic ever lavished voluntarily on a world leader. So much so those in the entourage feared the strain might impair further the President's health.

Robert J. Donovan's reportorial masterpiece for the New York *Herald Tribune* is resplendent with vivid verbs; specific, highly visual nouns; and imaginative, refreshingly descriptive adjectives. He combined these into a simple, chronological narrative which readers can follow easily. His first chronology runs through paragraph six. Others are from paragraph 7 to 15, 16 to 25, and 26 to the end. Donovan's story flows smoothly and interestingly, aided by introductory connective statements at the beginning of each new chronology. See how paragraph 7 picks up the thread of the previous paragraph, as does paragraph 16. A flashback in the next to last paragraph permits the writer to insert additional reference to the Pakistan and Afghanistan visits.

Donovan helped readers visualize the pandemonium by relating events to New York City thoroughfares (par. 11, 17).

This graphic story is easily one of the great crowd stories of all time.

By Robert J. Donovan
New York Herald Tribune, Dec. 10, 1959

India exploded last night with a welcome for President Eisenhower that was wild, massive and uncontrollable. Except for the fact that it was deliriously friendly, it would have been terrifying as well.

In a mob scene such as no other President of the United States has ever before experienced, a million or more screaming persons descended on Mr. Eisenhower on foot, on camel-back, on bicycles, in automobiles and bullock carts, obliterating all semblance of authority.

The crowds halted the President's car in the middle of New Delhi and deluged him with flowers.

Prime Minister Jawaharlal Nehru, who was riding in the open car with Mr. Eisenhower and Indian President Rajondra Prasad, tried frantically to wave the crowds back. Later he said it was the largest throng he had ever seen in New Delhi.

With thousands of hands clutching out at him, Mr. Eisenhower stood up through most of the tumult which went on continuously for the two hours and ten minutes it took his car to travel thirteen miles from the airport outside New Delhi to India's Presidential Palace.

'You Write It'

From the beginning to the end of the ride, he moved through a cloud of choking dust. The ordeal must have been exhausting, but Mr. Eisenhower was smiling at the end and when a reporter asked him what he thought of the demonstration he replied, "You write it."

The President's whole day yesterday was fantastic. His itinerary alone was prodigious.

He began the day in Karachi, Pakistan, concluding a visit that had begun Monday on the third leg of his 23,370-mile, eleven-nation trip.

From Karachi he flew to remote Kabul, Afghanistan. Despite the pronounced Soviet influence in that nation, he received a welcome that was only slightly less exuberant than the one in New Delhi.

Then later yesterday afternoon, he came to India for a four-and-a-half-day stay. He is the first American President in office to have visited the three that he has been in in the last twenty-four hours.

The mob scenes in New Delhi were indescribable. It was as if the morning rush-hour crowd at Fifth Ave. and 42d St. suddenly ran into the evening rush-hour crowd the very moment that the St. Patrick's Day Parade was passing through.

When it was all over, U. E. Banghman, chief of the United States Secret Service, which is responsible under law for the President, said: "Thank goodness, it was a friendly crowd."

James J. Rowley, chief of the Secret Service's White House detail, said: "It was the biggest crowd I ever saw."

President at Mercy of Crowd

It was indeed an extraordinary sight to see the President of the United States completely at the mercy of a crowd 9,000 miles from Washington. The crowd was so overwhelmingly friendly that there was no reason to be concerned, except for the wear and tear on the President. But there is no visible sign that he is not taking the taxing grind in stride.

There is a good deal of doubt among reporters accompanying the President whether he or anyone else fully realized in advance what an exhausting undertaking this nineteen-day trip is for a man who is sixty-nine and who has had a heart attack, a mild stroke and an operation for ileitis, all within the period of the last four years. It is nothing less than an impressive feat of physical endurance.

The reason for the chaos yesterday was that the crowds, despite some vigorous clubbing by the police, would not remain stationary. The people were not content to let the President pass. They were bent on following him. Thus the thousands who already had seen Mr. Eisenhower began piling upon the thousands who were just seeing him. In this way the density increased.

In no time at all this piling up of mass upon mass began to produce eddies, cross-currents and backwash. Traffic was moving in opposite directions in the same narrow thoroughfare. It was as if cars for New Jersey and cars for Manhattan both suddenly rushed into a one-way tube of the Holland Tunnel.

The only difference is that in this case there were bullock-drawn carts full of veiled women, and camels with two merry men aboard, pouring off the Jersey Turnpike.

Car Inches Forward

The upshot was that by the time the car with Mr. Eisenhower, Prime Minister Nehru and President Prasad reached the center of town it could move only inches at a time.

White House press secretary James C. Hagerty, who, like Mr. Eisenhower, was already two feet deep in flowers in his car, estimated that it took forty-five minutes for the motorcade to get around Connaught Circle, which the local cognoscenti say, is one mile around.

Throughout it all, the citizens of India who made up this throng were sublime. A million people never had so much fun all at once. They were really living it up in the donkey carts last night. Secret Service Chief Baughman may have been holding his head but they were holding their sides. Truckloads full of laughing people rolled up and down the streets, in conflicting directions, of course.

In their good will, they greeted the President with whatever English expressions they knew.

"Good morning," they shouted in the evening moonlight.

"Good morning," the President politely replied.

"Hello, hello," they responded. "Okay, Okay."

Kabul Crowds Delay President

Partly because of dense crowds in Kabul, the President was late arriving in New Delhi. This meant that it was dark almost as soon as he left New Delhi's Palam airport. The fact that the turmoil occurred at night made it all the more bewildering.

Until the motorcade reached the central parts of New Delhi the procession moved in darkness, except for light cast at intervals by torch-bearers and the pungent lanterns of banana peddlers. Thousands of people who had followed the President as far as they could would gradually fan out into the dark fields for home, and a stranger peering into the darkness would wonder where they were going and what their homes were like.

The excitement, the occasional qualms and finally the sheer zanyism of last night's proceedings overshadowed the rest of the day. But in any other circumstances the presence of the American President in Pakistan and Afghanistan all in the course of a couple of hours would have been an event of moment, indeed it was.

Mr. Eisenhower had a private dinner last night at the Rashtrapati Bhavan, President Prasad's official residence. He will occupy a suite there during his stay in New Delhi.

Can't See America For The Photographers

The year 1959 will be remembered, among other things, for Russian Premier Nikita S. Khrushchev's coast-to-coast barnstorming tour of the United States. The tour got off to a cold Washington and New York reception, threatened to erupt into an international crisis in Los Angeles, and finally warmed up in San Francisco.

James Reston, perhaps as no other American, recognized the real purpose of Khrushchev's visit and newsmen's role in it. His fast-moving, penetrating New York *Times* article, datelined Coon Rapids, Iowa, gains from his punchy quips,[1] keen observation,[2] and brief and pointedly clear sentences.

By James Reston
The New York Times, Sept. 24, 1959

COON RAPIDS, IA.—When Nikita S. Khrushchev arrived at Roswell Garst's farm here Wednesday, everything was wired for sound but the hogs.

The Associated Press had taken over one barn, United Press International another.

---

[1] Examples: "everything wired for sound but the hogs" (par. 1), "they changed everything at the Garst farm but the smell" (par. 10), "whoever said pictures don't lie is the biggest liar of them all" (par. 15), "this is the worst run political trip since Estes Kefauver ran for the vice-presidency" (par. 19).

[2] Examples: "Khrushchev cannot see America for the policemen and photographers" (par. 5), "there are so many reporters covering the story that they change the story" (par. 6), "the reporters are not covering this story, they are smothering it" (par. 8), "the reporters, photographers . . . are not only useful but indispensable" (par. 12).

Strange Birds

The upper pasture sported a new high steel television tower, and there were more photographers in the trees than birds.

Tall TV booms for high-angle cameras stuck up above a forest of new telephone poles, and while all this produced more corn—journalistic corn, that is—than normally grows in the whole state of Iowa, it also illustrates a problem.

It appears that Khrushchev cannot see America for the policemen and photographers.

There are so many reporters covering the story that they change the story.

They are not the obscure witnesses of history, but principal characters in the drama whose very presence is so ubiquitous that most of the time Khrushchev is addressing them, or addressing others with them in mind.

Smothering It

The reporters are not covering this story, they are smothering it and each other at the same time.

Never in the history of journalism have so many resourceful scribblers kept each other from following a big story closely, or written so much on a character they couldn't hear and often couldn't see.

There were so many of them around Wednesday that they changed everything at the Garst farm but the smell.

All this, mind you, gives Khrushchev no pain. He is less interested in seeing America than in having the world see him in America.

For this purpose, the reporters, photographers, technicians and all their gear are not only useful but indispensable.

The Film

Literally millions of feet of film have been taken on this astonishing odyssey. If it were all together it would produce a remarkably accurate but devastating record of the "new diplomacy."

But it will be interesting to see what comes out in Asia and Africa when the Soviets get through cutting it to size and shape.

You can bet your last ruble that it will show Khrushchev getting an enthusiastic welcome. Whoever said pictures don't lie is the biggest liar of them all.

For this film can be made to show anything—the silent crowds can be eliminated and the applauding crowds can be retained; Khrushchev's good jokes can be shown and his bad jokes cut; the simple people of this little Willa Cather town can be forgotten, and the Hollywood babes in their black lace tights can be immortalized along with the can-can.

Deadly Serious

In a worldwide propaganda battle, this is not frivolous nonsense, it is deadly serious.

For while it was inevitable that Moscow would be given much raw material during Mr. K's visit for propaganda in the neutral countries, it was not inevitable that clumsy administration should make things worse.

Washington did not minimize but actually doubled the damage. For this is, to put it mildly, the worst-run political trip since Estes Kefauver ran for the vice-presidency.

Khrushchev was President Eisenhower's guest, but the president's press secretary, James C. Hagerty, who knows how to avoid public relations disasters, ducked it after Washington.

This left the show to the state department, but Andrew J. Birding, who is in charge of the state's public affairs, ducked it too.

Up to Lodge

Thus the job fell by default partly to Ambassador Henry Cabot Lodge and his United Nations staff, and partly to the minor officials of the state department's press division.

The result has been turmoil, with nobody anticipating obvious problems, with the planes not arriving on time, with the Western European correspondents denied any chance to get close to the Soviet visitor, with local officials playing politics on the side, and the Russian delegation laughing contemptuously at America's reputation for efficiency.

Fortunately, Ambassador Lodge, though defensively sensitive and a little weary by now, knows what blunders have been made and intends to go over them in Washington when he gets back.

For the time being, his main task is to keep things in hand between Coon Rapids and Camp David. Then there may at last be a serious effort to devise a public relations policy capable of serving the nation's foreign policy.

Poor Man's George Bernard Shaw

Former Oklahoma Governor William H. "Alfalfa Bill" Murray rather typifies the bombastic, shoot-from-the-hip, sagebrush philosopher of an earlier era. This colorful old personality is about as out of place in the mid-Twentieth Century as would be a reincarnation of a dinosaur. But like the pre-historic mammal, he makes good copy.

Madelaine Wilson captured the personality of "Alfalfa Bill" in this interview story for the (Oklahoma City) *Daily Oklahoman*. It is largely his phrasing and her keen observation that make this story excellent. The first three paragraphs set the tone. Note, too, how she quoted him to illustrate his salty philosophical pronouncements and his rapid moving from one subject to another. (See fourth paragraph from the end.) This technique of "showing" instead of "telling" is worthy of emulation.

Here are a few of the passages deserving special attention: "Cluttered with man clutter" (par. 13); " 'I do thinking,' he bellowed. 'I don't guess at the damned thing.' " (par. 21); "You don't believe in world government? 'Oh, good God, no!' " (par. 38–39).

By Madelaine Wilson
The (Oklahoma City) Daily Oklahoman, Nov. 12, 1950

"No comment!" was former Gov. "Alfalfa Bill" Murray's gruff retort when asked for an interview.

Then he spent the next 1½ hours talking, reading aloud, quoting from his newest book, the Bible, the U. S. constitution, Arabian Nights and Ben Franklin's almanac.

And ended up by ordering the reporter out of the room and slamming the door till it fairly bounced on its hinges.

William Henry "Alfalfa Bill" Murray. There's nobody else like him in the world. A sort of poor man's
George Bernard Shaw.

Untidy, eccentric, almost blind and deaf, he still
has a mind and a will that are unbending to the
frailties of the 81 years which will be completed
November 21.

When he declared in defiance, "No comment," he
referred to the election victory of his son, Johnston
Murray, who will become Oklahoma's fourteenth
governor on Janury 8.

Sitting Up Late 'Foolishness'

An hour's conversation later, however, he chuckled
and confided, "I knew it was a cinch."

Recalling the night he, himself, was nominated
governor of Oklahoma, Governor Bill said, "I went to
my room in the old Threadgill hotel (now the
Bristol), told a few jokes to my friends and went to
bed." There was a time, however, when he sat up
all night. It was the Cleveland-Blaine contest for
presidency. "But sitting up late is all foolishness."

He spent election evening quietly in his room
alone, reading. Reading material that pertains to his
hobby—government. Then he went to bed about 10
p.m., and didn't learn the election outcome until he
read about it in Wednesday morning's paper.

"But I knew it was a cinch."

Oklahoma's father-son governorship is unusual
but not a "first." He cites the La Follettes of Wisconsin; the Conways of Arkansas, and the Talmadges of
Georgia.

Hotel Is Home

Governor Bill's Oklahoma City home is a two-win-
dowed west room on the second floor of the Clover
hotel, 307½ N. Broadway.

Apco Tower is seen through the metal venetian
blinds. A pale rose spread is on the iron bed. There's
a dresser (cluttered with man-clutter of papers, pipe,
medicine bottles, open pocket knife). And a ward-
robe with two mirrored doors, and a wash basin in
the corner.

But while you are observing his background, he
has started in on the second page of a five-page type-
written dissertation he had written against the long-
proposed constitutional convention.

It is an advertisement he had planned on placing in a newspaper until he decided it wasn't necessary.

If the people had voted for a constitutional convention to revise the constitution Murray helped write in 1907, Murray would have bought a hearing aid.

"I'd have gone as a delegate and I'd have made their heads swim," he vowed.

Deafness Has Advantages

But the question lost and Murray won't buy his hearing aid. "They're costly," he says, "and, besides, it is a pleasure not to listen to a lot of nonsense that goes on."

He sits in a brown wicker rocker, his back to the windows. A brown hat is pulled low over his thick eyeglasses. At his feet are a cuspidor and a twine-tied bundle of his books.

How did he arrive at all the flaws in the proposed constitution revision?

"I do thinking," he bellowed. "I don't guess at the damned thing."

His thin legs are encased in long underwear, and long white sox over which are pulled a pair of brown stockings with the feet cut off. He pulls up his pants leg to show you why the new cold weather won't bother him.

"Polio is principally caused by getting your legs too cold," he pronounces.

Cain and Abel Not Brothers

In the next breath he announces that Cain and Abel were not brothers, as it says in Genesis. Neither did the river Euphrates have four mouths, as the Bible says. It had only one. The other three were irrigation ditches dug by farmer Cain.

It isn't that his mind wanders. It's just the clash that occurs when you try to steer the conversation to something personal and he throws it back to Genesis or ". . . the court of appeals had learned about this treaty . . ."

He's probably as impersonal a person as you could find anywhere.

You wonder how his heart beats and you find only how his mind works. And it works, continually, at history or government.

Already author of several books "because that's the

only way I can get things I want to say in print,"
Murray is awaiting proofs on his newest book.

Another Murray-isms Book

He refuses to divulge its name. But, from hints in
his conversation, it will include Murray-isms on several things, including religion and the dire state of
government affairs.

And he can prove he knew all the time his son,
Johnston, was going to win the governor's election.
He is listed in his father's book as governor until Jan-
uary, 1955.

Proofs of the book will be ready about December 1.

By his own admission the only fiction he ever read
was four volumes of Arabian Nights, East Lynne,
Pygmalion and Peck's Bad Boy.

"I don't want to fill my mind with a lot of rot."
Anything that isn't history or government comes
under the classification of rot.

You note the right lens in his thick spectacles is
cracked. The laces in his black, patched shoes are
broken and spliced together in knots.

". . . Truman has set out to ruin the United States
by treaties."

U.S. in First Stage of Socialism

"England is in the first stage of communism. The
United States is in the first stage of socialism."

"The best governments in the world are those
where the people are cut along the same lines in
race, language, blood, religion. The Asiatic race will
never agree with the Caucasian."

You don't believe in world government?

"Oh, good God, no!" is his answer.

In Murray's opinion Roosevelt was a scoundrel,
Eisenhower would not make a good president and
your mind is clearer if you don't eat meat.

Given the privilege of naming the next president,
he'd list Bricker, first; Taft, second, "but I would
prefer MacArthur because he could win."

All of a sudden he rises from his chair, announces,
"You'd better go now, I'm done with you."

Then the door slams.

A Poet Talks Of Death And Life

The date, January 20, 1961. The event, inauguration of John F. Kennedy as president of the United States. Amid the traditional pomp and splendor a short, rather paunchy, white-haired New Englander—a poet—held front stage center as millions watched via television. Seldom in the Twentieth Century have Americans taken the time to pay such homage to a poet.

Almost fifteen months later Robert Frost was to celebrate his last birthday, his eighty-eighth. At that time, as newsmen are wont to do, Charles Whited of The Miami *Herald* interviewed Frost. His story, the next in this series, captures above all Frost's color and wisdom through the poet's rich, expressive language. Even Whited's descriptions, observations, and summaries retain the Frost flavor.

Almost never should a reporter lead a story with a full paragraph of direct quotation. Whited did it and it worked, this blind, sourceless beginning. Of course this quote packs high reader impact. A great man's comments on his death always do, especially when so uniquely expressed.

Whited repeatedly captured Frost's philosophy couched in his poetic expressions. A few samples: the whole of paragraph one; ". . . I would live a long time. A long, long time. Oh, a long time" (par. 3); "You fly in a plane over the country, and you look down and see all their rooftops. And every man you're looking on the roof of has his pleasures and his pains" (par. 27); "It's everywhere. All the time. Friendship and hostility and jealousy and compassion" (par. 32).

The writer draws on his own literary skills to maintain the story mood: ". . . and talked and sweated and talked" (par. 2); "He talked slowly, good talk, while his mind leaped ahead clearing a path for the words" (par. 12); "For Robert Frost is, after all, a farmer. A poet, philosopher, teacher, yes. But also a farmer" (par. 24).

Keen observations translated into words describe so vividly that the reader becomes a part of the scene, sits at Frost's right hand and sees and listens. Whited described the setting (par. 2), the man (par. 5, 7, 8, 28, 30), his apparel (par. 20), the house and garden (par. 21, 22, 24). Note, for example, the beauty of paragraph 28: ". . . all the warmth of a lifetime of gentle questions radiated from his eyes." And the alertness evidenced by paragraph 30: "A beam of afternoon sunlight stole through the half-closed venetian blinds and found the white, unruly hair, with its stray lock drooping down the forehead."

Finally, the reporter carefully tied together what could have been a loose bundle with the theme "he talked about." This transitional device, used expertly to compartmentalize the story into a flowing, unified, logical whole, appears throughout the story. He began with the topic "death" and led logically into Frost's age. Then, in paragraph 12, he introduced the "talked about" idea and used it as a connective in paragraphs 13, 16, 26, and 34.

By Charles Whited
The Miami Herald, March 16, 1962

"I thought I was going to die the other day. I thought, 'All right, good-bye.' Then I thought again, that I'd stay around and see who wins the next election."

Robert Frost, poet, relaxed in the small, hot living room of his New England cottage, set in a South Miami pine thicket, and talked and sweated and talked.

"It never occurred to me before that I might die. I was immortal. I would live a long time. A long, long time. Oh, a long time.

"Well, I know now that I can't live more than 150 years. After all, there is a limit."

Voice Like a Dump Truck

America's poet laureate, as he's sometimes called, is a thickset, paunchy man with a voice like a dump truck. A week from Monday, he will be 88.

And this was his first newspaper interview since pneumonia put him in South Miami Hospital for a month.

His hair is white as a wintry rooftop in Vermont. The heavy, broad face is etched with lines of fatigue and flecked with the brown spots of age.

But the eyes flash blue under straggling brows, and the words have a scalpel's cleanness.

"Eighty-eight? Why all the fuss about a man being

88? Ninety maybe, yes. Or a hundred. That would be something. But 88?"

To celebrate his birthday, they're planning a big shindig for him in Washington March 26. But the canny Frost isn't talking about that.

"It's a secret," he said with a sly grin. "I'm not supposed to know anything about it."

So he talked instead about a multitude of things. He talked slowly, good talk, while his mind leaped ahead clearing a path for the words.

'I'm Never Busy'

He talked about the slow life.

"I've always tried to get by, to make a living. But I get angry when people on the telephone say, 'He's busy,' I'm never busy!

"My friend Hemingway wrote tons of stuff that his wife has to sort through now. I've written five, six hundred pages in 70 years. That's all. About ten pages a year."

He talked about the fast life.

"I've been publicized more this year than ever in my life. It turns me outside in, or inside out. So much pleasant attention. But on the outside, that isn't where you write poetry."

The four-time Pulitzer Prize winner, whose work has brought him the world's honors, put his blunt fingertips together and looked at nothing at all.

He wore a faded blue shirt, open at the throat, and an old pair of loose white trousers. In the course of the conversation, he shucked his shoes and wiggled his toes in a pair of gray socks.

His house is simple, utilitarian, and screened from the world by heavy foliage behind the home of his son-in-law and daughter, Mr. and Mrs. Joseph Ballantine, 5240 SW 80th St.

He shipped his cottage by rail from New England years ago because author Hervey Allen talked him into having a winter home here.

"It's simple," said the poet. "The one thing I mind about Florida is people want to be too Floridan. Too much show. This is simple."

Room To Putter

Outside, he has plenty of room to putter with his avocados, his mangoes, and the other trees laden with fruit.

For Robert Frost is, after all, a farmer. A poet, philosopher, teacher, yes. But also a farmer. He farmed long before a line of his poetry was published. And his first book wasn't printed until he was 40 years old.

"If I have something to do, something to occupy my time," he said, "I'm happy."

Then he talked about people.

"You fly in a plane over the country, and you look down and see all their rooftops. And every man you're looking on the roof of has his pleasures and his pains."

The Frost face softened. The Frost voice deepened. All the warmth of a lifetime of gentle questions radiated from his eyes.

"No government can touch it. No psychologist can touch it. All the jealousy, the emotions that live and die, the little disloyalties—all are in the air. And with that, the great detachment."

Who Would Attack John Glenn?

A beam of afternoon sunlight stole through the half-closed venetian blinds and found the white, unruly hair, with its stray lock drooping down the forehead.

"Some boys attacked John Glenn, it says in your paper. Who the hell are they? What kind of boys are they? The minute anybody gets to be anybody, somebody else comes along and says, 'Who are you, to get so big?'

"It's everywhere. All the time. Friendship and hostility and jealousy and compassion.

"It's everywhere."

Then he talked of the moon, and of people going there some day. "And where will I be? With my toes turned up, my hands composed.

"There are many who were concerned with the world, now with their toes turned up and their hands composed, thinking of nothing—unless, maybe, they're looking in from another world."

PART 9

DEATH

April 14, 1865.
Nov. 22, 1963. . . .
These are the dates of our massive shame.

So wrote Kays Gary, columnist of the Charlotte (North Carolina) *Observer* the day after President John F. Kennedy was felled by an assassin's bullets in Dallas. Others referred to the heart-rending tragedy as America's "saddest hour," our "personal moment of infamy." New York *Times* Bureau Chief James Reston wrote, "somehow the worst in the nation had prevailed over the best." Ralph McGill, editor of the Atlanta *Constitution,* in one of the most moving pieces written on the assassination blamed "psychopathic hate" for the death and warned of the consequences in a column that began:

> A young President, husband, and father, now done savagely and pitilessly to death, is the latest harvest of psychopathic hate. Before we mourn, it seems necessary that the nation comprehend the fact that hate, whether of the extreme left or right, can destroy not merely the chief of state, but the state itself.

A torrent of words, pictures, emotions flowed from Dallas that awful day. Television and radio upon receiving the original bulletin from United Press International's Merriman Smith, immediately ceased all planned programming to cover the one big story and all of its ramifications. From noon Friday until sign-off Monday their full facilities were focused on the assassination, the assassin's assassination, the funeral, and the new Lyndon B. Johnson administration.

Schools and businesses and theaters closed, most sports events were postponed or cancelled, time seemingly stood still as a saddened nation mourned her lost leader and contemplated the despicable, unbelievable murder act. It was the death of Abraham Lincoln, James A. Garfield, and William McKinley re-enacted. Anguish similar to that of April 12, 1945, at the death of Franklin D. Roosevelt again lay heavy upon the land.

Six Hours When History Exploded

How does one report this tragedy, the greatest that many reporters will ever cover? The drama played out in full view, possibly in too full a view, as the accused assassin Lee Harvey Oswald, denied the usual police precautions, was in turn shot down—as a nationwide, Sunday morning television audience watched. It seemed every detail had been covered, every comment made and re-made. Yet it fell the lot of the Presidential press corps to record in permanent form for the present and future these dreadful events. And the pressures were great.

Just how great is illustrated by Mr. Smith's account of the tragedy as he lived it. No one, other than those personally involved, viewed the entire event from a more favored vantage point. As you read this story, note how you dash out of breath from one development to another, dial your office frantically, often almost futilely, in an effort to keep an anxious world informed. See how in the midst of dictating his story this veteran reporter absorbed the action surrounding him (pars. 25–29). His story reflects clearly his being caught up in the whirlwind of a momentous news event, so unexpectedly fast did the story break.

This, then, is an inside view of a great newsman in action. It is only one of many stories and bulletins he filed on the assassination and events that followed. But more, this skillfully written account covers extremely well the key action as it enveloped the late President, Mrs. Kennedy, President and Mrs.

Johnson, Governor and Mrs. John Connally, and those who surrounded them. Mr. Smith's first person story also brings into clear focus the drama of physicians and a hospital staff suddenly beseeched to do the impossible; this event's impact on one, then another, and yet another of those destined to play minor roles; the somber finality of the official notification of death; the swearing in of President Johnson; Mrs. Kennedy's vigil at her husband's coffin; the new President's consoling words to Mrs. Rose Kennedy and Mrs. Connally; and the methodical, step-by-step arrangements for what was to come in Washington.

It is indeed fitting that Merriman Smith, the dean of White House correspondents, relate the tragic end to President Kennedy's life. For Mr. Smith has been an intimate friend of this nation's political leaders since first becoming a United Press International White House correspondent in 1941. It is he who has signalled the end of Presidential news conferences for more than a decade with his "Thank you Mr. President."

But selection of his story is no hollow honor. Mr. Smith's story will live as his personal memorial to President Kennedy. The story moves rapidly; it is incisive yet detailed where details help transport readers to the scene (see especially pars. 12, 13, 18, 19, 24, 31, 40–44, 49, 52). Note how he set an appropriately slow, matter-of-fact pace in the opening two paragraphs, then built to a feverish pitch, beginning with paragraph three. Virtually every sentence thereafter contains elements of writing excellence, colorful and specific language, just the right words. From beginning to end (see last two paragraphs) this is a masterful report, one worth study by anyone who aspires to excel as a writer and reporter.

By Merriman Smith
UPI White House Reporter, Nov. 23, 1963

WASHINGTON, Nov. 23.—It was a balmy, sunny noon as we motored through downtown Dallas behind President Kennedy. The procession cleared the center of the business district and turned into a handsome highway that wound through what appeared to be a park.

I was riding in the so-called White House press "pool" car, a telephone company vehicle equipped with a mobile radio-telephone. I was in the front seat between a driver from the telephone company and Malcom Kilduff, acting White House press secretary for the President's Texas tour. Three other pool reporters were wedged in the back seat.

Suddenly we heard three loud, almost painfully loud cracks. The first sounded as if it might have been a large firecracker. But the second and the third blasts were unmistakable. Gunfire.

The President's car, possibly as much as 150 or 200 yards ahead, seemed to falter briefly. We saw a flurry of activity in the secret service follow-up car behind the chief executive's bubble-top limousine.

Next in line was the car bearing Vice-President Lyndon B. Johnson. Behind that, another follow-up car bearing agents assigned to the vice-president's protection. We were behind that car.

History Exploded

Our car stood still for probably only a few seconds, but it seemed like a lifetime. One sees history explode before one's eyes and for even the most trained observer, there is a limit to what one can comprehend.

I looked ahead at the President's car but could not see him or his companion, Gov. John Connally. Both had been riding on the right side of the limousine. I thought I saw a flash of pink that would have been Mrs. Jacqueline Kennedy.

Everybody in our car began shouting at the driver to pull up closer to the President's car. But at this moment, we saw the big bubbletop and a motorcycle escort roar away at high speed.

We screamed at our driver, "get going, get going." We careened around the Johnson car and its escort and set out down the highway, barely able to keep in sight of the President's car and the accompanying secret service car.

They vanished around a curve. When we cleared the same curve we could see where we were heading —Parkland Hospital. We spilled out of the pool car as it entered the hospital driveway.

I ran to the side of the bubbletop.

A Cradle of Arms

The President was face down on the back seat. Mrs. Kennedy made a cradle of her arms around the President's head and bent over him as if she were whispering to him.

Gov. Connally was on his back on the floor of the car, his head and shoulders resting in the arms of his wife, Nellie, who shook with dry sobs. Blood oozed from the front of the governor's suit. I could not see the President's wound. But I could see blood spattered around the interior of the rear seat and a dark stain spreading down the right side of the President's dark gray suit.

From the telephone car, I had radioed the Dallas UPI Bureau that three shots had been fired at the Kennedy motorcade.

Clint Hill, the secret service agent in charge of the detail assigned to Mrs. Kennedy, was leaning over into the rear of the car.

"How badly was he hit, Clint?" I asked.

"He's dead," Hill replied curtly.

Babble of Voices

I have no further clear memory of the scene in the driveway. I recall a babble of anxious voices, tense voices—"Where in hell are the stretchers. . . . Get a doctor out here. . . . He's on the way. . . . Come on, easy there." And from somewhere, nervous sobbing.

I raced into a hospital corridor. The first thing I spotted was a small clerical office, more of a booth than an office. Inside, a bespectacled man stood shuffling what appeared to be hospital forms. At a wicket much like a bank teller's cage, I spotted a telephone on the shelf.

"How do you get outside?" I gasped. "The President has been hurt and this is an emergency call."

"Dial nine," he said, shoving the phone toward me.

It took two tries before I successfully dialed the Dallas UPI number. Quickly I dictated a bulletin saying the President had been seriously, perhaps fatally, injured by an assassin's bullets.

Litters bearing the President and the governor rolled by me as I dictated, but my back was to the hallway and I didn't see them until they were at the emergency room about 75 or 100 feet away.

I knew they had passed from the horrified expression that spread over the face of the man behind the wicket.

Confused Panorama

As I stood in the drab buff hallway leading into the emergency ward trying to reconstruct the shooting for the UPI man on the other end of the telephone, I watched a swift and confused panorama sweep before me.

Kilduff of the White House press staff raced up and down the hall. Police captains barked at each other, "Clear this area." Two priests hurried in behind a secret service agent, their narrow purple stoles rolled up tightly in their hands. A police lieutenant ran down the hall with a large carton of blood for transfusions. A doctor came in, responding to a call for "all neurosurgeons."

The priests came out and said the President had received the last sacrament of the Roman Catholic Church. They said he was still alive, but not conscious. Members of the Kennedy staff began arriving. They had been behind us in the motorcade, but hopelessly bogged for a time in confused traffic.

Telephones were at a premium and I clung to mine.

My decision was made, however, when Kilduff and Wayne Hawks of the White House staff ran by me, shouting that Kilduff would make a statement in the nurses' room a floor above.

I threw down the phone and sped after them. We reached the door and there were loud cries of "Quiet!" Fighting to keep his emotions under control, Kilduff said "President John Fitzgerald Kennedy died at approximately 1 o'clock."

I raced into a nearby office. The telephone switchboard at the hospital was hopelessly jammed. I spotted Virginia Payette, wife of UPI's southwestern division manager and a veteran reporter in her own right. I told her to try getting through on pay telephones on the floor above.

Frustrated by the inability to get through the hospital switchboard, I appealed to a nurse. She led me through back stairways to another floor and a lone pay booth. I got the Dallas office. Virginia had gotten through before me.

I ran back to the conference room. There Jiggs Fauver of the White House transportation staff grabbed me and said Kilduff wanted a pool of three men immediately to fly back to Washington on Air Force One, the presidential aircraft.

"He wants you downstairs and he wants you right now," Fauver said.

Down the stairs I ran and into the driveway, only to discover Kilduff had just pulled out in our telephone car.

Charles Roberts of *Newsweek*, Sid Davis of Westinghouse Broadcasting and I implored a police officer to take us to the airport in his squad car. The secret service had requested that no sirens be used in the vicinity of the airport, but the Dallas officer did a masterful job of getting us through some of the worst traffic I've ever seen.

As we piled out of the car on the edge of the runway about 200 yards from the presidential aircraft, Kilduff spotted us and motioned for us to hurry. He said the plane could take two pool men to Washington; that Johnson was about to take the oath of office aboard the plane and would take off immediately thereafter.

I saw a bank of telephone booths beside the runway and asked if I had time to advise my news service. "For God's sake, hurry," he said.

Then began another telephone nightmare. The Dallas office rang busy. I tried calling Washington. All circuits were busy. Then I called the New York bureau and told them about the impending installation of a new President aboard the airplane.

Kilduff came out of the plane and motioned wildly toward my booth. I slammed down the phone and jogged across the runway. A detective stopped me and said, "You dropped your pocket comb."

Shades Were Drawn

Aboard Air Force One on which I had made so many trips as a press association reporter covering President Kennedy, all of the shades of the larger main cabin were drawn and the interior was hot and dimly lighted.

Kilduff propelled us to the President's Suite two-thirds of the way back in the plane. The room normally could accommodate eight to 10 people seated.

I wedged inside and began counting. There were 27 people in this compartment. Johnson stood in the center with his wife, Lady Bird. U.S. District Judge Sarah T. Hughes, 67, a kindly faced woman stood with a small black Bible in her hands.

Johnson was worried that some of the Kennedy staff might not be able to get inside. He urged people to press forward, but a signal corps photographer, Capt. Cecil Stoughton, standing in the corner on a chair, said if Johnson moved any closer, it would be virtually impossible to make a truly historic photograph.

White-Faced, Dry-Eyed

It developed that Johnson was waiting for Mrs. Kennedy, who was composing herself in a small bedroom in the rear of the plane. She appeared alone, dressed in the same pink wool suit she had worn in the morning when she appeared so happy shaking hands with airport crowds at the side of her husband.

She was white-faced but dry-eyed. Friendly hands stretched toward her as she stumbled slightly. Johnson took both of her hands in his and motioned her to his life side. Lady Bird stood on his right, a fixed half-smile showing the tension.

Johnson nodded to Judge Hughes, an old friend of his family and a Kennedy appointee.

"Hold up your right hand and repeat after me," the woman jurist said to Johnson.

Outside, a jet could be heard droning into a landing.

Judge Hughes held out the Bible and Johnson covered it with his large left hand. His right arm went slowly into the air and the jurist began to intone the constitutional oath. "I do solemnly swear I will faithfully execute the office of President of the United States. . . ."

The brief ceremony ended when Johnson in a deep, firm voice, repeated after the judge, ". . . and so help me God."

Johnson turned first to his wife, hugged her about the shoulders and kissed her on the cheek. Then he turned to Kennedy's widow, put his left arm around her and kissed her cheek.

As others in the group—some Texas Democratic House members, members of the Johnson and Kennedy staffs—moved toward the new President, he seemed to back away from any expression of felicitation.

'Let's Get Airborne'

The two-minute ceremony concluded at 2:38 p.m. Central time and seconds later, the President said firmly, "Now, let's get airborne."

Col. James Swindal, pilot, cut on the starboard engines. Several persons, including Sid Davis of Westinghouse, left the plane. The White House had room for only two pool reporters on the return flight and these posts were filled by Roberts and me, although at the moment we could find no empty seats.

At 2:47 p.m., the wheels of Air Force One cleared the runway. Swindal roared the big ship up to an unusually high cruising altitude of 41,000 feet where at 625 miles an hour, ground speed, the jet hurtled toward Andrews Air Force Base outside Washington.

When the President's plane reached operating altitude, Mrs. Kennedy left her bedchamber and walked to the rear compartment of the plane. This was the so-called family living room, a private area where she and Kennedy, family and friends had spent many happy airborne hours chatting and dining together.

Kennedy's casket had been placed in this compartment, carried aboard by a group of secret service agents.

Her Vigil Shared

Mrs. Kennedy went into the rear lounge and took a chair beside the coffin. There she remained throughout the flight. Her vigil was shared at times by four staff members close to the slain chief executive—David Powers, his buddy and personal assistant; Kenneth P. O'Donnell, appointments secretary and key political adviser; Lawrence O'Brien, chief Kennedy liaison man with Congress, and Brig. Gen. Godfrey McHugh, Kennedy's Air Force aide.

Kennedy's military aide, Maj. Gen. Chester V. Clifton, was busy most of the trip in the forward areas, sending messages and making arrangements for arrival ceremonies and movement of the body to Bethesda Naval Hospital.

As the flight progressed, Johnson walked back into the main compartment. He came up to the table where Roberts and I were trying to record the history we had just witnessed.

"I'm going to make a short statement in a few minutes and give you copies," he said. "Then when I get on the ground, I'll do it over again."

It was the first public utterance of the new chief executive, brief and moving:

"This is a sad time for all people. We have suffered a loss that cannot be weighed. For me it is a deep personal tragedy. I know the world shares the sorrow that Mrs. Kennedy and her family bear. I will do my best. That is all I can do. I ask for your help—and God's."

A Special Call

When the plane was about 45 minutes from Washington, the new President got on a special radio-telephone and placed a call to Mrs. Rose Kennedy, the late President's mother.

"I wish to God there was something I could do," he told her, "I just wanted you to know that."

Then Mrs. Johnson wanted to talk to the elder Mrs. Kennedy.

"We feel like the heart has been cut out of us," Mrs. Johnson said. She broke down for a moment and began to sob. Recovering in a few seconds, she added, "Our love and our prayers are with you."

Thirty minutes out of Washington, Johnson put in a call for Nellie Connally, wife of the seriously wounded Texas Governor.

"We are praying for you, darling, and I know that everything is going to be all right, isn't it? Give him a hug and a kiss for me."

It was dark when Air Force One began to skim over the Washington area, lining up for a landing at Andrews Air Force Base. The plane touched down at 4:59 p.m.

I thanked the stewards for rigging up a typewriter for me, pulled on my raincoat and started down the forward ramp. Roberts and I stood under a wing and watched the casket being lowered from the rear of the plane and borne by a complement of armed forces body bearers into a waiting hearse. We watched Mrs. Kennedy and the late President's brother, Atty. Gen. Robert F. Kennedy, climb into the hearse.

The new President repeated his first public statement for broadcast and newsreel microphones, shook hands with some of the government and diplomatic leaders and headed for his helicopter.

Not With His Chief

Roberts and I were given seats on another 'copter bound for the White House. In the compartment next to ours in one of the large chairs beside a window sat Theodore C. Sorensen, one of Kennedy's closest associates. He had not gone to Texas with his chief but had come to the air base for his return.

Sorensen sat wilted in the large chair, crying softly. The dignity of his deep grief seemed to sum up all of the tragedy and sadness of the previous six hours.

As our helicopter circled in the balmy darkness for a landing on the White House south lawn, it seemed incredible that only six hours before John Fitzgerald Kennedy had been a vibrant, smiling, waving and active man.

*　　*　　*

As Merriman Smith's story reported, the President's body was flown to Washington the day of the assassination. The closed casket was placed on view Saturday morning in the East Room of the White House where the family, close friends, and high government officials were invited to pay their respects. Early Sunday afternoon the casket was borne by horse-drawn caisson to the Capitol Rotunda where it lay in state on the catafalque built for America's first assassinated President, Abraham Lincoln. An estimated 240,000 persons filed past the bier in a steady stream throughout Sunday afternoon, Sunday night, and Monday morning. Millions more watched on television this the most extensively covered news event in history. Meantime, Jack Ruby, a Dallas nightclub owner, gunned down the accused assassin in the Dallas city hall as police were transferring him to a maximum security cell in the county jail.

His Servant Commended To The Lord

Newsmen from throughout the United States and the world were in Washington to cover the slain President's funeral Mass. Much brilliant writing flowed from their typewriters. The most outstanding found after an extensive search was by veteran newsman Bob Considine, an International News Service byliner retained by the Hearst Headline Service after I.N.S. was sold to United Press International in 1958. Selection of Mr. Considine's story ran counter to the author's pledge that no writer would be represented by more than one story in this book. Both the Kennedy assassination and this story were selected, however, after the remainder of the manuscript was in type, including Mr. Considine's account of America's first air drop of the H-Bomb. So powerful is his funeral story that it could not be overlooked.

From the impressive lead in which Mr. Considine lifted a phrase from a prayer at the funeral Mass—"Thy faithful servant John"—to the end this story reverently, yet tastefully, recounts the tribute the world paid a fallen leader. This is no maudlin piece, not given to faint, transparent clichés. Rather, it is reporting at its best, reflecting careful attention to a myriad of important details. The report is complete, as complete as one would desire.

The writer moved rapidly through the highlights in the first eleven paragraphs. Otherwise, the scene at Arlington would have been delayed too long. After this essentially chronological fragment, Mr. Considine began a second chronology that runs virtually to the end of the story.

Let's briefly consider some of the other strengths of this story: He wisely focused early paragraphs on Mrs. Kennedy and the children (pars. 2–5). He described Mrs. Kennedy as "erect as a medieval queen, with only the whiteness of her face betraying inner emotions" (par. 12). The limousine in which the two Kennedy children rode "rolled slowly, as if held back by some gigantic weight" (par. 15). "They [world leaders] came to pay tribute to the man some of them loved, a man they all respected." (par. 26). He reminded us of Mr. Kennedy's triumphal Texas tour that was disrupted by his assassination and added "today they (the cheering crowds) wept for him" (par. 31). He selected from the Bishop's eulogy the quotation that probably will accompany Mr. Kennedy into the history books, "Ask not what your country can do for you, ask what you can do for your country" (par. 38).

Mr. Considine ended his story with a reminder that this was the President's greatest tribute, greater even than those accorded to him in life. Throughout, he inserted specific details and description to add to the story's solemn impact.

By Bob Considine
Hearst Headline Service Special to the
N. Y. Journal-American, Nov. 25, 1963

WASHINGTON, Nov. 25.—Prince and pauper, commoner and king said farewell today to our martyred President, commending his body to Arlington Cemetery and the soul "of Thy faithful servant John" to the hands of Almighty God.

Eight hundred thousand Americans, many of them weeping without shame for John Fitzgerald Kennedy, watched his sorrowing but courageous widow, Jacqueline, follow on foot the caisson upon which his casket lay.

Only once this awful day did her emotions betray her. Leaving the church in which the President's funeral Mass was offered, she lifted the heavy black veil that had partially covered her face, then pitched her head forward, sobbing into a white handkerchief.

The President's daughter, Caroline, 6, also was overwhelmed by tears as she left the church for the journey to Arlington.

"John-John," who had cried upon entering the church, stood rigid after the service, and raised his hand to his forehead in salute at the sight of his father's casket.

In Arlington's Fields

In Arlington's fields, on the hill behind Mr. Kennedy's grave, cannon boomed at 21-gun salute, the sounds echoing across the Potomac, bright today with sunshine.

Taps was sounded—each note hanging in the crisp air. The honor guard stood as if frozen.

Military jets racing over the site in tight formation shattered the stillness. Their sounds faded and a prayer was heard—

"I am the Resurrection and the Life . . . "

The casket was lowered; the flag that had covered it was presented to Mrs. Kennedy. An "eternal flame" blossomed at the head of the grave.

Suddenly, it was finished; and Mrs. Kennedy went home to the White House.

In the funeral procession earlier, she was erect as a medieval queen, with only the whiteness of her face betraying inner emotions. She walked between Sen. Edward Kennedy and Attorney General Robert Kennedy, who clutched her hand.

Behind this grief-stricken trio walked the late President's mother, Rose, and his three sisters and their husbands. With them were President Lyndon Johnson, who has picked up the torch wrested from Mr. Kennedy's hands, and Mrs. Johnson, herself a tragic figure in black.

The High and Mighty

Quietly, behind the Kennedy family, came the great from foreign nations—Prince Philip of Great Britain, Queen Frederika of Greece—close to 100 in all. Leading them was the tall, stately figure of French President Charles de Gaulle.

To the rear of these statesmen a black limousine rolled slowly, as if held back by some gigantic weight. Inside were Caroline and young John, both dry-eyed then, keeping their promise to Mrs. Kennedy "to be brave like Momma."

And so the funeral procession wound through Washington on its mournful journey that began at the Capitol, paused briefly at the White House, then continued to St. Matthew's Pro-Cathedral.

The overwhelming silence that enveloped this stronghold of liberty was broken only by muffled drums, the funeral dirges of bandsmen, and the clopping of horses' hoofs—

And, of course, by the muted sobs of those who bowed their heads in grief as John Fitzgerald Kennedy neared his final resting place in Arlington Cemetery.

Cushing Greets Widow

At the great stone steps of St. Matthew's, where President Kennedy often heard Sunday Mass, Boston's Cardinal Cushing awaited the woman he had joined in holy wedlock with John Kennedy 10 years ago.

The bright November sun glistened off the copper dome of the edifice and reflected off the tall, gold mitre which His Eminence held clutched in his right hand.

At the Cathedral, the President's widow was joined by her two children, both of whom were dressed in blue. The Cardinal spoke a few words to them. The sun caught Caroline's blonde hair for a moment. Then the children and their mother filed between the doors of the church, to be followed by other members of the family.

None of the mourners already inside the edifice turned. There were no curious here today, only the sorrowing.

Then, slowly, the nation and the world's people of greatness walked down the broad aisle, touched with areas of sunlight that filtered through stained glass windows, and took places in assigned pews . . .

Former Presidents Eisenhower and Truman, Chief Justice Earl Warren, Senate Majority Leader Mike Mansfield, House Speaker John McCormack, members of Congress . . .

Emperor Haile Selassie of Ethiopia, the front of his tunic agleam with ribbons and decorations; other leaders from Africa, some of whom wore scarlet sashes and gold epaulets . . .

So they came to pay tribute to the man some of them loved, a man they all respected.

Caroline rocked back and forth gently in her seat as a choir sang. Outside the Cathedral, the casket was sprinkled with holy water by Cardinal Cushing. The honor guard formed. The choir stopped and the first strains of organ music filled the church. Caroline sat still.

The procession down the aisle of the Cathedral was

led by three priests, one carrying a cross, the other two bearing candles.

A few moments later the Cardinal, vested in black, walked upon the altar and intoned the words:

"I will go to the altar of God . . ."

It was 71 hours and 30 minutes from the moment President Kennedy had been struck by an assassin's bullet as he rode through downtown Dallas at the head of a motorcade, waving and smiling to the thousands who cheered his presence. Today they wept for him.

For the fallen President, the Pontifical Mass of requiem offered for the repose of his soul contains basically the same prayers accorded the humblest in the Roman Catholic Church.

"We pray that John Kennedy may be spared all punishment and taken into Paradise," Cardinal Cushing said at one point.

The Cardinal's hands were strong and steady as he extended them from time to time in his offering of the Mass.

Receive Holy Communion

Following the Consecration, Jacqueline Kennedy and the President's two brothers moved to the altar rail to receive Holy Communion—

The sacrament whereby bread and wine is changed into the Body, Blood, Soul and Divinity of Our Lord, Jesus Christ.

At the conclusion of the Mass, the congregation rose as His Eminence left the altar. He changed vestments, then returned to hear a 10-minute eulogy by Bishop Philip M. Hannan, Auxiliary Bishop of the Washington Archdiocese.

The bishop concluded by quoting some of the memorable phrases from the inaugural address "ask not what your country can do for you, ask what you can do for your country."

Last Words Of Church

Now the Cardinal rose from his throne and moving slowly behind an acolyte carrying a crucifix came down from the altar to the place where the coffin rested between six tall candles.

In Latin and the vernacular, with holy water and

incense, he said the last words of the Church over the stilled body. The crowded congregation, some of the dignitaries in the fez and burnoose that symbolize centuries of religious warfare involving Christianity, joined the Cardinal in the recitation of the Lord's Prayer.

Then, the final prayer:

"In Thy Hands, O Lord, we commend the spirit of Thy servant John."

As the flag-crossed coffin moved slowly down the aisle toward the door of the cathedral, preceded by the Cardinal and followed by the widow and children and all the others, the band in the street outside played "Hail to the Chief," as a dirge.

Then as the remains of John Fitzgerald Kennedy emerged into the sunlight and were borne down the steps to the caisson, the band moved into one of the most majestic hymns of the Church, "Holy God We Praise Thy Name."

The widow stood at the foot of the steps. Caroline huddled close to her on her right. John-John cried briefly. His mother leaned over the child to speak to him, and as she did her black veil covered the upper part of his blue-coated body.

Salute From Son?

When the veil was lifted, little John-John seemed to come to a form of attention and salute, though he might have been simply brushing away a tear.

The final leg of this terrible journey had begun. The President was being brought to a place of peace and rest in Arlington Cemetery, a quarter-mile from the Tomb of the Unknown Soldier, where he had joined with other American leaders in tribute just two weeks ago today.

The entire funeral, with all its mournful magnificence and splendor, had taken just about five hours. But to many, it seemed like five years since the cortege had moved from the Capitol Rotunda, where it had lain in state, to Pennsylvania Avenue.

Actually, the procession had started at 10:52 a.m.

For the most part it was a silent crowd that watched, a crowd of bowed heads and tears.

But at one point, as the caisson turned the corner by the Treasury building a woman broke into a high pitched wail, "President Kennedy is gone. Oh Lord, Lord." She kept up her cry but the words trailed off and soon were indistinguishable.

Rank on rank the military came, representing all the services, saluting their Commander-in-Chief.

The Greatest Tribute

Church bells pealed in the distance and the crowd watched in utter silence.

It was the greatest tribute ever paid John Fitzgerald Kennedy—

Greater than the roar which greeted his nomination for President in 1960—

Greater than the roar which had greeted him when he was sworn in as President of the United States.

A hero in life, a martyr in death—

John Fitzgerald Kennedy—

May he rest in peace.

The Alluring Assassins

Alton Blakeslee of The Associated Press ranks as the dean of science, including medical, writers. His three-part feature on "The Alluring Assassins" details the suspected causes of heart attacks and strokes, causes of two of every five deaths in the United States.

Blakeslee documented his story with voluminous medical evidence, yet translated it into language understandable to laymen. When he used medical terms, he defined them (par. 3). His skill brings to life what might have been a dull statistical report—"many men and women are eating and lazing their way into the hands of the assassins" (par. 6), "twiddling TV dials" (par. 14), "piggy bank excess weight" (par. 15). Too, his personifying suspected causes as "assassins" (par. 9), even a "syndicate of assassins" (par. 1), helps popularize an important story subject.

By Alton Blakeslee
AP Science Writer, Jan. 22, 1961

A syndicate of assassins stalks this land, stilling 1,300 human hearts each day, almost one a minute.

This deadly syndicate causes heart attacks, the greatest single killer of Americans. It also causes 500 fatal strokes a day, thus accounting for 40 per cent of all American deaths.

The syndicate has a name—atherosclerosis, a process in which vital arteries become narrowed or clogged.

Few if any doctors think there is only one cause of atherosclerosis. Rather, they suspect a syndicate of causes.

And expert suspicions are pointing, among other things, to two of the most alluring aspects of American life—our rich diet and our soft living.

They suspect many men and women are eating and lazing their way into the hands of the assassins.

They think—but cannot yet prove—that some changes in diet and exercise habits might greatly reduce the risk of heart attack. Part of their advice is "Stop gorging and start moving."

Taking Own Advice

Very significantly, many heart specialists and general physicians are taking their own advice. It's less and less a case of a chubby physician, for example, telling his patients THEY should reduce.

The alluring diet assassin involves as prime suspects too many calories, too much of certain fats in our food, obesity, and cholesterol in the blood stream.

Indeed, says one researcher, Soviet doctors are becoming worried that heart attacks will soar in the Soviet Union when and if Premier Khrushchev makes good his boast of matching America in rich and plentiful food for all.

It's far easier to ride than to walk; to watch than to do.

This soft living cloaks another assassin, many authorities think.

They point to acres of excess American weight, flabby muscles, potbellies, spreading rears, creeping obesity after age 25.

They worry over habits of too little exercise, of

activity limited at day's end to twiddling TV dials, or pressing power brakes on cars.

Saving and Spending

Calories can be spent or saved like money, they stress. Save too much, and you grow fat. Spend some extra calories each day in movement, and the piggy bank of excess weight can grow slimmer.

Not all heart authorities, be it clear, agree that diet and inactivity are important assassins. Nor can they promise that changes would disarm them.

But many agree moderate changes might do much good, and cannot do harm, particularly for middle-aged men now dying of heart attacks at an appalling rate.

They'd like to see young men start these changes early, before atherosclerosis—which is a long-term process—snuffs out their lives in their 40's or 50's. Autopsies find that atherosclerosis already has started in the arteries of 60 per cent or more of young men killed in accidents or war.

Suspected Agents

All authorities point to other suspected agents in the syndicate:

HEREDITY: Risk of coronary attacks appears higher if a close relative died prematurely of a heart attack—before age 50 or 60. Heredity cannot be changed. But it can put a man on notice to take special precautions.

TENSIONS: Medical opinion is divided on the role of tensions and pressures. Humans in every age have lived under tensions, some point out. Others think stress is involved, in part perhaps by making blood tend to clot faster.

HIGH BLOOD PRESSURE: Chances of a coronary are higher if blood pressure is high. Modern drugs often can reduce it.

SMOKING: Most statistical studies link excessive cigarette smoking with increased risk of coronaries.

Syndicate members can gang up.

Dr. Jeremiah Stamler of Chicago's Board of Health puts it this way:

A man has only one chance in 20 or even 50 of dying of a heart attack before age 65 if he has normal weight, average or low amounts of blood cholesterol, no damage to kidneys, no high blood pressure or diabetes, is not a heavy cigarette smoker and is moderately active.

But his chance of escaping a heart attack in middle age is only one out of two if he's been tagged by two or three members of the syndicate, such as high blood cholesterol, high blood pressure, or obesity.

Diet and Inactivity

This article concerns only diet and inactivity as suspects in atherosclerosis.

The heart is a powerful and near-tireless muscle, squeezing blood from its chambers to circulate through the body.

The heart muscle itself receives nourishing blood from two pencil-sized arteries, the coronary arteries.

Fatty plugs and blood clots forming in these arteries can block the flow, and this starves some of the heart muscle tissue. If the blockage is severe enough, a heart and a human being die.

Cholesterol, a waxy substance, and fatty materials in the blood are known to form part of the artery deposits. Hence the suspicions concerning diet.

But the heart fights for life. It can develop extra, or collateral, little blood vessels to nourish the heart muscle.

Exercise helps a heart develop this ability, and may even reduce the risk that plugs or deposits will form in the first place.

Atherosclerosis, with its toll of the heart and brain, now is called the nation's gravest chronic epidemic.

Leonard Warren Dies At The Met

Among the best and worst-written stories appearing in newspapers are those based on deaths. The great majority of obituary stories are absurdly stereotyped, more so than any other single type of news content. Conversely, stories based on deaths of famous people often are moving, interesting memorials.

Such is Sanche de Gramont's Pulitzer Prize-winning story on

the death of Metropolitan Opera star Leonard Warren. One gains the impression de Gramont was in the audience when Warren was stricken. Actually, he was dispatched from his re-write desk at the New York *Herald Tribune* after Warren collapsed.

Regardless, the writer set the scene skillfully (pars. 3–6, 9–14, 18–28). He treated sympathetically, yet factually with the subject's life and integrated into his story pertinent background information. Despite the polished product, de Gramont had less than 90 minutes in which to go to the Metropolitan Opera, gather all information, return to his office, and write the story.

The major strengths of this story lie in its completeness; simple, dignified language; the drama of Mr. Bing's announcement.

By Sanche de Gramont
New York Herald Tribune, March 5, 1960

Leonard Warren, leading baritone of the Metropolitan Opera, died last night on the stage where he had sung for more than twenty years.

The forty-nine-year-old singer collapsed as he was ending the second act of Verdi's "La Forza del Destino." He fell forward as he was making his exit at 10:05 p.m. and twenty-five minutes later the house physician pronounced him dead, victim of a stroke.

There was an awesome moment as the singer fell. The rest of the cast remained paralyzed. Finally someone in the capacity audience called out "For God's sake, bring down the curtain."

The curtain came down, ambulances were called, and a member of the cast tried mouth-to-mouth respiration. A priest arrived to administer the last rites to the singer, who was a recent convert to Roman Catholicism.

Members of the staff who came from the stage weeping announced that the opera star was dead.

The news was met with hushed consternation by many in the opera house who had come backstage after the curtain was lowered.

In the audience were many critics who came to hear Mr. Warren and Renata Tebaldi, making her first appearance this year. Mr. Warren was acknowledged to be the world's best dramatic baritone. He had a repertoire of twenty-six operatic roles.

A member of the Metropolitan staff said Mr. Warren had appeared in perfect health when he came to sing last night.

At the time he collapsed, Mr. Warren had just finished the aria "O fatal pages of my destiny." He was singing the role of Don Carlo in the opera, set in Italy and Spain, and was dressed in the colorful uniform of a Spanish grenadier. The opera has a tragic ending in which Don Carlo is killed by an erstwhile friend.

The surgeon, in the opera, played by Roald Reitan, a baritone, sings to Mr. Warren: "E salvo (He's well).

Mr. Warren responds: "E salvo, e salvo, O Gloria. (He's saved, he's saved, O joy.")

He turned to his left, and prepared to make his exit, which ends the act, and collapsed. Some thought he had tripped. The conductor, Thomas Shippers, froze. Mr. Reitan raced to Mr. Warren's side as the curtain fell. He was followed by Richard Tucker, who was playing Don Alvaro and was watching from the wings.

Mr. Tucker said: "Lennie, Lennie, what is it?"

They turned him over.

Wife in Audience

The singer's wife, Mrs. Agatha Leifflen Warren, was watching from a parterre box with her brother, Roy Leifflen, a Washington attorney, and Msgr. Edwin Broderick, of St. Patrick's Cathedral, a friend of the Warrens.

Mrs. Warren saw Mr. Warren's face and gasped. Msgr. Broderick went backstage. Dr. Adrian W. Zorgniotti, the house physician, also went backstage.

Mr. Warren remained unconscious. The physician said he thought the singer suffered a massive cerebral vascular hemorrhage. His respiration stopped two or three minutes after he collapsed. He was pronounced dead at 10:15 p.m.

Half an hour after Mr. Warren collapsed, the warning buzzer sounded in the foyers and lobbies of the packed house. The audience returned to its seats.

The audience chattered until the house lights dimmed and a moment later the spotlight hit the curtain and Rudolf Bing, general manager of the Metropolitan Opera, stepped out.

With his hands clasped in front of him he announced: "It is one of the saddest days——"

At this point the audience broke into shouts of "Oh, No. Oh No."

Tribute by Bing

Mr. Bing continued, "I ask you to stand . . ."

The audience again moaned and whispers went through the audience, "He's gone. He's gone."

". . . In tribute," Mr. Bing continued, "to one of our greatest performers, he died as I am sure he would have wanted to die.

"He died in the middle of a performance."

"Cannot Continue"

"I'm sure you will agree that under these circumstances we cannot possibly continue."

Mr. Bing made an about face and returned backstage.

The audience left the theater in visible shock and disbelief.

Ambulances from at least three hospitals and oxygen from a police emergency squad arrived at the opera too late to help.

Audience Stunned

The audience emptied into Broadway and stopped momentarily in front of the W. 40th St. exit, its red light flashing. Police blocked the backstage entrance. In the theater, musicians talked quietly among themselves, recalling the singer's career.

Mr. Bing called the singer's last performance "one of his greatest."

A spokesman for the Metropolitan Opera said it was believed to be the first time in the opera house's existence that a star had been fatally stricken on stage in the middle of a role.

Mr. Warren was taken to the dressing room he occupied for many years, and from there to the Abbey Funeral Home, 66th St. and Lexington Ave.

Mr. Warren made his debut at the Metropolitan on Jan. 13, 1939. He was to sing another Verdi role,

"Simon Boccanegra," in Philadelphia Tuesday, and had been scheduled for the title part in the company's first production of Verdi's "Nabucco" for the Metropolitan's fall season.

In 600 Performances

Mr. Warren had sung a total of more than 600 performances of twenty-two roles, more than a fifth of them as Rigoletto.

Like most top-flight singers he was temperamental. He told other singers how to sing, conductors how to conduct, directors how to direct, photographers how to make pictures, recording engineers how to record and costumers how to costume.

He was forgiven for all this because many regarded his as the greatest baritone in Italian repertory, a "human bellows mounted on matchsticks." He had a fifty-one-inch chest (unexpanded), a size 17½ collar, a massive head, almost six feet of height and well over 200 pounds of weight—all supported on thin legs.

At the time he was engaged by the Metropolitan he had seen only one opera in his life, "La Traviata," when he was twenty-two. He had no definite idea of making a career in music, and began his career in his father's fur business.

In 1935, he went to Radio City Music Hall, went backstage, asked for an audition and got it and a job. He stayed at Radio City for three years, spending all of the time in the chorus. He never got a chance for a solo turn.

Mr. Warren went to the Met by way of the "Auditions of the Air" in 1938, when he was dared into entering by fellow chorus members at Radio City. When he auditioned for Wilfrid Pelletier, the conductor thought a ringer had been brought in.

He did not have a single operatic role at that time, and he went to Italy to prepare some repertoire. Working under Giuseppe Pais and Ricardo Piccozi in Rome and Milan, he learned seven roles in seven months.

Mr. Warren was born in the Bronx, and attended Public School 11 and Evander Childs High School. For a year he studied business at night at Columbia University, preparatory to entering his father's fur brokerage business.

As a hobby he began studying music at the Greenwich House Music School, and sang lustily while counting muskrats and minks in his father's establishment.

After his audition with the Radio City Music Hall, he studied voice production with Sidney Dietch.

Besides the Metropolitan Opera, Mr. Warren appeared with the San Francisco Opera, the Chicago Opera and the Cincinnati Summer Opera and sang concerts extensively throughout North and South America.

He also appeared often on major radio and television programs, including "Voice of Firestone" and "Toast of the Town." His extensive list of recordings for RCA Victor included a wide variety of music from "Falstaff" to sea chanties and Kipling ballads.

'Twas A Good Clean Fight

Two world champion boxers were dethroned within a year—by death. Benny (Kid) Paret, welterweight champion, died April 3, 1962, from brain injuries suffered in a title match with Emile Griffith on March 24. Almost a year to the day later, on March 25, 1963, Davey Moore, featherweight champion, died after a brain injury in a title fight with Ultiminio (Sugar) Ramos.

Both deaths brought heated demands that prize fighting be outlawed. As Jimmy Murray, columnist of the Los Angeles *Times*, asked March 24, 1963, "Does a 'sport' which has been on parole deserve a full pardon when it proves again it hasn't changed?" Robert L. Teague, The New York *Times*, wrote March 27, 1962, as Paret lay unconscious on his deathbed, "Once again boxing suddenly has become an ugly word." Other noted sports writers, among them Red Smith, the New York *Herald Tribune*, defended boxing. Regardless of demands by such personages as Pope John XXIII, Tennessee Senator Estes Kefauver, and Governor Edward G. Brown of California for an end to legalized prize fighting, the sport probably will not be outlawed. Boxing faces its greatest threat from television through convenient exposure to millions at virtually no cost.

These, the first and second fatalities to defending champions, recall a piece about a lesser "club fighter" that appeared in The Milwaukee *Journal* April 23, 1948. Richard S. Davis clearly placed the blame for ring fatalities where it belongs—with the crowds who demand slugging matches rather than those based on skill (par. 11).

Davis combined "fight" ring language with an informal conversational tone to create the illusion he is talking directly to each reader. That gives his essentially chronological story real impact. Even so, it is no loosely written, verbose article. Every phrase adds to the mood.

He certainly proves the wisdom of letting the news event dictate how a news story should be written. For certainly Davis violated some of the sacred "rules" some writers revere above all else. This clever story accomplishes something, however, all news stories should; it holds up to clear view a piece of essential truth.

By Richard S. Davis
The Milwaukee Journal, April 23, 1948

Say it again, maybe a little louder, so the lady can hear. Put on that Sunday look and make it good and strong. Now then:

"It couldn't be helped. It was a good, clean fight all the way—no fooling, lady, we cer'nly wouldn't kid you at a time like this—and it was just one of those things. It might happen to anybody, honest to God it might."

Get it in all the reports, and put it in the paper nice and pretty, and keep on saying it, loud and often. That'll be swell. She's only going to be here a couple of days and it sure will make her feel a lot better.

Who is she? Why, she's the kid's mother. Name of Mary Darthard, a colored lady from Kansas City. That's right, the mother of the kid fighter who got his brains knocked out Wednesday night—boy, what a lulu of a fight that was!—and died in the morning. You know, busted blood vessels, or something.

Seems like this colored lady hears over the radio that the kid has been carried out of the ring in a coma. So what does she do? She calls the kid's wife, and she calls her cousin, who has a green Buick, and at 1:30 in the morning there's six of them starting off for Milwaukee.

Wife Can't Come

Not the wife, though. The wife is seven months pregnant. Naturally she can't take the trip, because all the other three times she was pregnant something went wrong. She's only 18, just like her husband was. When she hears what's happened, she collapses. Johnny, her brother-in-law—he's the kid who drove the car—says she collapses six times and it's dangerous. OK, she stays home.

So the six in the car come tearing along to Milwaukee and here they are, Thursday afternoon, sitting in the district attorney's office. The colored lady's married daughter—Inez Drizzle, her name is —is dabbing at her mother's forehead with a handkerchief, and they're both crying and shaking, sort of, and it gets you.

Just between us old fight customers, it don't seem right for a kid like that—just 18 and going to be 19 in May—to be lying down there in the morgue, and his mother upstairs trying to talk to the D.A., and reporters there, and people standing around, and all for what? A funny ending, what I mean, for good clean sport.

D.A. Tries To Make It Easy

"A good, clean fight," that's just what the D.A. says, "not like the fight I understand they had in Kansas City." He's trying to make it as easy as he can, the gray-haired D.A., but it don't go over.

The eyes of the colored lady look like they're made of wood—wet wood soaked in rain. She's a kind of an invalid, seems as though, and she's had a terrible time bringing up those kids, three boys and a girl. Housekeeping, washing and ironing, when she was strong enough.

It's a good thing the colored lady don't know what us old customers know—that fighters like her boy, Jackie, have got to be sluggers or else. If they're clever, they get booed out of there. They got to be "club fighters" and get their brains scrambled.

All the colored lady knows is that her boy didn't get much out of it. He cer'nly didn't do much for her down there in K.C. Sure, he had an apartment for his kid wife, and he bought her a lot of pretty things, but he didn't even have a car. Sixth middleweight in the country, according to the books, and he didn't even own a car. It's a laugh.

When They Got Married

A reporter is talking to the colored lady and asking her questions that hurt, like when did Jackie get married. She says he got married to Ernestine Alexander, who was just a baby like he was, because they had to get married. That was in 1945, just after the eighth grade. She and the other people gave their consent.

"My husband," the colored lady says, and she looks like somebody has stabbed her, "I can't rightly say where he is. We just don't live together any more. He up and left me when Jackie was a baby."

The colored lady said what a fine, strong boy Jackie was, how he was good at football and basketball in that Wendell Phillips grade school, but how he liked boxing best. A Golden Gloves champion, he was.

"I never wanted him to be a fighter, though," the lady says. "Seems like I knew all the time that something would happen. Even the other night, before this last fight—what day is this, Thursday?—that means it was Tuesday night I had my dream. I dreamed I saw them carrying Jackie out of the ring. He was hurt awful bad, but not—but not the way it was. No, not like that, because he knew me."

'His Heart Set on It'

And the colored lady tells the reporter that the reason she don't argue when Jackie starts to fight professional is because "his heart was so set on it—getting to be the champion and making a lot of money." She says she always hated it herself. She's shaking as she remembers and the tears trickle down her thin cheeks like crooked tracks on a window pane.

It's not so bad when she talks about the way her

boy went all his life to Sunday school—to the Centennial Methodist, it was—and how even last Sunday he went to church.

"That's where we'll have the services," she tells the reporter. "As soon as my oldest boy—Edward Lee Darthard his name is—as soon as he gets here from New York City, we'll decide just when."

The colored lady don't want to say any more. She gets led away, out of the D.A.'s office, and into the elevator. She sort of weaves like a punchy fighter. Us old customers hate to look. It's too familiar.

Out there in the lobby is sitting this fighter, Lytell. He's sitting there smoking a cigaret and it looks like a white match in his big hand. He don't move, he just sits there and what he is thinking hurts.

Wants To Aid Widow

It's funny about this guy. He's got a flat nose, like all fighters, and big ridges over his eyes, and it's easy to see he packs a terrible wallop, but when he talks it's in a quiet, gentle voice, you might say like a woman's. He says he would like to fight for nothing in Milwaukee and give all the dough to Jackie Darthard's widow.

Seems like that 18-year-old widow with a baby on the way can use a piece of change. You know how it is with fighters—colored fighters more than anybody—how they get their money cut up like a honey dew.

Only a Club Fighter

The reporter on this job talks to a sports writer in K.C. about young Darthard and the sports writer tells him: "Naw, he didn't have anything. Not much, anyway. You see he was only a colored club fighter around here until just lately. No money in that, y'understand."

Sure, us old customers understand. It's a laugh, in a way, but not too funny when you think what can happen, the way it did to this kid. Ironical, is that what they call it? Seems as though it's plenty ironical.

After you knock around a while you see lots of things that are ironical for colored folks. For instance, there's this Dorothy Byrd, a round-faced dolly who has plenty of mileage, as the boys say. They say she's the madam of a couple of bawdy houses. And that's why you'll get a kick out of this.

This Dorothy Byrd was at the fight when the kid got his. It cut her all up. So she gets into her car and drives out on highway 41, and stays there all day Thursday until she spies a car with a Missouri license plate and colored folks in it.

A Friend in Need

Then she stops the car and tells the colored lady what has happened to her boy. And she sticks right with the crumpled people from K.C. all the way along. She takes the mother home with her—no, of course, the mother doesn't know what line of business this Dorothy is in—and tries everything nice she can think of to put that broken heart together again.

The reporter asks this Dorothy how come she takes such an interest in perfect strangers. And Dorothy says, no fooling: "If I was in trouble like this, and didn't have no friends, I would want somebody to do at least this much for me."

Is that ironical, too? Does it hand you a laugh? You can write your own ticket, all the way through.

REPORTING
AT ITS BEST

PART 10 ──────────── ★★★★★★★★★★

Life's Fabric

HUMAN INTEREST STORIES are those which present a bit of life's fabric rather than record major "hard" news. Yet these items about people and animals and things a bit "off beat" fulfill a valuable news media need. They provide spice, the dessert for the daily news diet. Those worthy of the human interest classification produce a chuckle, a sigh, a lump in the throat, a tear.

The format—limitless. Here all is sacrificed to a simple, usually unadorned telling. For if the event lacks punch, the cleverest of writers can't create it. Possibly this is the secret— in the best human interest stories the writers stand aside and let the story come through.

The writer's major contributions, then, are (1) being constantly alert for items that merit human interest treatment and (2) using imagination in selecting the method of presentation, choosing the one which will best tell the story. This requires writing skill of the highest order.

Of Zoos And Gnus

Note how Charles Maher of The Associated Press did just that in this brief item. His play on words grows naturally out of this news event.

By Charles Maher
The Associated Press, Oct. 28, 1960

LOS ANGELES, Oct. 28—The zoo knows it and the gnu knows it: It takes a he-gnu and a she-gnu to produce a new gnu.

That's why Griffith Park Zoo is making a deal with the Fresno Zoological Society.

Griffith Park has several she-gnus but no he-gnus. At Fresno, she-gnus are rare but there are no he-gnus to spare.

The news is that the two zoos will be making gnus by mating gnus.

(Written by gnus man Charles Maher.)

Daddy's A Hero

The Seattle *Post-Intelligencer* gave Mel Meadows' feature on a minor human tragedy best page one play, and for good reason. Meadows humanized deftly this father and son so they come through as people, not merely a prisoner, a statistic. This is just another reminder that we all live on the "people" level with our personal problems and joys. Well written copy aimed at this appeal seldom misses.

Meadows intelligently wrote this from the child's viewpoint, "Eight months is forever" (par. 4). Even so, one understands the heartache of the parents, the all-too-brief happiness. The story gains by its simplicity—he developed only three central characters and let the little drama unfold easily, chronologically. He wisely withheld until the end why Billy and his mother are separated from daddy.

Here, again, is an example of the reader appeal based on the faceless crowd. For Billy and his father exemplify the thousands of young sons and fathers separated by prison bars.

By Mel Meadows
Seattle Post-Intelligencer, Oct. 31, 1958

Seattle is far away . . .

In Spokane, Billy Mims, Jr., two and a half, doesn't really know how far away but that's where Daddy's going to be and that's where he wants to be.

In the world of a small boy, seeing Daddy isn't a matter of time, or distance, or money.

Eight months is forever . . .

Billy's mother, Jodine, remembers the day last March when Billy's father, William T. Mims, 22, went away. Mostly, she remembers Billy wondering why she was crying.

Billy doesn't really know how far away or how long ago. All Billy knows is:

Daddy's the best football player in the whole world . . .

William T. (Bill) Mims, a first string end, is six feet tall, slimmed down now to 160 pounds.

He has brown hair, brown eyes and the Montgomery, Ala., birthright of a Southern Gentleman, case-hardened at the core by a hitch with the United States Marines.

The Ramblers would be tough, and him with two fingers taped. . .

A kindly neighbor drove Jodine and Billy from Spokane to West Seattle Stadium. From 50-yard-line seats, Daddy was big as life to Billy and no one tried to stop him when he toddled onto the field.

Bill Mims was Number 23, benched by a knee injury.

He caught Billy in both arms, the best catch a man ever made, and he and Billy played out the rest of the game; Billy in his Daddy's helmet and—when he tired—on his Daddy's knee, arms around a football.

Mommy stayed in the stands, so Billy went back to get her. She hugged him and cried a little and brought him a bottle of pop and down on the field the coach put Mims in for a last-minute play, just so Billy will always know:

Daddy is the best football player in the whole world. . .

A gun ended the game and other men with guns kept spectators off the field and Billy couldn't see his Daddy . . .

Patiently, Mommy explained to Billy that Daddy's team was traveling and Daddy had to leave right away with the other players . . .

. . . for a far away place . . .

. . . a place called Monroe . . .

. . . where William T. (Bill) Mims, the star end, will spend 3½ years in Washington State Reformatory for fumbling—with bad checks.

A Night For Drama Lovers

Accuracy is to a reporter as piety is to a clergyman. But accuracy involves more than getting facts straight, spelling names correctly, giving disputants fair treatment. It includes evaluating a news event insightfully so this event may be reported in its proper context.

Carl Gartner must have asked himself "What is this really all about?" when he covered the appearance of the wrestler Gorgeous George for the Des Moines *Tribune*. Obviously, the *Tribune* drama critic saw this as a spectacle, a performance. Why not treat it thusly? The strength of this whimsical article lies largely in his light-handed reminiscences of other dramatic performances at the KRNT theater and his gay phrasing, which appears throughout the piece. Even though a highly featurized style was used, the report includes the essentials, the outcome.

Interesting comparisons abound: "rasslin's answer to Hedy Lamarr" (par. 1), "almost as pretty as a basket of fresh pine shavings" (par. 8), "detachable like a strip-dancer's kimono" (par. 9). Repetition of "trod" (par. 1–2), helps the lead set the mood for the story. Gartner's descriptions of George and Jones help retain that mood. The story has no weak spots, as so often occurs when a reporter attempts this type of composition. The last seven paragraphs are delightful.

It is worth recalling that "professional" wrestling was at its apex of popularity when this story was written.

By Carl Gartner
Des Moines Tribune, November 19, 1950

Gorgeous George, rasslin's answer to Hedy Lamarr, Wednesday night joined the illustrious list of great actors who have trod the boards of KRNT theater.

He also trod the face of Farmer Jones.

It was a brilliant night for lovers of the drama.

More than 5,000 gentlefolk of the community attended, and an estimated 1,500 others, who thirst just as eagerly for culture but who lacked the foresight to obtain tickets ahead of time, had to be turned away into the chill winter night. Many of them went up to Louie's.

(This compares with 4,000 who saw Leslie Howard in an elaborate production of "Hamlet" at the theater in 1937.)

It was a night to bring back memories. No sooner had Gorgeous George's gentleman's gentleman started spraying the stage with a tankard of under-privileged perfume, preparing the way for his employer's entrance, than veterans of the drama fondly recalled the opening performance of the 1931 season: "Blossom Time."

Then George came glittering down the aisle, and another theatrical milestone had been passed. Ever since it was presented here in 1937, "The Great Waltz" had been considered the most beautiful production ever to be unveiled in KRNT theater, but now "The Great Waltz" was in second place.

George's daintily curled blond hair was almost as pretty as a basket of fresh pine shavings.

Riding in dignity atop his silken robe was a gleaming white ermine collar, detachable like a strip-dancer's kimono, and in his haughty eye was the look of a man who knoweth that pride goeth before the best two out of three falls.

One look at George's raiment and you knew he had nominated himself as man most likely to succeed the rainbow. He already has the pot of gold.

("You Can't Take It With You" was a major success on this same stage in 1938.)

Meanwhile, George's co-star, Farmer Jones, a red-blooded American boy with whiskers down to here, was already on stage, tenderly giving his pig its 10 p.m. bottle.

Jonesy was garbed in somewhat more informal attire than was George. A gray, cotton sweatshirt, ultra-smart in its simplicity, covered his rugged shoulders, and a well-experienced pair of delicate Delft-blue jeans, torn off at the fashionable pedal-pusher length and tastefully held up by a length of clothesline, covered the rest of him.

His rich-but-honest feet were quite bare, but he had fetched along a pair of brogans, with which he good-naturedly clubbed George between falls.

("Tobacco Road" first played this theater on Dec. 20, 1935.)

In the midst of this romantic setting, the house lights dimmed, Mr. Jones put away his pig, the referee advanced to inspect George for concealed mirrors or other dangerous weapons, and our hero eloquently snarled his best line of the night:

"Get your filthy hands off me!"

(Gorgeous George professes to be deathly frightened of germs, unless they are attached to banknotes of large denomination.)

A compromise was effected whereby George's gentleman's gentleman was allowed to remove his master's cape and robe. Thereupon Jeeves gathered up his liege's combs, mirrors, bobby pins and robes and departed, a gong clanged, and the stars moved into the first of their many embraces.

("The Hour of Charm," directed by Maestro Phil Spitalny had been presented on this exact spot Dec. 11, 1946.)

From here on it was just like Sadie Hawkins' day.

There were times when to the untutored eye proceedings looked rougher than nine dollars worth of sandpaper (wholesale), but they really weren't, and eventually George won the first fall by a dropkick or something.

The time was 15 minutes and 50 seconds, which included the 30 seconds Farmer Jones took on one occasion to whip out a red bandana and blow his handsome nose.

Between falls George sniffed smelling salts affectionately tendered by his lackey. Jones didn't sniff a thing, not even his pig, but bounced back at the gong to take the next fall in only five seconds, with a graceful hookslide.

By now it was noisier than Mule Train with all the whips out.

There was organized cheering ("Yea, Farmer") by the audience, which had worked itself up into a loving hatred for the Gorgeous One and his city slicker ways.

But the drama had a tragic ending. The cheering didn't do a modicum of good.

George was still in there shining. His strength was as the strength of 10 because his heart was approximately pure, or because it was his night to win, and by 11 p.m. it was all over.

Georgeous George was the winner and still fragrant.

Once again the house lights came on, the police

appeared to see George safely to his dressing room,
and all the eccentric people who had just worn
ordinary clothes took their way sorrowfully home.
Many was the mind that turned nostalgically back
as this performance was compared to such others in
the past as:

"The Corn Is Green" (Dec. 26, 1943).

"Kiss the Boys Goodby" (Apr. 25, 1939).

"Idiot's Delight" (1937).

Winnie Ille Pu

To write interesting features one must assume an attitude
proper to the news event. He then must translate that mood
clearly, appropriately, accurately without submerging the event
into a morass of stylized jumble.

Todd Simon interwove imaginatively Latin phrases, nu-
merals, references into his story about "Winnie Ille Pu." Even to
one who does not appreciate the subtleties of Latin, the piece
communicates clearly. Note the crowning stroke in this delightful story: Simon's byline appears at the end.

By Todd Simon
The (Cleveland) Plain Dealer, Dec. 28, 1960

This is a little bear tale. It begins at the end and
goes frontward, being rather vice versa by nature.

THE END

And so you can buy the Latin version called
"Winnie Ille Pu" some time between the ides of January and the calends of February, if you still love
the small bear and didn't find Caesar's Gallic War
too traumatic an experience in your youth.

Right now there are no copies, but, after doing a
double take, the Dutton publishing house is scurrying to print up a big second batch of them.

The Publix Book Mart, somewhat stunned, sold
CXXV copies and couldn't get more no matter how
it hollered. Dutton had underestimated the egg-head-
edness of the public.

It was a sneaker. Unballyhooed and brought out too near to Christmas, "Winnie Ille Pu" was gobbled up like Saturnalia cakes. It could have been the top juvenile book of the gift season.

Divided Into Partes Tres

Who were these customers grabbing for it? The bookseller found they were divided, like Gaul, into partes tres:

(I) People who had been reared circa MCMXXVI and would like Pooh Bear whether he lived under the name of Sanders or under the name of Ursus Pu.

(II) People who met Pooh when young and whose children are currently hating Cicero in school.

(III) Some who thought it chi-chi; "Who ever heard of translating a book INTO Latin, instead of out of it?"

Publix Book Mart sold XXV then L, then a second L. Both it and the publisher were obstupefaeti, as the Latin Winnie would say. Os hians, pedibus planibus, we dare say. We dare say it because that's how our Latin dictionary talks when it means open-mouthed, flat-footed.

The owner of the Publix Book Mart read a half-column review—in Latin!—in the London Times literary supplement in September. Being no bear on Latin but a shark at spotting a good, offbeat commercial possibility he sent for the American edition. The London Times had reviewed an edition by Methuen & Co. Ltd.

Swedes Buy MM Copies

The Latinized Winnie the Pooh had already scored successes in Sweden, where MM copies sold out in no time.

The first edition of "Winnie Ille Pu" was published in Sao Paulo, Brazil, by the multlingual translator himself.

He is Dr. Alexander Lenard, M. D., who is farming and teaching in a town near Sao Paulo. He came from Hungary.

Now the Romans, as well as friends and countrymen, can be charmed by A. A. Milne's Winnie the Pooh, thanks to a Magyar-Brazilian linguist.

E. P. Dutton & Co., which brought out the first

Pooh books in America, published his "Winnie Ille Pu."

It is wrong to presume that Americans know no Latin beyond et cetera and bona fide.

Homo may be much more sapiens than we all thought.

By TODD SIMON

Sell Us Anything

The Holy Bible remains as many writers' model for literary excellence. It is little wonder, then, that reporters have attempted to adapt parts of the Bible to news events. Virtually always the result has seemed forced, often because no realistic relationship existed between event and Biblical reference. In other instances the event was lost sight of, buried under an illfitting literary style. Some have suffered from the opposite, failure to retain the writing theme throughout.

Robert W. Wells of The Milwaukee *Journal* selected the birth of the Christ child for the theme of his "last minute shopper" article. His allusions are entirely natural, thanks to his keen observations and imagination. Fiction you say? Not on your life. This happens and happens and happens. Therein lies much of its charm. Any writing which strikes a memory chord common to the many has stroked writing's most responsive key.

Word selection, restrained use of repetition, real life experiences add to the warmth, the humanness of this witty morsel.

By Robert W. Wells
The Milwaukee Journal, Dec. 23, 1960

And it came to pass, the season of the last minute shopper having come, that it was Friday. The time of desperation was upon the land and lo, there was wailing and gnashing of teeth.

The wise shoppers departed homeward, trampling each other, striking out joyfully with the elbows, bearing with them gifts of exceeding worth, to be paid for no man knew when. The pleas to do such shopping early had resounded loud in the land, being cried from the housetops and trumpeted from the loudspeakers.

And it happened that the wise shoppers had heeded these exhortations so that in the time of desperation their teeth should remain ungnashed and their garments unrent.

But it was not so with the prodigal shoppers. In the time when the wise ones had been trampling each other and striking out joyfully with the elbows, the unwise men had stayed behind in their tents, sulking or playing at sheepshead, hardening their hearts against the prophets who cried woe.

Woe to those who put off until the morrow the mailing of packages! Woe to those who wait, hoping these things shall pass and depart from us! Woe to those who heed not the prophecies!

Woe to those who wait until the last minute to seek out gifts of plastic! Woe, and again woe, to those who delay the assembling of presents for the little ones, following those instructions laid down by scribes gifted in tongues, none of them understandable.

But the last minute shoppers heeded not the warnings, and it came to pass that it was the Friday before the Sunday and they were cast down into the pit, which was loud with the sound of gnashing incisors.

And their women berated them, saying: Go to the market place, thou clown, and return not without golden baubles to lay at my feet or the skins of minks for my shoulders. For my neighbor's husband has met with the money lenders and is in hock to them forever and why should the wife of my neighbor have a chance to lord it over me when the gifts are opened?

And so it was that the prodigal shopper appeared at the gates, wild of eye and trembling, crying aloud to the merchants.

Sell me anything, he was crying, sell me whatever is left. Sell me cashmere with collars of animal skins. Sell me, oh, merchant, whatever you have not yet unloaded. For I have not heeded the warnings of the prophets and the sands are running out and I am not ready.

Sell me sequined babushkas. Sell me toys with three screws missing. Sell me the gifts the wise

shoppers cast aside as unworthy, for there is no time
remaining.

For while I was sulking in my tent playing sheepshead, the hour has waxed late and lo, I have been
found wanting.

And it came to pass on the last Friday before the
Sunday that is called Christmas that there were
legions of such prodigals abroad in the land, each
trampling the other and striking out with his elbows.

And the wise men heard the noise and saw the
confusion and were exceedingly content.

Old Times In A Picture Book

Every mortal doubtless harks back to joyful times when a
less complex universe seemingly rendered life less challenging.
Only fleetingly may man re-experience anything akin to the
lost past. Robert J. Lewis did. And at a time when doubtless a
million others bypassed this "pleasure" with oaths for an incon-
veniencing snowfall. Possibly Mr. Lewis' deeper message sug-
gests we need be alert to savor "Old Times in a Picture Book."
At any rate his story for The Washington *Evening Star* gave
thousands a chance to reminisce.

Imagination? Doubtless. Yet it was all there for anyone to
see, to record. This four-mile forced walk home in deep snow
would embitter most. Not Mr. Lewis. He saw this as a rare
opportunity, a delightful experience. His story literally reflects
enjoyment with each step. And why not?

The description is clear, accurate, and interesting, primarily
because it deals in specifics: initials in a heart (par. 9–12), a
display window (par. 15), a neighbor by name (next to last
paragraph), etc.

By Robert J. Lewis
The Washington Evening Star, Jan. 27, 1961

I walked all the way home last night.

The cars couldn't take it, physically or spiritually.
So they deserted the town and left it for human
beings. Pedestrians, remember?

It was old times in a picture book.

Snowflakes in your face. A blanket of them, dry and squeaky, underfoot. The lights glowing bright—beckoning beacons, inviting and gay. The air crackling and tingling the skin.

But the city is magically warm, for all that. It's full of the nostalgia of things-as-they-used-to-be. And as they could be again.

It's a sidewalk world. The boulevardiers are out in force. Snow narrows up the walking space. The paths are cozy. You have to say "Excuse me" as you pass others going in the opposite direction.

And you learn so many things as you walk the 4 miles, all the way home.

Love In Bloom

Love, for example, blooms in a driving snowstorm. You know that, for sure.

Do you believe that people draw hearts in the fleeting snow, shot through with an arrow and labeled with initials like "E.R." and "W.M."

You do, indeed, because you see them there on Connecticut Avenue, just above R.

Gentle flakes, silent and growing deeper, soften the outlines of those sentimental graven hearts. Soon they'll give way to a bland, poker-faced billow of white.

But they prove while they're still there that walkers in love were out this night, thrilled, no doubt, as you are by a city miraculously changed and made better.

All the usual hectic quests are forgotten. Nobody even seems to be hurrying home any more. What are all these people doing downtown?

They're window-looking for one thing. The cruise clothes are marvelous this winter.

Lobsters, Oysters and Snow

And, somehow, flakes of snow are drifting into the display space of Harvey's Restaurant. There they nestle among the bright red lobsters, unshucked oysters and the usual garnish of tomatoes—intruders in a work of art.

As you walk you wonder.

Why is the city different?

How has six inches of snow changed it so much?

Tire chains of a passing taxi tinkle an answer. The muffled rasp of a distant snow shovel add a word or two.

The city's reborn, they seem to say.

It's a place for people again. It's smaller.

It's cleaner.

It's quieter.

It's snug and bright.

It's fun to walk where you want to go.

But are these things just echoes of other words you've been hearing lately? That downtown should be refashioned in scale for walking human beings?

A tougher stretch is ahead—the hill from Florida avenue to California street. Here the sidewalk disappears altogether. But soon you're up the hill, and on your street.

As you reach your house, after those four miles, a real surprise. Your neighbor, Dr. Stone, is shoveling a path across your sidewalk.

Good cities make good neighbors. That figures, too, you guess.

———————————

Others Seek Their Place in the Sun

MORE so than during any other era Americans after World War II recognized their true role in the community of nations. Many were coming more nearly to accept the late Wendell Willkie's one-world concept.

Newsmen alertly probed the struggles of others for their place in the economic and political sun. From the great outpouring two stories were selected for consideration here, one on India and the other on Africa.

It Can Be Done

In the mid-1950's Americans wondered if communism were inevitable in Asia. Or could these peoples build their economy under democratic forms of government? Or was some other form of government, say dictatorship, to take root? One newsman who sought an answer was Saville R. Davis. Mr. Davis conducted an intensive on-the-spot study preparatory to writing a series that appeared in The *Christian Science Monitor*.

This is a thorough reporting job, enriched with factual data, specific examples, and informed interpretation. Only one as well read, as perceptive as Mr. Davis could write such a piece.

By Saville R. Davis
The Christian Science Monitor, Oct. 23, 1956

The most exhilarating news that can be brought back from Asia today is that "It can be done." There is no fatal barrier, either technical or economic or in the primitive inexperience of the people themselves, that can block Asia from coming promptly into the modern age. In India the industrial revolution is already taking hold. In other Asian countries the foundations for it are being laid. Most everywhere the agricultural revolution is beginning to blossom. A release from the worst blights of hunger and poverty and ignorance are no longer beyond the horizon of hope.

The job can be done.

There have been grave doubts on this point, and still are. Travel through Asia today and you will find an impressive jury of pessimists for each man who offers some corner of proof to the contrary. The beaten path through Asia, the ordinary sort of inspection tour examining local politics, talking to businessmen both Asian and western, studying business conditions, is enough to discourage anyone. The sheer lack of all kinds of talent—technicians, administrators, managers, investors willing to take risks—is enough to take the heart out of all the most sturdy.

The job, after all, is stupendous. It is to find drastic shortcuts through a process of economic growth that took a century and a half in the West. It is all very well for civilians to talk glibly about annihilating time, and for politicians to wave grandiose paper plans like banners. But the experts in economic development and the businessmen know too much for comfort about the hard actualities of "capital absorption," as they call it. There is little atmosphere of enterprise except of the practical sort, little climate of that self-reliant ingenuity that built the American West.

There is far too much listless leaning on government. Most Asian governments are a morass of incompetence and bureaucracy from the western business point of view; one of the mildest descriptions I heard in southeast Asia was "hideous." There are many areas where government corruption is spectacular. And while this last might have a stimulating effect economically—it played no small part in the building of the American West—the social and political effects of corruption are very dangerous in these times.

Passport to Pessimism

So the ordinary kind of travel in Asia is a passport to pessimism. It is necessary to go off the beaten track, search out those cases where expert and intelligent effort is being made on specific projects. Then examine them in the light of each article of doubt:

Can such people who are innocent of any technical know-how, any mechanical flair, any common sense ingenuity, make a rapid transition to being managers and workers in an enterprise system? Can they make the transition at all? Can private ownership function, despite the tentacular grip of government inertia or venality? Can the grip of government be loosened? Can it be cleansed and made efficient in relation to business? Can planning contrive to mesh all the various rapidly expanding elements in this bootstrap lifting process—supplies of capital, power, transport, raw materials, technicians, managers and the like—so some do not run behind others and cause terrible bottlenecks? Can businessmen forego quick exorbitant and often corrupt profit for a slower but responsible and legitimate gain? And so the questions go.

After nearly a year of special inquiry, this reporter would answer, always speaking generally, in the affirmative. It can be done. It is being done in enough specific cases to establish over-all possibility.

I saw successful projects in most every kind of development ranging from big dams and big industries down through marketing systems, small industry, radically improved farming methods and the training of managers, foremen and workers, as well as projects to overhaul government departments and regulatory bureaus. I came away convinced that these things can be multiplied in spite of the negative atmosphere in Asia, and that the atmosphere itself is already changing.

A new kind of economics is in the making. A new profession of economic developers is taking shape out of the Asian economists and planners, the western economists, technical experts and business advisers, the organizations where all these come together and discuss; such as the United Nations ECAFE—the Economic Council for Asia and the Far East.

Why should this rather weighty economic question be raised here, in a group of articles on the mental attitudes and forces bearing on the emergence of Asia?

Because one golden thread binds together all the cases where experts and businessmen broke through the inertias of Asia and reached success. It was conspicuously absent in the many observed failures. The moral it points is as close to a valid rule as one can make in a field as broad as economics:

Where the organizers and trainers and experts refused to accept the typical pessimism of the East about the common people and their capabilities, where they genuinely believed in the inherent worth of men and women, where they taught and trained confidently, they succeeded.

Where they were assailed with doubts, where they felt frustrated by the obvious limitations of Asian people, where they did not know that men and women out of the jungle or out of eastern city slums could, in fact, be trained and the forces of self-improvement released inside them, they had indifferent success or failed.

Mental Attitude Governs

The attitude, the mental approach, governed. If the constructive attitudes I found were merely roseate optimism, they would doubtless have been useful. The American system was built by people who wouldn't accept limitations and figured the job could somehow be done. But what I observed was something deeper. Those western businessmen and experts from technical assistance, those Asian officials and businessmen and teachers who got the job done and knew how to liberate workers from the past, were usually crusaders in their way. They were in line with something fundamental. They believed in the capabilities of these people, either because of their experience in training or their faith in the future of Asia and Asians.

To this should be added one other element of near genius: they usually managed to free their development jobs from the worst of bureaucracy. In countries where the hand of government was so heavy that western moderate socialism would be pallid by comparison, the experts told their government bosses, "Here is a technical job that needs to be done; you can't do it the old way. This is the age of technicians, and business managers are a kind of technician just like engineers. You can't interfere with them too much. Watch us if you will, see that we don't cheat the government or the public. But if you want the job done, liberate us and let us do it."

This was a work of education which cut two ways: up the ladder to government and also down the ladder to the workers. Both had to be freed from the habits of the past and given a new concept of the work to be done.

Scores of individual memories illustrate: A keen and experienced Danish instructor of mechanics for airplane engines in Indonesia, holding up a neatly tooled steel part and saying proudly, "The boy who made that was up in the palm trees a few weeks ago." A teacher of English which is required for technical study in Thailand saying, "They just eat it up." An American chief engineer in India's Damodar Valley where one big dam was just being finished and another started, "We have all Indian engineers in charge now; I'm the only American left."

Abilities Unlocked

The most moving sights I saw were those where the thinking capacities of individual men and women were suddenly unlocked by experts who knew how, and in a very short time were fulfilling themselves in jobs where they could afford to feed and clothe themselves and their families decently for the first time. It was poetry to see them as I went from one technical assistance project to another, at their benches and desks. They shone with unmistakable gratitude.

But the less personal side of the picture is no less fascinating.

Governments like those of Burma and India and Indonesia have all started down roads that they idealistically label socialist. In the change-over from colonial to free status, the governments took over a good many enterprises. They have embarked on others. But they are having trouble.

Consider for a moment: What does the West

chiefly object to in socialism? It is concentrating too much power in the state, bureaucracy, arbitrary decisions imposed by government. But these are the standard diet in the East. Nowhere has government traditionally been more arbitrary or more hopelessly bureaucratic—either colonial government or the indigenous varities. To be sure, the aim of this arbitrary power was not socialist—not for the benefit of the many, it was used to protect the few.

So bureaucracy is not what Asia is in danger of. Asia has had it. And a less efficient, more dense, and inept variety could not be imagined. To say this is not, I hope, to hurt the feelings of anyone in the East; they themselves are the first and loudest to complain.

The reformer in the larger Asian countries dreams of a new kind of government which would use its vast power for the people. And he is not without some justification.

For quite different reasons, every western economist I met agreed that much of the development job would have to be done by government in the early years, merely because there isn't anyone else on the scene yet. There is a great shortage of risk capital and managerial competence. And there are great nation-building jobs to be done on the scale of the TVA or Grand Coulee, which were government-built even in the United States.

So these governments have tried to use their historic power in new and modern directions, now that their countries are free. But it couldn't work well much of the time—not as planned anyhow. The heavy hand of government was just too heavy. However they sought to retool the state machinery it creaked and broke down. This was too much of a change of personality to expect from such a rigid and stodgy character as the Asian state. The ingrained habits of those who hold and wield authority have not been transformed overnight—partly because they still hold and wield authority, even though the aims of the regime have been broadened.

Many of the first hard lessons of experience in India, Burma, and Indonesia have therefore been disappointments, and it is probable that as more state enterprises are completed and start to function, more disappointments are in store.

So in Indonesia and Burma, for example, though

less uniformly in India, there is a lot of second thought going on. And even in India with its superior tradition, the rigidities of the civil service are admirable in preventing fraud to the state—but they don't know much about how to make decisions and take risks and shift direction quickly when something fails, and bulldoze a job through until it works.

Enterprise Fostered

In Jakarta and Rangoon I found vigorous legislation, just completed, to reserve major sectors of the economy for private enterprise. Foreign capital will have specific rights to withdraw dividends and repatriate itself in a fairly short period. In India, when I arrived, a similar effort was in process to draw a much more sharp line defining the limits of the state, the areas of mixed economy where the state promises to stay out. And in each of these countries I talked to key central planners who helped draw up these new blueprints for a divided economy, with public, mixed, and private sectors, and who thoroughly understood the need for them.

Just as British and German socialism has gained experience with a government bureaucracy and retreated from its more advanced ideological positions, so south Asian socialism shows signs of doing the same at an even earlier stage. Perhaps that is because they feel in their bones that they may have reformed the aims of government but not its methods to anything like the same degree.

There is a marvelous impersonality about enterprise, nowadays. It is so technical—even in its management—that governments increasingly have to treat it with respect. And do.

There is a trend toward something like economic realism. Nobody has bothered to give it a fancy title with slogans and battle flags, but it is gaining converts as the great pressure for action intensifies, under India's passionate struggle for economic democracy, and as results sometimes lag, India is becoming more pragmatic, which is a virtue close to the American heart.

In New Delhi I was given some facts by an objective American business source for which the usual descriptions of India had not prepared me:

About 40 per cent of all government expenditure

in India is made by the 20 local state governments—
a concept of states' rights that has considerable backing among conservatives in the United States.

All expenditure by government in India—state as
well as national—amounts to less than nine per cent
of national expenditure. The proportion in the United
States is double: about 18 per cent.

Agriculture is wholly in private hands. It contributes nearly half of the national product. There
was some talk of cooperative farms but it hasn't
gotten anywhere.

Small industry is wholly in private hands.

Most of medium and large industry is still in private hands. What the government has reserved is
the right to nationalize in cases of paramount public
interest (with compensation required by the Constitution) and to control new investment in certain key
industries. But relatively little has yet been done
under these provisions. On the contrary, while a
number of new government plants are going up, private capital is also taking part in the expansion of
steel and oil—both "key industries"—on terms which
obviously have satisfied the private investors. The
government has no plan to take over existing plants
even in key industries because its resources are far
too preoccupied with expansion.

Development Fostered

An aggressive program for stimulating private investment is part of India's second five-year plan,
through tax benefits, credit facilities, and subsidies
—not unlike those which the United States Congress
initiated in Puerto Rico and which have been spec-
tacularly successful.

In sum, while the government will concentrate on
capital goods industries, utilities, and essential services, private enterprise is assigned all the rest from
heavy and consumer industries on down. By the end
of the second five-year plan the private sector will
still account for about 90 per cent of national expenditure and 75 per cent of the nation's employment.

This is what India calls the "socialist pattern."

Figures, of course, shouldn't be taken too seriously,
even when prepared by outside and objective sources.
There is a lot of doctrinaire talk being flung around,
along with some virile counter argument, a surpris-

ing amount of it, in the free mart of ideas which India keeps wide open. There is a vaguely defined socialist attitude which goes well beyond these facts recited above and will undoubtedly cause attempts by government or politics to interfere with the conduct of business.

But in all these three countries I talked to American businessmen who were convinced they could do business there. They were enough impressed by the trend toward an open economic system, and even more important, they were sufficiently unafraid of what the future might bring, so they were committing their companies and capital and doing good business. I found no one who was doing bad business, although there had been some which earlier gave up and pulled out.

It is impossible not to be impressed by these facts. India's is surely the boldest effort ever made by a parliamentary democracy to throw all its resources into sudden economic development, while still preserving a fair-sized economic framework of individual freedom, and a full freedom of political choice.

The verdict that "It can be done"—that rapid economic development is possible in Asia under a democratic process and without Communist compulsion—is good news for the free world.

Africa Races The Clock

Saul Pett is one of the most skilled news writers in the business. The Associated Press regularly assigns him to the top news of the day. Such was his assignment in the autumn of 1960 when he wrote this well-documented story.

Mr. Pett has the ability to zero-in on the real significance of complex events and to communicate this clearly. His interpretative story is built on the theme "Africa slept late." Note how he carried this highly appropriate theme through his story, adding impact and interest. He spelled out Africa's dilemma in terms vividly understandable to westerners (par. 5). Elsewhere, he gave anecdotes and examples to support his interpretations.

Hence, his article is a fitting one to conclude this anthology. It combines writing excellence, imagination, and thorough reporting into one significant interpretative story.

By Saul Pett
The Associated Press, Aug. 7, 1960

In the history of men and nations, Africa slept late, very late. It awakened only yesterday with the sun high in the sky. Like most people who oversleep, it got up with a jolt and rushed out of bed with a frantic need to catch up with whatever it missed. It is rushing into the world and the 20th century only half-dressed.

Africa capsulized the bookshelves of history into one hurried paragraph and defies the law of evolution for nations. Africa has no time for evolution or natural birth.

New nations are being born overnight, with all the dangers of forced delivery to both mother and child, and it is still too early to tell whether the offspring will be weak, half-formed or deformed.

There is no parallel in history to match the awakening of this huge continent of 250,000,000 people, to whom the wheel was a novelty only yesterday and freedom a novelty today.

Gauls to DeGaulle in Generation

We might have had something like it if Europe, by speeding up the film of time to a crazy comic pace, had moved in a single generation from the ancient wandering Gauls to DeGaulle, from the Celts to Macmillan, with no Voltaire or Magna Carta in between. We might have had something like it in North America, if George Washington and Benjamin Franklin and Thomas Jefferson had been the sons of illiterate Indians, if only a generation had separated 1492 from 1776 and 1776 from 1960.

The paradox of Africa is that it must leap directly from the Stone Age to the Atomic Age. The tragedy of Africa is that it must do this self-consciously in a glass cage, with all the divided world looking over its shoulder.

Each new development is watched carefully by

Russia, the United States and India, by the liberals of New York and London, the propagandists of Moscow and Peiping, the racially sensitive neutralists of New Delhi and Jakarta, the white supremacists of Mississippi and Africa itself.

Can't Delay Independence

Thus, a Western European power might think, for the best, most unselfish reasons, that independence for a given colony in Africa should be delayed. But before coming to such a decision, it would have to consider the screams of "imperialistic enslavement" sure to come from Russia and China, the urbane but suspicious questions sure to come from India and other nations lately freed of colonialism themselves.

And the screams came on schedule in the Congo. A week after that colony became independent, Belgium rushed troops back in to protect the white population from violence.

Russia promptly cried out that the Belgians with American support were trying to re-establish control of the Congo. The United Nations was called in and immediately East and West chose up sides.

Thus, overnight, what was a simple question of law and order versus primitive chaos became a complicated problem in world power politics.

Within Africa itself, opposing sides feed on each other's moves. Thus, Tom Mboya finds fuel for his Kenya nationalist movement in the race riots of South Africa, bitter-ender white settlers of Kenya find their rationalization enforced by the nightmare of the newly independent Congo, and the rigid Afrikaner of South Africa points to an undemocratic process of Ghana and says, "See, give them independence and they create a dictatorship."

But the most striking thing about Africa to the visitor is its hurried compression of time, the bewildering primitive anachronism trailing it into the 20th century.

Chain Reaction of Terror

Less than a week after independence in the Congo law and order collapsed in a chain reaction of terror, murder and rape. The black man turns on the white man, his former ruler. The black man also turns on other black men, exploding tribal feuds that were never settled in 80 years of Belgian colonialism or the last two years of spreading Congolese nationalism.

Why the terror and chaos?

Because an area 80 times larger than Belgium and one-third the size of the United States suddenly became independent without the least understanding of the world. No one had really prepared it for freedom, neither the Belgian colonials nor the Congolese nationalists.

Among millions of illiterate Congolese, there was the notion firmly rooted by ignorance and wishful thinking that independence meant the gates of Heaven would open. Independence, many thought, would mean that the black man would inherit the white man's business, car, home, even his wife.

Independence, thought the native army, would mean that every soldier would start making much more money and every private would be well on his way to becoming a general. Less than a week after independence, the Congolese army mutinied and went out on a rampage.

The terror of the Congo was entirely predictable but still the colony moved relentlessly toward independence and no one seemed able to stop or even slow it down.

Paradox of Compressed Time

Africa contains many other examples of the paradox of compressed time.

Telephone service in Tanganyika is interrupted because elephants knock over the poles. In the suburbs of the modern city of Durban, South Africa, warring tribes still fight with spears, clubs, knives and the evil spirits enlisted by opposing witch doctors.

Lions and giraffes still stop traffic in the suburbs of Nairobi, a modern cosmopolitan city of glass buildings; and a modern cosmopolitan white woman, who was educated in the best schools of Europe, says she's less fearful of finding a leopard in her garden at night than an unexpected native with a panga knife.

In the Congo, there is a week's delay in collecting

the results of the first national elections—a mass pin-up contest, in which the largely illiterate electorate voted for the picture of their favorite candidate. Why the delay? Thousands of marked ballots were lost because a boat carrying them sank in a crocodile-infested river, because many, many other votes were stolen, burned, slashed or just switched by warring tribes swooping down on the polling places with bows and arrows, spears, machete knives.

Superstitions Plague Africa

In Johannesburg, a native houseboy recalls that some days you just can't win. Before going to a poker game one night, he paid his witch doctor to guarantee him luck by rubbing hippo fat in his palms. Then he played poker and lost. Then he beat up the witch doctor. Then he was arrested and fined.

Near the base of beautiful, snow-capped Kilimanjaro, where rich white hunters from the cafe society of Hollywood, New York, London and Paris stalk their game, native cattle die of disease. But the native farmers refuse to allow the government to dip the cattle in chemicals for fear they'll become bewitched.

In Kenya, the Masai tribe still largely exists on a diet of cow blood and milk curdled with urine. In many areas of black Africa, native girls are still subjected to dangerous, painful circumcision on the theory that a killed sexual appetite reduces infidelity.

In many country and urban areas, modern, educated Africans as well as the primitives still pay a bridal price of 11 cattle for their wives.

In the rising racial tension of South Africa, white men are carrying guns and at the first sign of trouble farmers herd their families into the towns the way American pioneers used to race for the nearest cavalry fort ahead of an Indian attack. In the renewed racial tension of Kenya, white men and white women carry guns again midst unsubstantiated rumors of a Mau Mau revival.

Tribal Customs Continue

In Ghana, President Kwame Nkrumah returns from a meeting of the British Commonwealth in London, where he played a highly articulate role, and is given a rousing welcome in his own capital of Accra. And a white lamb is killed in gratitude for his safe journey.

In humid, exotic Dar es Salaam, the modern capital of Tanganyika, there is a big ornate welcome for Julius Nyerere, the literate, urbane young politician of 38, who is expected to become his country's first prime minister. He is returning from a posh tour of the United States and among those welcoming him home is his mother, who wears no shoes.

In Nairobi, nationalist and labor leader Tom Mboya, who studied at Oxford, meets with assorted constituents in his modern offices. Most wear Western clothes, not quite as Ivy-Leaguish as Mboya's but one constituent is a tall, sinewy old warrior with misty eyes.

He wears a skullcap and a white gown under an ancient British army coat of khaki. The tops of his ears are pierced to hold large rings and the lobes have huge holes from which silver trinkets dangle. He is barefoot and carries a slender but menacing black ebony club and a long hand broom of animal hairs for swatting flies.

Father Was a Cannibal

In the Central African Republic, the late Barthelmy Boganda, prime minister, used to charm his European visitors with his culture and intellectual distinction. And then he enjoyed seeing their expression change as he casually remarked, "My father, you know, was a cannibal."

In many places in Africa, leadership is falling to or being grabbed by a small intellectual elite who are usually the first generation in their families and their countries to have been educated. Illiteracy remains staggeringly high and preparation for self-rule, except for this narrow elite, staggeringly low.

In the entire native population of 8,780,000 in Tanganyika, where independence is only a year or two away, there are no African lawyers, only 15 doctors, 70 college graduates and 214 students now in college.

In the entire native population of 13,000,000 in the Belgian Congo, which became independent June

30, there isn't a single official previously trained for high office, not a single lawyer or doctor or engineer and only 16 college graduates.

The statistics can be repeated in many places in Africa and they are repeated night and day by the white settlers of Kenya, fighting a losing battle against African independence, and the Afrikaners of South Africa, fighting a rigid battle against equality for Africans.

One can agree with their premise—that, by the standards of history, most Africans are ill-prepared for independence—without accepting their conclusion—that Africans should not get independence. But, in any case, the argument seems academic.

Africa Sweeps Toward Independence

Ready or not, Africa sweeps toward independence with an overwhelming, increasing force. Ten years ago, the continent had only four independent nations—Ethiopia, Liberia, the Union of South Africa and Egypt.

Eventually, Africa may produce some 40 independent nations, and if each joins the United Nations, they would hold one-third of its seats.

White resistance to the emergence of the black man varies with the depth of the white man's entrenchment and the size of the native population outnumbering him.

The least resistance and the least racial tension have occurred in Tanganyika, where the blacks outnumber the whites 430 to 1. There was more resistance in the Belgian Congo, where the blacks outnumber the whites 130 to 1. There was and is still more in Kenya, where the ratio is 93 to 1, where the white man has dug in deep, where he has invested his capital in the land, where he makes a handsome living out of his investment and fears it will be expropriated by a native government.

And finally, the greatest fortress of white resistance in all Africa—and surely it will be the last to fall—is South Africa. Here, the white man tells you, with almost as much emphasis as if he were claiming a majority, that the ratio is only three Negroes for every white man.

White Man Here 300 Years

Here, the white men have lived for 300 years, have built the strongest, wealthiest nation in Africa.

But the native in South Africa cannot vote or join a union or strike or hold a skilled job in a white area (black areas produce little demand for skilled workers) or own his own home in the new housing locations or use the white man's elevator or bus or theater or park bench or washroom or restaurant or even the same counter at the post office.

He must get the white man's permission to travel, to choose jobs, to visit his wife (if they work in different areas) or just to be out on the streets after 11 at night. And at all times he must have and be ready to show the first cop who demands it his passbook of identification.

Ironically, in touring Black Africa from the equator south, I heard the word "revolution" used only twice.

Once was in the highlands of Kenya where a white settler said he would, if he had enough followers, lead a revolution against the approach of black rule in Kenya. He is not likely to.

In Johannesburg, South Africa, several Negro students and teachers said, "If the guns come from the north, we'll lead a revolution." They are not likely to—not in the immediate future.

The Afrikaner government of South Africa remains remarkably rigid on apartheid. It remains confident, despite the riots of some months ago, that the black man in South Africa will not revolt.

Will Shoot All Whites

A visitor exposed to the rising hate, the tension, the widening schism between black and white in South Africa is not so sure. Somehow, one feels, the "wind of change" sweeping Africa will sweep all the way to Capetown some day, and when it does the rigid Afrikaner government, because it's so rigid, will come down in a thousand pieces.

"And the worst part of it," said a young native writer in Johannesburg, "is that when we get the guns, we will become blind. We'll shoot the whites we like and the whites we don't like. There will be no time to distinguish."

Everywhere in Africa, even where he has been

told independence is on the way, the black man is increasingly impatient. Even in Tanganyika, where there is little tension and no segregation.

There the British are preparing the natives for independence in a remarkable plan of gradual stages—first more seats in Parliament, then several ministries in the cabinet, then full internal self-rule and, finally, with authority over defense and foreign policy—complete independence.

A senior British official said, "We have Tanganyika on the end of a long rope and we are letting it out slowly. At least, we're trying to let it out slowly but the Africans are pulling harder every day.

They're pulling harder everywhere in Africa, the last inhabited continent of the world to join the 20th century.

Index